The

Dis

M000232668

2006

UPPER
ROOM BOOKS®
NASHVILLE

An Outline for Small-Group Use of Disciplines

Here is a simple plan for a one-hour, weekly group meeting based on reading *Disciplines*. One person may act as convener every week, or the role can rotate among group members. You may want to light a white Christ candle each week to signal the beginning of your time together.

Opening

Convener: Let us come into the presence of God.
Others: Lord Jesus Christ, thank you for being with us. Let us hear your word to us as we speak to one another.

Scripture

Convener reads the scripture suggested for that day in *Disciplines*. After a one- or two-minute silence, convener asks: What did you hear God saying to you in this passage? What response does this call for? (*Group members respond in turn or as led.*)

Reflection

*   What scripture passage(s) and meditation(s) from this week was (were) particularly meaningful for you? Why? (*Group members respond in turn or as led.*)
*   What actions were you nudged to take in response to the week's meditations? (*Group members respond in turn or as led.*)
*   Where were you challenged in your discipleship this week? How did you respond to the challenge? (*Group members respond in turn or as led.*)

Praying Together

Convener says: Based on today's discussion, what people and situations do you want us to pray for now and in the coming week?
Convener or other volunteer then prays about the concerns named.

Departing

Convener says: Let us go in peace to serve God and our neighbors in all that we do.

Adapted from *The Upper Room Daily Devotional Guide*, January–February 2001. ©2000 The Upper Room. Used by permission.

Cover design: Ed Maksimowicz
Cover photo: Susan W. N. Ruach
First printing: 2005

Lectionary texts from *The Revised Common Lectionary* copyright © 1992 by The Consultation on Common Texts (CCT), P. O. Box 340003, Room 381, Nashville, TN 37203-0003 USA. All rights reserved. Reprinted with permission.

Scripture quotations not otherwise identified are from the New Revised Standard Version Bible, copyright 1989, Division of Christian Education of the National Council of the Churches of Christ in the United States of America. Used by permission. All rights reserved.

Scripture quotations designated RSV are from the *Revised Standard Version Bible*, copyright 1952 (2nd edition, 1971) by the Division of Christian Education of the National Council of the Churches of Christ in the United States of America. Used by permission. All rights reserved.

Scripture quotations designated NIV are from the *HOLY BIBLE, NEW INTERNATIONAL VERSION.* NIV.® Copyright © 1973, 1978, 1984 International Bible Society. Used by permission of Zondervan Publishing House. All rights reserved.

Scripture quotations designated KJV are from the King James Version of the Bible.

Scripture quotations designated NKJV are taken from the New King James Version.® Copyright © 1982 by Thomas Nelson, Inc. Used by permission. All rights reserved.

Scripture quotations designated JB are from THE JERUSALEM BIBLE, copyright © 1966 by Darton, Longman & Todd, Ltd. and Doubleday, a division of Random House, Inc. Reprinted by permission.

Scripture quotations designated NLT are taken from the *Holy Bible, New Living Translation,* copyright ©1996. Used by permission of Tyndale House Publishers, Inc., Wheaton, Illinois 60189. All rights reserved.

Scripture quotations designated AT are the author's translation.

Scripture quotations designated AP are the author's paraphrase.

Scripture quotations designated *The Message* by Eugene H. Peterson, Copyright © 1993, 1994, 1995, 1996, 2000, 2001, 2002. Used by permission of NavPress Publishing Group. All rights reserved.

ISBN: 0-8358-9899-7

Printed in the United States of America

Contents

Foreword

As the new year approached, my young adult daughter said over the phone with a big sigh that she wanted to get more discipline in her life. That sigh indicated both desire and ambivalence. Her expressed longing gave me a chance to share my favorite definition of "discipline": discipline is remembering what you want.

I don't know if my daughter took comfort in that definition, but for me it takes matters out of the realm of "shoulds" and "oughts." If I want to make music on the piano, I practice. If I want to win games of tennis, I practice. If I want to grow in my faith and relationship to God, I practice those things that help me develop and advance in that area.

In my own life I want to know God more deeply and live more faithfully. But I get involved in the ups and downs and the dailyness of life; I forget my desire. I've learned that in a relationship of continued growth, I need to open myself to God on a daily basis. So I have developed practices, or spiritual disciplines, over the years that help me remember what I want, that help me stay open to God.

One of these practices is daily devotional reading. Many people discover that daily reading of scripture and other brief devotional works helps them start the day well. Other people prefer to spend this kind of devotional time around their lunch hour or at a break. Still others choose an evening time when the reading helps them reflect on the day and begin to think about the next day.

Such daily reading becomes a useful way to focus or refocus on God in the midst of life. Amazingly, the ideas and thoughts from the daily devotional time will invite further reflection even a day or so later.

When I first began the practice of a daily devotional time, I struggled to remember to do it. To help me remember I put the Bible and the devotional resource in a place where I would see it. I also covenanted with a friend to ask each other every two weeks how our daily devotional times were going. Often I thought about skipping the daily devotions until I remembered my friend's upcoming inquiry.

Committing daily devotional time and remaining accountable to another person or group of persons for that practice can be a life-transforming choice. One pastor ordered a number of copies of *The Upper Room Disciplines* daily devotional guide and gave a copy to all the church leaders. He asked them to join him in reading both the scripture and the short devotional each day. At various church meetings he invited participants to share how God had spoken to them through the reading or their reflections related to the readings. The pastor and members of the congregation discovered that the readings spurred interesting thoughts and encouraged them to reflect on their faith more deeply, which led them to perceive the exciting work of God among them. The practice of reading the same devotional guide together changed their lives and the life of the church.

Some positive results of daily devotional practice that I've observed over time in my own life are these:

- I *consciously* connect with God at least once a day.
- I am more grateful.
- I receive support and encouragement in tough times.
- I am held in a more grounded, peaceful place.
- I am nudged to be a kinder, more faithful, and more fruitful person.
- I am reminded who I want to be.
- I am coming to know God more deeply.

My prayer is that this book will inspire, challenge, strengthen, and support your spiritual journey and help you remember who you want to be.

—SUSAN W. N. RUACH
Director, Conference Spiritual Leadership Development
General Board of Discipleship of The United Methodist Church

The Mystery of Christ

January 1, 2006 • Jennifer Grove Bryan[‡]

SUNDAY, JANUARY 1 • Read Matthew 25:31-46; Ephesians 3:1-12

"In [Jesus] we have access to God in boldness and confidence through faith in him" is how the writer describes humanity's gain since Jesus' birth. Given opportunity to grow in wisdom and stature, Jesus was allowed to accept or reject his charge as God's anointed one, Messiah, Christ for all.

Just as Jesus' baptism clarified his identity and spiritual task, we also begin a New Year in our own lives. Will the mystery of Christ claim us, as God's will claimed Jesus? Will we live as though we share in the divine promises?

Matthew reminds us that Christ's throne of glory will also be a judgment seat, where the glorified Christ condemns or vindicates, based on our love of neighbor as expressed in practical ways. Will it be revealed that, like the writer of Ephesians, "I have become a servant according to the gift of God's grace that was given me by the working of his power"?

Jesus sent his Spirit to enable the righteous to continue his work until he returns again. Those who "go away into eternal punishment" are those who refuse to participate in the "mystery" of Christ. They have not been motivated to merciful deeds and compassionate actions generated by God's Spirit. Like Simeon and Anna, Mary and Joseph, each of us chooses whom we serve. Let the Holy Spirit clarify your identity and spiritual tasks. We enter into oneness with Father, Son, and Holy Spirit when we participate in the "mystery of Christ" that is passed along to those who receive the gospel.

PRAYER: Holy Spirit of Christ, strengthen me as your servant. Enable me to share the gospel. Amen.

[‡]Deacon, The United Methodist Church; serving at Lenexa United Methodist Church, Lenexa, Kansas.

God's Creative Love

January 2–8, 2006 • Wilkie Au‡

MONDAY, JANUARY 2 • Read Genesis 1:1–2

God is present at Creation's beginning with the earth as a formless void, as well as at the beginning of our lone nativity when God "created my inmost self, and put me together in my mother's womb" (Ps. 139:13, JB). As John's Gospel puts it so poetically, "In the beginning was the Word, . . . and the Word was God" (1:1).

A new child. A new job. A new year. Our human journey consists of endings and new beginnings. Newness can add excitement to our life, bringing opportunities for joy and happiness. Yet, new beginnings can also be scary because of the many unknowns they entail. Whenever we find ourselves resisting change and new beginnings because of fear, we need to hear anew the good news proclaimed in scripture that God is present in all the beginnings of our lives.

God is present even in troublesome new beginnings. Jacob, caught in the middle of a family crisis that he had brought upon himself, had to escape in a hurry and take refuge with his mother's family in a far-off land. On the road at night, he finds himself alone and fearful about his uncertain future. However, in a vivid dream that floods him with fresh hope, he hears God's affirmation: "Be sure that I am with you; I will keep you safe wherever you go" (Gen 28:15, JB). The God of Jacob is also our God who promises to remain always with us and to keep us safe on our journey.

In all of our beginnings, the Word is present as the abiding source of life and light. God's presence bathes us in a light that no darkness can overcome (John 1:1–5).

PRAYER: Good and gracious God, may we journey through life with courage and hope, relying on your loving presence. Amen.

---

‡Associate Professor of Theological Studies, Loyola Marymount University, Los Angeles; California; Roman Catholic lay author.

TUESDAY, JANUARY 3 • Read Genesis 1:3-5

"God saw that the light was good." Throughout this first creation account in Genesis, we hear God's resounding affirmation of creation's goodness. After each element of the universe is created, we witness God's delight in the goodness of everything divinely fashioned. At the beginning of a new year, we could benefit from asking ourselves two questions: (1) Do we delight in and appreciate the created things that fill our lives? (2) Do we take time to evaluate our works, like God evaluated the works of creation, to see if our works too are good?

Both questions contribute to our maintenance of a vital spiritual life. We easily become accustomed to possessions and take things for granted. Spiritually, we are called to recognize and appreciate all the gifts of the earth and to let our hearts fill with gratitude for God's bountiful love. The created universe of light and darkness, sea and sky, male and female is a cornucopia of gifts from a generous and loving God. Expanding our gratitude for God's many good gifts deepens our love of God.

Periodic evaluation of our works can give us a fresh chance to prioritize our time and energy and to assess anew how we, as people called to be cocreators with God, can best contribute to the world by bearing fruit that evokes both our and God's delight. To see our daily labor as part of God's ongoing creative love in the world endows our ordinary efforts to love and serve with great significance. Renewed gratitude and meaning can get our new year off to a vibrant start.

PRAYER: Good and gracious God, thank you for your marvelous love made manifest in your wonderful gifts to us. Help us always to delight in your gifts and to enjoy them in a way that deepens our love for you and for our brothers and sisters in the world. Amen.

As we begin this new year, let us pause to praise God for the wonders of creation. Let us stand in grateful awe before the dazzling colors of a rose garden or the majestic shapes of Yosemite's stone monuments. Let us take delight in a sunset and marvel over the sparkling beauty of a star-studded sky. Let us gaze admiringly at a favorite stretch of beach and look fondly at the face of someone long loved. These "wonder-filled" acts are simple ways of worshiping God, the generous Source of everything.

The cultivation of wonder can give our new year a shot of spiritual vitality because wonder expands our awareness of the divine. As adults, too many of us have lost our childlike capacity to wonder. Frederick Buechner in his book *Wishful Thinking* says it well: "Using the same old materials of earth, air, fire, and water, every twenty-four hours God creates something new out of them. If you think you're seeing the same show all over again seven times a week, you're crazy."

Creation is no accident. And it didn't just happen once. It is ongoing, a continuing act of God's creative, deliberate will. And it is good. It is good because through God's gift to us, the future is new and open to us every day. It all depends on what we do with what God gives us—every day

The openness of the future, the magnitude of God's gifts to us—these are the things that lead to wonder. Wonder is that sense of radical amazement over the very existence of things. When we pray with wonder, we attempt to enter into the garden of creation reverently and gratefully, there to witness the presence of God, who at every moment sustains us and all things in existence.

PRAYER: Good and gracious God, we thank you for all the gifts of creation and especially for the gift of life, for it is in you that we live and breathe, move and have our being. Amen.

Titled "Hymn to the lord of the storm" (JB), this psalm reminds us of God's sovereignty over all things. The voice of God commands "the multitudinous waters," "shatters the cedars of Lebanon," "sets the wilderness shaking," and "gives strength to his people." Because God reigns in everything, we can believe with Paul "that by turning everything to their good, God cooperates with all those who love him" (Rom. 8:28, JB). Or as Ignatius of Loyola states in his *Spiritual Exercises*, God's presence in creation is dynamic, not merely inert. Ignatius directs us "to consider how God works and labors" for us and all creatures upon the face of the earth. God is ever in our midst working powerfully on our behalf. "In the heavens, the elements, the plants, the fruits, the cattle, etc., [God] gives being, conserves them, confers life and sensation, etc." (#236).

God's ongoing labor in the world invites us to live with greater trust. In everything, we must rely on God "whose power, working in us, can do infinitely more than we can ask or imagine" (Eph. 3:20). The problem with most of us is that we push ahead alone, relying solely on our own power. Spiritually, we are challenged to give up our pretension of self-sufficiency and admit our need for help. In the spirit of the first three steps of 12 Step spirituality, we are called (1) to acknowledge our powerlessness to make it on our own and to let go of our resistance to rely on God; (2) to admit our dependence on the power of God; and (3) to surrender our lives to God's care, confident that support will come "from above," as Jesus promised Nicodemus (John 3:3), if we continue to do our responsible best.

PRAYER: Good and gracious God, help us in all we do to trust in your power at work in our world and lives, and help us also to rely more trustingly in each other. Amen.

FRIDAY, JANUARY 6 • Read Acts 19:1-7

EPIPHANY OF THE LORD

Through the instrumentality of Paul, the disciples of John at Ephesus receive the precious gift of the Holy Spirit that comes with baptism. The book of Acts illustrates God's reliance on the disciples to embody the real, though imperceptible, presence of the risen Jesus. The spirit of Jesus is given flesh-and-blood reality in the lives of his disciples: in Peter who cures the paralytic at the Temple gate called Beautiful (3:1-10) and in Stephen who prays that those putting him to death will be forgiven (7:60). Peter's cure of the lame beggar and Stephen's prayer of forgiveness both trigger vivid memories of Jesus' own words and actions. They proclaim the good news that Jesus' spirit continues to be active in history—but now embodied in the lives of his disciples.

Similarly, our call to discipleship entails embodying the spirit of Jesus for others. Like the disciples of John at Ephesus, who numbered a highly symbolic twelve, we are called to minister as a community. In our efforts to give human form to the Spirit's presence in the world, we are called to collaborate with others. We cannot embody the compassionate presence of Christ for a suffering world by ourselves.

A young boy strained to move a large rock. Walking by, his father asked him, "Son, are you using all your strength?" "Yes, I am," replied the exasperated boy. "No, you're not," the father continued, "because you haven't asked me for help."

Scripture makes clear that God intends that we work together. Yahweh said, "It is not good that the man should be alone. I will make him a helpmate" (Gen 1:18, JB), and Jesus sent the seventy-two disciples on their first mission in pairs so that they could labor with mutual support.

PRAYER: Good and gracious God, we thank you for calling us to serve you in companionship. Help us to be generous in allowing you to use us in whatever way to embody the presence of the risen Christ today. Amen.

As part of the Trinity, the Holy Spirit often seems like a forgotten middle child. Like the disciples of John at Ephesus who were never told that "there is a Holy Spirit," we sometimes do not realize the importance of the Holy Spirit in our lives. The Holy Spirit is the Paraclete or the Advocate whom Jesus promised to send to his disciples from the Father (John 15:26-27). This Advocate, Jesus reassures his disciples at the Last Supper, will support them in their walk of faith. "When the Spirit of truth comes he will lead you to the complete truth" (John 16:13).

Reflecting on the etymology of the words *Paraclete* and *Advocate* can renew our appreciation of the gift of the Spirit. Literally, the words *Paraclete* (from the Greek) and *Advocate* (from the Latin) have similar meanings: "along side of" and "to call." A lawyer, for example, is an advocate, someone we call to stand alongside of us in support. To call upon the Holy Spirit in prayer is to call upon God to stand by our side when we need guidance and support.

Spiritually, we may profit by thinking of the Holy Spirit as the one who stands by our side calling us to ongoing growth and renewal. The new year frequently prompts us to make resolutions to improve our lives in some way: to be better persons, to live healthier and fuller lives. Maybe these promptings for improvement arise from the Holy Spirit who remains ever at our side to empower our "hidden self to grow strong, so that Christ may live in [our] hearts through faith" and that we might more and more each day be "filled with the utter fullness of God" (Eph. 3:17-19, JB).

PRAYER: Good and gracious God, open our hearts to the Holy Spirit whom you send into our lives, and let that Spirit guide and support us in all we do. Amen.

Contemplating Jesus' baptism in the Jordan by John reveals to us our basic identity as Christians. When Jesus emerges from the water, he sees the heavens torn apart and hears a voice from heaven affirming him as the Beloved. Significantly, Jesus receives this gift of divine affirmation prior to the start of his public ministry. In other words, God affirms his lovableness based on his being, not his doing. As brothers and sisters of Jesus, we too claim our fundamental identity as the beloved of God.

God's unconditional love for each of us comes as a gift. It does not depend on our attributes, talents, or achievements. When we forget the gift of God's love for us, we sometimes find ourselves trying to prop up a shaky and insecure sense of self by accumulating possessions and achieving success. Faith, however, reassures us that God's creative love is what brings us into being. We close the week as we began, recalling the words of the psalmist, "It was you who created my inmost self, and put me together in my mother's womb; for all these mysteries I thank you: for the wonder of myself, for the wonder of your works" (Ps. 139:13-14, JB).

Prayer gives us the chance daily to enter into God's presence and to hear once again the voice that addressed Jesus saying to us: "You are my beloved one in whom I take great delight." Our daily life in family and community, on the other hand, gives us the chance to remind one another by word and action who and whose we are as the beloved of God. To live each day of the new year with a greater consciousness of God's unconditional love for us is to be truly blessed.

PRAYER: Good and gracious God, help us receive the free gift of your love and to live peacefully and lovingly together as your beloved children. Amen.

You Know Me

January 9–15, 2006 • *Connie Nelson*[‡]

MONDAY, JANUARY 9 • **Read 1 Samuel 3:1-4**

As I write this, my city is reeling from a weekend of violence and fear: a federal judge and three other innocents killed, an assailant who eluded authorities for almost twenty-four hours, an entire metropolitan area in "lockdown" mode. We all breathed a collective sigh of relief with the capture of the accused.

We regularly read or hear breaking news stories from around the world: a roadside bomb in Iraq, an assassination in Lebanon, a church member who killed eight in his congregation, ongoing genocide in Sudan, the deadly tsunami.

"The word of the LORD was rare in those days," today's text says. It wouldn't be a stretch to want to apply those words to our age, our time. A natural disaster strikes. Where is God? Random violence claims a loved one. Where is God? The world seems to spiral into chaos and confusion. Where is God?

Although Samuel had been dedicated to God from the moment of his conception, had been mentored by the priest, Eli, made his home in the "temple of the LORD" with the ark of the covenant right under his nose, the text says that he lived in an age when "visions were not widespread." God was all around him, trying to get through to him, but he had no clue. He couldn't see. He couldn't hear.

And yet, God was there. And God is here, in our world, in our lives, all around us, breaking through the darkest moments with sustaining love. It's up to us to open our eyes and to listen.

PRAYER: Help me listen—to myself, to others, to you, O God. Help me to remember always that you know me and love me fiercely. Amen.

---

‡Ordained United Methodist elder, staff member of The Carter Center in Atlanta, Georgia; former conference communications director, and staff member of the General Board of Global Ministries.

There have been moments in my life when I've experienced what I consider to be divine revelation—an "aha" moment, a clear knowledge that the spirit of the Holy was moving within my psyche, my soul, guiding me toward a decision, leading me to a different path—by myself. But more often than not, that "sense" has not been uncovered or understood alone. I've sought out a guide, a friend, an *anam chara*—soul friend.

Just before sunrise, Samuel hears a voice calling his name. Thinking his teacher Eli is calling, he responds, only to be sent back to bed. Finally, when he hears the voice calling the third time, "Samuel, Samuel" and repeats his predawn visit to Eli, the old priest perceives that "the LORD was calling the boy."

Eli, in that moment of Samuel's calling, acts as midwife to help birth Samuel's awareness of the Holy, of God's voice, of God's call. Even this young man who from his conception has been dedicated to God, whose entire life has been spent in study and prayer, can't hear, doesn't understand. Samuel needs the guidance of a wise one to walk him through this experience of the Holy, needs an *anam chara* to remind him to listen. Without a guide, Samuel might have missed the moment.

A soul friend can be a colleague, a minister, or perhaps someone completely outside the church who possesses a depth of God's spirit and understanding. Or a soul friend can be a more formal relationship—a spiritual director, a pastoral counselor. During the many different phases of my own life—teenager, university student, pastor, single mother—I have been graced by the wisdom of women and men who walked with me and helped me hear God's voice and who reminded me to listen. Without these soul friends as guides, I might have missed the moment.

PRAYER: For those soul friends who guide us to you and who help us hear your voice, O Holy One, we give you thanks. May we be present to do the same for others when you call. Amen.

Psalm 139 has been a favorite of mine from my college days. Although they follow today's text, verses 7-10 encapsulate the entire psalm for me: "Where can I go from your spirit? Or where can I flee from your presence? . . . If I take the wings of the morning and settle at the farthest limits of the sea, even there your hand shall lead me."

I have held fast to the words of the psalmist, particularly during times of transition—from seminary to pastoral ministry, from Texas to England to New Mexico to Georgia, through personal and professional upheavals. They have reminded me again and again of this important truth: God knows me, and God is with me. Not only does God know and love me, but God created me just as I am. I am no accident; I am beloved and never alone.

The psalmist writes, "O LORD, you have searched me and known me. You know when I sit down and when I rise up; you discern my thoughts from far away."

I do not read these words as an expression of fear that God maintains some great cosmic database, recording every negative thought or act we commit. I read them as an acknowledgment of being intimately known, of never being in a place where God is not, either physically or psychologically. "You hem me in, behind and before."

Once when I was on retreat, a spiritual director encouraged me to close my eyes and imagine myself with God. As I meditated, a profound image entered my mind—so strong an image I could feel it physically. I saw myself as a small child strapped with brightly colored fabric onto God's back. The image of an African mother going about her daily duties with this child—me—securely fastened to her body disclosed my experience of God in that moment. I was hemmed in, safe, secure.

PRAYER: O God, may I always remember that there is no part of my life where you are not. May I draw strength from the knowledge that I am never alone. Amen.

God knows us. Some years ago, I made a pilgrimage to Iona, a small island off the west coast of Scotland, which once served as the cradle of Christianity in northern England. In a time of professional transition I wanted a place to pray, to listen, to simply be with God. I wanted answers, and I knew they were on Iona.

The retreat I had envisioned, however, never happened. I felt physically uncomfortable for the first few days, so cold that no amount of layering helped; the candle I had brought from Atlanta, the one I use when I pray, sat unlit the entire week—no candles in the abbey, I found out. But most disconcerting to my well-laid plans was the lack of "a word from the LORD." Nothing. Nada. I listened. I prayed. Oh, I "sensed" an answer; but it wasn't what I was looking for, so I dismissed it.

As I journaled on my final day there, I realized that the answer to the questions I had scripted for God—what job should I pursue, what city should I be in, where should I go next—was not at all what God was trying to get through to me. What I had sensed all along wasn't static, internal dissonance but what I needed to hear: "Be yourself."

"That's it?" I asked, both in my writing and out loud. "What does that mean?"

And in the weeks and months—and now years—that have followed, I understand more clearly what that means: It's not about where I am or what professional role I've taken on or might have even felt called to—it's about who I *am*. I plumb the depths of this self, embrace both the gifts and the foibles, and live out of the knowledge that not only am I God's child—knitted by God "in my mother's womb"—but that I am the only "me" there will ever be. To be my authentic self is the most powerful expression of faithfulness I can make.

PRAYER: Beloved Creator, for answering our prayers in unexpected ways, for empowering us to be ourselves—the unique daughters and sons you created us to be—we give you thanks. Amen.

When I felt called to ministry at the age of seventeen, initially it felt like a solitary path. Although my denomination had been ordaining women for almost twenty years at that point, I had never met a clergywoman. Yet I did not doubt that I was following God's voice. When I met the campus minister at The University of Texas—a woman ordained in the United Church of Christ—I felt a sense of both emotional and physical relief. *Oh. There you are. I know you. You know me.*

I've experienced this phenomenon at other important times in my life: in a community of clergy in inner-city Leeds, England; as part of a group of women who have made an annual beach pilgrimage for twelve years; when I joined the staff of an international peacemaking organization. "Aha" moments happen when we meet kindred spirits: it's a shorthand, a fast-forward, an instinctual knowing.

In today's text, Nathanael sits under a fig tree, minding his own business, when Philip calls out to him. Nathanael mutters the infamous question, "Can anything good come out of Nazareth?" Jesus responds (and I love the sarcasm both of them display here), "Here is truly an Israelite in whom there is no deceit!"

And then Nathanael asks Jesus the question: "Where did you get to know me?"

Jesus caught him off guard, saw right through him. Jesus got him with just one look as he sat under the fig tree. But the reverse was also true for Nathanael: in that moment, he understood that he had met a kindred spirit. Of course, this kindred spirit just happened to be the son of God.

Oh. There you are. You know me. I know you.

PRAYER: Gracious God, for those moments when your Spirit brings kindred souls together, souls that know the other and understand that we are part of you, we give you thanks. Amen.

In today's text Paul responds to the gnostic tendencies of the believers at Corinth. The gnostics—a body of Christians who believed in a dualism of body and spirit and the inferiority of the physical realm to the spiritual—practiced spiritual piety but felt they had carte blanche as far as the body was concerned. Convinced of their secure salvation, they took the approach of "all things are lawful for me." *Gnosis*, knowledge, and not the physical realm was sacred for them.

Paul has two problems with this line of thinking: he understood the whole person—body and soul—to be a member of Christ and therefore sacred; he also believed in the physical resurrection of the body with the return of Jesus. "Do you not know that your bodies are members of Christ?" he asks. "Should I therefore take the members of Christ and make them members of a prostitute? Never!" To have sexual relations with a temple prostitute, Paul knew, was to be joined with—to be in communion with—the god served by the prostitute. A false god.

The body-soul dichotomy embraced by the Corinthian Christians is one all too often embraced today, separating the spiritual from the physical, the mind from the body. Yet the scientific community tells us that the two are intricately connected: mental outlook profoundly affects physical well-being, and the reverse is also true. Each depends on the other for wholeness.

SUGGESTION FOR REFLECTION:
- How do I honor and care for my body as part of a whole, sacred self?
- How do my actions or inactions serve a "false god"?
- In what part of my life do I declare, "All things are lawful for me?" How does this reflect my life as part of God's realm?
- At what times do I best experience wholeness, integration of my mind, spirit, and body?

PRAYER: **Help me remember that my whole self—body, mind, spirit, all—belongs to you, O God. Let my every act reflect that knowledge; let my every word reflect your love. Amen.**

In *The Book of Hours*, poetic "love letters to God," Rainer Maria Rilke expresses a deep love for the divine and God's understanding of all creation—the physical, the spiritual, the pain, the joy—as sacred. Nothing lies outside the realm of the Holy; pain and darkness can draw us closer to God's spirit.

In the intimacy of our creation, God speaks to us, whispers our names, and accompanies us on our way. God knows us. Rilke writes, "These are the words we dimly hear: . . . go to the limits of your longing. Embody me."

Imago Dei. In the image of God.

This week we have meditated on the reality of being known: known by ourselves, by others, and by God. I find it hard to comprehend or imagine that this aging body with graying hair and a brain that increasingly fires on fewer than all cylinders (to this, my daughters will testify) bears any relationship to the realm of the sacred. How can I dare to believe that my thoughts and actions, my words and silence have any greater import than a solitary attempt at living a life.

Yet the Holy uses this very body, this very spirit, this very mind in ways that continue to surprise—in ways nothing short of grace. Because of this, Paul's first letter to the Corinthians proclaims with certainty that we are not our own. It proclaims with certainty that we belong to God. Because of this, the scripture tells us that we must seek honor in everything we do—with our bodies, our minds, and our spirits. We are united as one with Christ because we belong to God.

God knows me. God knows you. Thanks be to God.

PRAYER: In this moment, Beloved One, enfold me in the knowledge that I am your child. Help me always to remember that you know me, that you created me to be who I am—to be yours—and that I am never outside the realm of your profound love. Amen.

The Ultimate "News"

January 16–22, 2006 • *Ray Waddle*[‡]

MONDAY, JANUARY 16 • **Read Jonah 3:1-5, 10**

I thank God for the book of Jonah. It's surprising to find this strange little story in the Bible at all, because it paints an unflattering portrait of a biblical prophet. But it's a consoling story. Jonah sulks, yet God never gives up on him or anyone else.

God chooses Jonah to deliver a warning of repentance to the enemy city of Nineveh. Jonah wants no part of it. He flees God by ship, gets tossed off and swallowed by a fish who vomits up Jonah after three days. Back on his feet, Jonah begrudgingly delivers the warning to the Ninevites, who wisely repent. This act of piety angers Jonah; he wanted them destroyed. God, unflustered, spares everyone. You can read the whole story in six minutes.

I hunger for details of Nineveh's mass conversion, a city of 120,000. But what matters is God's care for people beyond Jonah's world. The scope of God's salvation cannot be humanly defined or contained.

Scholars sternly insist that the story of Jonah is a legend, a tale with no basis in historical fact—as if that settles it. What's true is that the story is in the Bible, and it fills me with wonder and gratitude to read it. Despite its mopey main character, the book of Jonah has a message with a big soul. God embraces the whole world of people—animals too. We're all inhabitants of Nineveh at one time or another—alien, offtrack, displeasing to God. But God wants us back. People can be repaired and restored. There's hope for everybody: all those other people and Ninevites and my noisy neighbors and me.

PRAYER: Thank you, Eternal Spirit, for the refreshment and wonder I find in the Bible. Keep me open to its power. Amen.

[‡]Veteran religion writer and columnist, author of *A Turbulent Peace: The Psalms for Our Time* and *Against the Grain: The Unconventional Wisdom of Ecclesiastes*; member of Christ Church (Episcopal), Nashville, Tennessee.

For years I worked in the newspaper business, where deciding what's newsworthy is the obvious daily focus. Sometimes I wrote fast-breaking stories about religious controversy, other times features about compelling personalities. If it affected people's lives, provided information, or stirred emotions, it was news.

Reporters don't set out each morning to write "bad news" but to tell the best story they can that day—one that grabs readers and relays information they didn't know or identifies a trend that defines their world. News ought to satisfy the readers' questions, address their predicament, engage their sense of wonder.

In Mark, Jesus proclaims news—the good news of the kingdom of God, the ultimate story. It stopped his earliest disciples in their tracks—brothers Peter and Andrew, brothers James and John, sons of Zebedee. The news and newsbearer were so compelling that these Galilean fishermen dropped their nets and never looked back. "Follow me and I will make you fish for people." This astounding declaration—Jesus called it the nearness of the kingdom—penetrated them to the core. It filled the void they had been carrying inside whether they knew it or not. This was news to them.

Everybody carries the same void. Call it whatever: the human condition, the taint of sin, the dull ache of alienation, loneliness, dread, restless boredom. A fundamental uneasiness isn't overcome until we hear the right news and realize it's the news we've been waiting for.

The everyday news of journalism causes a brief sensation until the next day, when the furious process of fact-gathering starts again from scratch. The news encountered by fishermen on an ancient Judean shore was different—eternal, ever-renewing. It filled the disciples' deepest longing for a lifetime and beyond.

SUGGESTION FOR MEDITATION: **Ponder again why the gospel's good news is the solution to our predicament—why it's the ultimate "news."**

Psalm 62 is one of the great hymns of trust in God, a declaration of confidence in God's providence. "He alone is my rock and my salvation." Yet the idea of providence fades from society's daily grasp. The rhetoric of individualism says I'm supposed to control my own destiny, make my own reality, and be my own financial adviser. Indeed, all the roadside casinos and lotteries declare: Take fate into your own hands.

Where is God in all that?

Providence means God's plan is unfolding. God cares. Everything that happens makes sense in the end. "For my hope is from him," the psalm affirms. This is useless false piety unless I feel its truth deep inside. But how?

The psalm offers a clue: "For God alone my soul waits in silence." It's not a matter of reading the top ten theological classics for the guaranteed, well-rounded answer. I learn to trust God by keeping it simple, in good times but also in the testing times, the seasons of suffering in the dark. I approach in silence, looking neither left nor right, not comparing myself to others. Silence is the place where the truth has a chance to talk back—the truth of God the Creator holding down the fort, calling us to our better impulses, connecting us to the miraculous surge of life. That confidence crowds out other things that are eager to fill the hole—resentment, exhaustion, fear of the future, fear of one another.

God is the presence still energizing the universe even at the end of the day, long after all the high-flying answers of society (technology, fame, individualism) have collapsed in inadequacy or skipped town.

PRAYER: God of life, thank you for your gift of stillness that builds stamina and courage to face again the work of the world. Amen.

Shelves of books have been written in hopes of figuring out what Jesus meant by the kingdom of God. Did he mean a present-day reality? a future event? Is the kingdom the church itself, or a quality attainable within the very souls of believers?

In this passage from Mark, Jesus speaks plainly and from the heart. He states what is central to his message: God's reign, the rule of God, the kingdom of God has come near.

Whatever else it is, Jesus implies the kingdom is available if we get our priorities straight. The kingdom of God is not an airy metaphor but a personal and political possibility right now. That's good news. It's also hard to face.

In church life, the kingdom of God usually stands for a distant future scenario, an abstraction, a mere phrase. It's easier to be distracted by a hundred other disputes and controversies than to get down to kingdom business. When I clear away the clutter and actually read the Gospels, I realize the kingdom of God is persistent and unavoidable. Jesus refers to it some fifty times in the New Testament.

How do I find this kingdom? Jesus says it's a matter of faithful preparation: repentance and obedience. It's also a matter of opening my eyes. The kingdom is vast enough to stretch across present and future. Every day offers a new shoreline of the kingdom, a place to plant a foot, practice goodness, glimpse the divine potential. The ground rules of this kingdom are not of this world—lose your life to save it, the last shall be first, love your enemies. We're invited to leave the old assumptions behind like unneeded baggage at the border, cross to the new frontier, and take up citizenship.

These words in Mark arrive across twenty centuries—fresh, mysterious, urgent.

SUGGESTION FOR MEDITATION: What are the marks of the kingdom of God? How do I recognize them?

The Corinthians press Paul for answers: If Jesus' return is near, how must we live in the meantime? Do we carry on normally? Should we marry?

As far as we know, Paul was unmarried. Believing the Second Coming is just around the corner, he advises the Corinthians to stay unmarried if they can. But married or not, remain as you are, he tells them. Don't make big plans in the old way. The times call for a new set of values. Expect Christ to return and turn the world upside down for good and forever.

The end didn't come as Paul envisioned it—not yet, two thousand years later. Every generation is tempted to think it lives in important, world-shattering times with a ringside seat on ultimate events in the history of God's universe.

But is this the Bible's message—permission to give up on the hopeless world because the end lies just around the bend? It's hazardous to cite any biblical passage in isolation. The Bible contains its own reality checks. In John's Gospel, Jesus' first public miracle occurs at a wedding in Cana. He is among the guests when he turns water into wine. He sees no need to break up the festivities or warn people off the ceremonies of life. Jesus' message that day was that God's glory shone through him.

Psalm 62 from this week's readings also comes to mind: "Trust in him at all times, O people." That's an answer to anxiety about the future and a rebuke to one of society's great pastimes—predicting Armageddon by decoding biblical prophecy. Trust the Lord, the Bible says, not our own shaky, complicated expectations of doom—our modern tower of Babel.

Nevertheless, Paul makes his point: the times are out of joint, then and now. But God is in control of the story's beginning, middle, and end. We aren't.

SUGGESTION FOR MEDITATION: What do I fear? How do I allow my fears to affect my religious outlook?

I confess I neglected reading the prophets for years. They were too strange, intense, discomforting. Eventually I realized that was the point. They're in the Bible to tell difficult truths. They point to the irresistible reality of God, the blinding light of God's expectations, the unavoidable political and ethical dimensions of belief. It's not easy to be told I'm worshiping false gods and ignoring social justice. Amos, Isaiah, Jeremiah, Ezekiel—real prophets manage to insult pretty much everybody. Because they tell the truth.

Even Jonah, the not-ready-for-prime-time prophet, tells God's truth, despite himself. He was in no mood to bother warning the city of Nineveh to repent. But the Lord's urgency shown through him anyway: It unleashed a dramatic chain reaction of repentance and fasting among the Ninevites, starting with the king.

Today some commentators say our country is experiencing a revival of faith, spirituality, a keen interest in biblical values. A new Great Awakening might be stirring. I notice the prophets are seldom quoted. Other parts of the Bible are—by left and right, depending on the moral issue of the hour. But discomfort with the prophets continues. Their sound bites are too harsh. Depend only on God, they say, or face future judgment. Return to the true faith. Stop the oppression, stop the injustice—now.

The prophets are not all gloom. Their truth offers hope too. The book of Jonah tells the truth of God's compassion. Earlier in his adventure, reluctant Jonah converts the heathen sailors by telling the truth of his own faith in God. Later, Jonah confronts God with emotional truth, admitting his own anger about Nineveh's repentance. God answers not by smiting Jonah but by showing the divine love for all creation.

It takes courage to read the prophets. But stick around for the happy ending.

SUGGESTION FOR MEDITATION: What truth from the prophets do I need to hear today?

When will Jesus return? The subject flusters nearly everybody. Paul expected the end-time any minute ("the appointed time has grown short"), though he admitted he wasn't sure. Even Jesus himself said he knew not the hour or day of the final judgment. Only God does. The rest of us must live with uncertainty, and nobody likes uncertainty. So, since Paul's time, much anxious labor has gone to the guesswork of predicting the time of the second coming of Christ.

This speculation has caused embarrassment and heartache for the faith, driving Christians into opposing corners. One side spends great energy making precise predictions of Christ's return. The aim is to find cosmic clues in daily headlines and link them to biblical prophecies. I remember hearing the end would arrive in 1973. Correction: 1988. Correction: 1992. Surely year 2000. When the dates quietly passed, many people were disillusioned. But the disillusionment never stops the next breathless round of dramatic predictions.

Another group of Christians (mainline churches) usually keeps an awkward silence on the subject. It ought to reconsider, step into the conversation, and help the millions in the middle who aren't sure what to think. Instead, a void of silence is filled by Chicken-Little doctrines that whip up fascination and fear.

At the church I attend, the weekly public profession of faith includes the words, "Christ will come again." We should face that prospect without nervously changing the subject. Elsewhere the New Testament says the end-time will bring a new heaven and new earth, a brilliant transformation of what we know. We don't know the details. All we need to know is the news of resurrection, God's triumph over present and future darkness.

With every new sunrise, God offers us another chance to do some things right. It's another day for praise, not dread.

SUGGESTION FOR MEDITATION: What does Jesus' second coming mean? How do I find a balance of attitude between predicting it and ignoring it?

Authority and Fear

January 23–29, 2006 • *Patricia Wilson*[‡]

MONDAY, JANUARY 23 • **Read Deuteronomy 18:15-20**

We like an authority: someone who has the knowledge, education, or experience to tell us what we need to know. We're more likely to listen if she's appeared on *Oprah* or written a book or been on the cover of *Newsweek*. If he's spoken in front of huge audiences, met with popes and presidents and prime ministers, or won the Nobel Prize, that's the person we will listen to.

Authorities spring up whenever an opportunity presents itself. In today's passage, Moses tells the people who is authorized to be a prophet. Prophesying will not be a fixed office like that of the priests, but rather, a role legitimized by authority, authority given by God to the prophet. Any "unauthorized prophesying" will carry a heavy penalty.

As Christians we are "authorities." We have been given that authority by God to tell others about divine love and saving grace. We need to know that our role on this earth involves the task of being authorized prophets in God's name. Yet we fear speaking up and fulfilling this role in case we will be considered "unauthorized" in comparison to those who have letters after their names or who write the books or who appear on popular talk shows.

Does being an authorized prophet seem a little far-fetched to you? Then consider who has given you this authority—the God of gods and Lord of lords. The Alpha and the Omega. How powerful that was and still is!

PRAYER: Heavenly Father, give me the courage to speak with the authority that you have bestowed on me. Help me to move beyond my fear into the power of your spirit. Amen.

[‡]Author of eight nonfiction books published by Upper Room Books, including *Quiet Spaces*, a book of prayers for women; active member of The Anglican Parish of Port Dufferin, Nova Scotia.

"Awesome!" Two teens busily flipped through the clothing racks in the store. One pulled out a bright pink T-shirt. "Awesome!" she said. "Totally awesome!" The other girl agreed.

A pink T-shirt. Awesome. No . . . make that *totally* awesome.

No doubt, if the two girls saw a movie: awesome; a fast car: awesome; a cute boy: awesome; a new hairdo: awesome. Everything of note is now "awesome."

Awesome often appears in scripture as a word to describe God. God is awesome! The dictionary tells us that awe is a profound and humble fearful reverence inspired by a deity or by something sacred or mysterious, a submissive and admiring fear inspired by authority or power, or a wondering reverence tinged with fear inspired by the sublime. Awe and fear go hand in hand. Notice the connection between awe in verse 9 and the fear of the Lord in verse 10.

As you read Psalm 111, note adjectives used to describe God and God's works. What qualities do you notice? Do the descriptions inspire you to praise and worship God in response to God's wondrous works? Read the psalm aloud, imagining congregations singing the words in worship.

Old Testament passages often remind us of the Almighty's power. How can we function if we are experiencing such awe and fear? How can we imagine approaching the heavenly throne, even in prayer?

Jesus acts as our advocate with the Father. Through him we can stand before God, not as pitiful subjects but as God's children, welcome to take our place in the kingdom.

The awe remains, but the fear is calmed by the assurance that Jesus stands beside us.

PRAYER: **Dear God, thank you for sending your Son to be my advocate so that I may live my life in joy rather than in fear. As I walk my daily path with Jesus by my side, help me remember that he carries the burdens of my fear. Amen.**

Some people like fear. They like that swoop of terror; the on-rush of adrenaline; the heart-stopping, pulse-pounding, mind-altering feeling of fear that blots out all other thoughts. They jump off bridges, tumble out of airplanes, climb up mountains, hurl over waterfalls, and speed around racetracks. They love roller coasters, fast cars, high peaks, and dark places.

Some people allow fear to limit their lives. Phobias large and small keep them inside the house, off of airplanes, away from dogs, out of elevators, or on dry land. Snakes, spiders, and mice can reduce them to quivering masses of terror.

Today's passage suggests that fear is neither a pastime nor a straitjacket but may actually serve as a teaching tool. Through our fear of a consequence we learn to act wisely. Fear of a traffic accident will keep us driving in a safe manner. Fear of burning ourselves gives us the wisdom to put on oven mitts; fear of getting lost gives us the incentive to bring a map when we go hiking; fear of being mugged keeps us out of dark alleys late at night.

Our fear of the Lord is a fear based on the consequences that will follow if we stray from God's path—not the hellfire-and-brimstone kind of consequence that many people advocate but the consequence of being rudderless, adrift on the sea of life with no captain at the helm. Without God, we fall prey to the whims and terrors of the world around us. We have no compass to guide us, no safe harbor to shelter us. We are alone.

Such a thought is hard to imagine. So we move away from this fear toward a growing wisdom as we understand God's purpose in our lives and our place in the universe.

PRAYER: **God of all power and might, be with me this day. Continue to guide and lead me. Give me wisdom to walk the path you have chosen for me. Amen.**

There's what you know. There's what you don't know. And what you don't know you know. And what you don't know you don't know! The last of these is the most dangerous. In our arrogance and pride, we like to think that we know it all—especially when it comes to living a Christian life. After all, we tell ourselves, I've been at this game for some time now. I read the Bible. I go to church. I pray daily. There's not too much that I don't know; and since I'm aware of the small shortcomings in my knowledge, I'll continue to study and pray until I've filled those gaps too. Then I can share my wisdom and knowledge with the less fortunate.

"Know-it-all" Christians are commonplace in our churches. They feel that they have a divine right to tell others how it should be. They like to make up rules for their churches, limit freedoms, suppress thinking outside their own boundaries, and judge others. In so doing, they stroke their own egos and give themselves a pat on the back for their efforts.

However, their words and actions may turn off those who are aware of the limits of their own Christian knowledge. Their rules and guidelines may drive away the timid seekers, alienate church members, and cause factions to develop in the community. As the authorities on all things spiritual, they stifle Christian growth in others.

This passage reminds us that our knowledge will always be limited by what we don't know we don't know. If we think we know it all, we've still got a lot to learn! Paul reminds us that love, not knowledge, is the key to Christian living. If we love God, we are known by God. If we love others, we express God.

By loving, not pontificating, we drive out fear and build up our community.

PRAYER: Heavenly Father, remind me today to hold back my words when I think someone else is wrong and needs my correction. Instead, help me show that person your face by the love I express for him or her and others. Amen.

Some Christians like to live on the edge, daring to go just a little beyond the standard for Christian behavior. They might watch an X-rated movie or read a trashy novel, telling themselves that it won't affect their Christian walk. That may be true for them, but what if someone new to faith knows that they do this? That knowledge could become "the thin edge of the wedge" that leads others away from God.

Sound a little far-fetched to believe that your acts might lead someone away from faith? might cause them to stumble and fall? Impossible to think that your acts could become a catalyst for others' downward spiral? It's not a new concept.

Paul talks about the meat left over from ritual sacrifices to pagan idols. This food was often available to others in dining areas attached to the temples. Even those who didn't frequent the temple would dine there.

Paul worries that some Corinthian Christians are dining at the temple restaurants. He agrees that the sacrificial food has no power of itself. However, the notion of its sacrifice to an idol may have power over a weaker Christian who eats at the temple and then suffers pangs of conscience for doing so. If a person weak in the faith eats the food (following the example of those more mature in the faith) it may jeopardize his or her faith. The example of the more experienced Christians who seem to be authorities in matters of spirituality can imperil the faith of others.

As Christians, we must be sure that all we do, say, read, hear, or experience reliably reflects our faith. There is no room for gray areas, not because we cannot handle them in our maturity but because others may not have the same capacity or understanding that we do. Jesus himself told us that if we cause a little one to sin we might as well be thrown into the sea with a millstone around our neck!

PRAYER: Father God, help me to be aware of everything I do today, looking at these acts with an understanding of how they may affect other Christians around me. Amen.

Most people like rules. Rules make life a lot easier. In fact, one of the first things we want to know in any new situation is "what are the rules"? How long is coffee break? What time do I start? When is the report due?

Churches like rules too: who sits where, what comes when, who speaks, who doesn't, which songs are acceptable, what rituals are in place.

The rules soon turn into unquestioned, firmly entrenched laws. Obey the law, and you will be safe. Break the law, and you will suffer the consequences.

In Jesus' time, the many laws governing the lives of the Jews required professional interpreters. When these scribes disagreed, confusion among followers would result. Which interpretation was right? Who was the real authority? The laws had to be obeyed, or divine retribution would follow. Many pious Jews lived in fear of making a mistake and suffering the consequences. Jesus acknowledged this problem when he told the "experts in the law" that they burdened the people with a load they could not carry and took away the key of knowledge.

When Jesus teaches in the synagogue, the listeners immediately recognize his true authority. Jesus himself says that his teaching comes from God. What a breath of fresh air this must have been to a confused congregation. Here at last is someone who can set them on the right path.

Jesus took the laws of the Jews and reinterpreted them into a code of love that all could embrace and follow. His great commandment that we love one another supercedes all the laws and sets us free.

PRAYER: Holy Lord, help me to obey your great commandment during this day. Teach me to love as you do, and give me the grace to see your love in those around me. Amen.

Have you ever wondered about the possessed man in this story? He may have been a member of the congregation, perhaps a well-respected elder, or a mainstay of the synagogue. Perhaps he was known as difficult, prone to angry outbursts, overbearing, or demanding. Maybe he was withdrawn, sullen, morose, or anxious. Surely something about him caused others to fear him or to feel uncomfortable with him.

Until Jesus arrives on the scene, the man's demon seems well-hidden. But Jesus' appearance triggers a reaction from the demon within who recognizes the power and authority of the Holy One of God. The demon uses the pronoun "us" when he asks Jesus what he is going to do. The powers and principalities of darkness recognize the arrival of the enemy.

The demon fires the first shot in the great battle, trying to undermine Jesus by claiming to know who Jesus is, for intimate knowledge of another was believed to give power. Jesus responds by taking command of the situation. With the authority that rests on him, he exorcises the demon with a single sentence. The battle now escalates.

We have only to read the newspapers, watch the late-night news, or look around our neighborhoods to see that the battle continues today. The forces of evil still strive to undermine Christians, still continue to disrupt lives, split congregations, and destroy peace. Rather than moving toward one powerful body of Christ, we find ourselves fractured and splintered into smaller and smaller groups of self-interest and self-righteousness.

Where will it all end? We don't know. All we can do is continue to fight the powers of darkness, oppose evil, stand up for what we know to be true, and hold out against the darkening world around us. The victory will be ours; this we have been promised, but the battle is far from over.

PRAYER: Powerful God, be with me today and give me courage to continue the battle. Shield me with the power of the Holy Spirit as I go forth in your holy name. Amen.

Serving God in Times of Change

January 30–February 5, 2006 • *Dent C. Davis*[‡]

MONDAY, JANUARY 30 • **Read Isaiah 40:21-28**

On an everyday basis how can persons become aware of God's presence and guidance? How do we *know*? Knowing involves a process of becoming aware of something, often as a person ponders some experience and makes a connection between that experience and some knowledge or other experience. It is a way of finding out. How do we know of God's work in our lives?

The prophet gives us three clues: listen, look, understand. *Listen*—a common activity; but think for a minute, how carefully do we listen, really listen to those with whom we talk? Many times we don't listen well, especially when facing daily pressures. *Look*, the text says. Most of us are always looking around, but how much do we really see of the world around us? We often go through our days focusing on the next task and problem.

Understanding may hold the clue to this kind of knowing. Parker Palmer, in his book *To Know as We Are Known*, underscores the importance of understanding. Understanding is the process of learning to "stand under" an experience or phenomenon with humility, respect, and expectation. Knowing God means learning to stand under perplexing experiences, challenges, difficulties, failures, and successes with humble openness to the lessons they may teach us and the ways they may mirror God's call to us. Though God is present everywhere and in every experience, we sometimes fail to see that presence. Sometimes we have to "stand under" an experience a long time before it becomes clear, before we know that "the LORD is the everlasting God."

PRAYER: Today, O God, help us to listen, to pay attention in new ways, and to stand under the mysteries of life. Teach us your grace. Amen.

[‡]Presbyterian pastor; Director of Continuing Education, Columbia Theological Seminary, Decatur, Georgia.

Scott Peck begins his book *The Road Less Traveled* with the observation, "Life is difficult." Often a person need not look far to know the truth of this statement. For the original readers of Isaiah that was especially true. They lived in an uncertain and rapidly changing world filled with political unrest and international intrigue, warfare and violence, prosperity for some and poverty for others.

Many today also know the challenges involved in life's uncertainties at work, with family, and the spiritual life. Ours is an uncertain and often difficult world. In these verses Isaiah gives us a glimpse of God's presence in the midst of a life of difficulty. As hard as it may be to know God's presence in such times, God's grace and mercy surround us in each of the seasons and circumstances of life. Given to all, young and old, rich and poor, the prophet describes a vision of a time of renewed energy and strength even in the midst of difficulty. Strength is promised, not to fix the difficulty but to see us through: strength for the journey, energy for the long haul, hope for the future.

The Hebrew word for waiting and hoping is the same. Hope is not rooted in unrealistic optimism but in faithful activity and an active faith. Faithful perseverance and patient endurance matter. But we do not wait or hope alone. Although life is difficult, we are surrounded by strength and energy rooted in the grace of God, a grace that knows no bounds. "Lift up your eyes on high and see," the prophet says.

PRAYER: O Lord, as we experience the difficulties of life, help us to lift up our eyes. Give us strength for the journey, energy for the challenge, and hope for the future. Amen.

"Praise the LORD," the psalmist writes. *Praise* is an important word in the psalms. Often associated with worship, it has to do with glorifying God. Hallelujah means to praise God, pointing to the greatness of God often with joy and gratitude. Praise focuses on God and expresses confidence in God. We often use the word in a flippant way associating it with some momentary exultation at a sense of good fortune, sometimes not even aware that we are referring to God.

The focus of praise in the psalms is not on our good fortune or our experience—but on God. When the psalmist says, "Praise the LORD," he is acknowledging the reality of God's presence in life and expressing confidence in God's grace and mercy. When we read the word *praise* in the text it should remind us of God and of the fact that God is different from us—powerful, merciful, and just. Yet praise also reminds us that God is a part of all life. In some ways this psalm echoes a theme that would later be captured in the Doxology, arguably the most frequently sung hymn in the Christian church:

> Praise God from whom all blessings flow;
> Praise God all creatures here below;
> Praise God above, ye heavenly host;
> Creator, Son, and Holy Ghost. Amen.

The importance of praise is not the word itself or the gestures used to express it or even how often we say the word. What is important is our attitude. We tend to think of life in self-centered ways. We focus on our problems and what we believe are the solutions. Another option exists—God's option. "Praise God" is a way of saying that whatever our experience, whatever our perspective, there is more, always more. There is God. Praise God.

PRAYER: Teach us, O God, how to praise you, how to focus on your grace and majesty and not just our needs. Amen.

Living in our world as parents, supervisors, coaches, and employees we learn to measure success by results: such things as production, grades in school, and good behavior. According to the psalmist God takes pleasure in those who fear God and hope in God's steadfast love. Note what is *not* said—no reference to success, good grades in school, or even good behavior. Success, measurable outcomes, and results are less important than fear and hope.

The Hebrew word for fear can refer to fear as we commonly understand it, but it also refers to a process of revering; of respect, awe, and even amazement. Fear in these verses is not rooted in judgment but in awe and amazement at the gracious mercy of God. To fear God is to focus on God, first and foremost.

Hope is the process of living into the future even when the reality of the present doesn't quite measure up. The amazing message of this text is that God takes pleasure not in what we do or accomplish but in the mere fact that we focus on the mercy, grace, and loving-kindness of God. Awesome!

PRAYER: Gracious God, help us not to judge others or ourselves as the world does: by the outcomes of our efforts. Rather fill us with fear that we may see your grace and possibility in our lives and the lives of others. Give us hope that we may know your love. Amen.

This passage offers a blueprint for ministry, service in the name of Christ. Ministry is the responsibility and calling of all—young and old, ordained and lay—who are disciples of Jesus. How does Paul suggest that we approach ministry?

Of the many themes in these verses, four stand out: humility, service, accommodation, and focus. *Humility*, the bedrock of Christian service, acts without intent to seek reward, compensation, or recognition. *Service* is the basic activity of discipleship. In talking about service, Paul uses the word *slave*, a person who is compelled to act for others. Paul saw himself as a slave of Jesus Christ. Paul believed that he was compelled to act by his allegiance to Christ.

Service addresses the needs of others, not ourselves. Learning to attend to others, the process of *accommodating* oneself to their needs and circumstances, becomes important. So Paul can be as a Jew to win Jews; he can make himself weak to win the weak. In each case he puts himself at the service of others. He can engage in an extraordinary flexibility of activity and service because of his *focus* in ministry. Paul's focus on the gospel provides the lens through which he views his life and the needs of others. Directing his actions through the lens of the gospel, he can accommodate himself to people in varying situations. His message is clear: under the guidance of the law of Christ and with clear focus on the gospel, we are to serve others in humility, accommodating ourselves to their needs in order that they might hear the gospel and believe.

But there is more. Paul uses his own life story as an example for his reader. Ministry is more than words. It is how we live. What we do this day will be an example of who we are and what we really believe. What will people say about us?

PRAYER: Lord God, in our service give us humility of intention, willingness to accommodate ourselves to the needs of others, and a steadfast focus on the good news of Jesus Christ. Amen.

This text is about service and compassion. Those touched by the grace of God are called to touch others, and that touch can be the context for healing. Life delivers us "chance cards," events and experiences we don't count on—like illness.

Peter's mother-in-law lies ill. Most know the challenges of illness, either personally or in the lives of friends and loved ones. Illness often comes at the most inopportune time, even for Jesus. But Jesus responds. He takes Peter's mother-in-law by the hand and lifts her up, just as friends have done for us and we have done for others. Healing comes through touch. It is personal.

Today physicians, medications, and procedures that would have seemed miraculous to ancient people assist in our healing. But the personal touch remains central to the healing process. The text also reminds us that compassion and service are more than occasional projects or activities. No sooner does Jesus address the need of Peter's mother-in-law than here comes a dozen more, in fact dozens more, in fact all the sick in the whole town.

Imagine what it would be like to have the whole town crowding around your door. Sometimes life feels that way. Healing happens in the synagogue, at home, and on the street corner. In the story, healing happens because of Jesus' compassion and his willingness to get involved, extending himself unselfishly for the benefit of others. Over and over we are given opportunities to respond by serving. In serving we often have the opportunity both to heal and to experience our own healing. When an occasion arises for you today, will you see it? How will you respond?

PRAYER: Lord God, help us to learn compassion. Help us to see the needs of others. Help us learn what it means to respond in a personal way. Give us awareness, commitment, and perseverance. Amen.

Discipleship and ministry embody compassionate service. But faithful ministry requires more than service. Reflection also plays a part. In the midst of the busyness of ministry Jesus seeks time alone, time for prayer and renewal. In the morning, long before dawn, he leaves the house, going off to a lonely spot to pray.

Many times when my children were younger and our family went on vacation, I looked forward to driving in the darkness before dawn. In the midst of the activity and excitement of vacation, these early-morning hours lent themselves to quiet reflection and a time of renewal. Some of life's lonely spots are places we seek; some are places we encounter. Some lonely places are made lonely because of our experiences of loss of loved ones or jobs or changes in health. Whether the experience is of our own choosing or not, Jesus' example suggests that the lonely places in life can become places of prayer and renewal.

Renewal can occur in many ways. In these verses Jesus engages in prayer, the act of placing oneself at the disposal of God's Spirit. Prayer takes many forms: active or reflective, spoken or silent. Whatever the form, prayer is often a time of reflection, a time of new awareness, a process that helps us see things differently.

Time away from routine and moments of quiet make space for us to hear what God may have been trying to communicate for a long time. But we missed God's voice because we were too busy to hear. These verses call us to take time apart from the busyness of life. God speaks to us in many such times—a trip, a moment of silence, a new routine, a time of challenge. Look for God's presence in times of change.

PRAYER: Lord God, in the busyness of life help us to take time away. Renew us in prayer and rest. Strengthen our resolve to serve and our passion to know you. Amen.

The Race of Faith

February 6–12, 2006 • *Kyunglim Shin Lee*[‡]

MONDAY, FEBRUARY 6 • Read 1 Corinthians 9:24-25

Paul uses a metaphor of athletic games that was well-known in Corinth to instruct the Corinthians about Christian living. "Everyone who competes *for the prize* is temperate in all things" (1 Cor. 9:25, NKJV)." The New International Version translates this verse: "Everyone who competes in the games goes into strict training." Paul does not speak about how to *run* the race but how to *prepare* for the race. The athletes develop self-control and self-discipline prior to the race. This training allows them to run the race in such a way as to win it.

In the Christian life we cannot expect victory over temptations and difficulties unless we have prepared ourselves through ongoing discipline. We need not wait until we actually face problems to work on self-control and self-discipline. When we discover a need for it, it may be too late. As in athletic contests, the outcome of the race of life depends on preparation.

Paul counsels discipline and self-control "in all things," not just in specific areas. Athletes know the importance of strengthening *all* muscles, so they may focus on developing a weaker area. It is also true in the Christian life. The *Book of Discipline* of The United Methodist Church encourages us to "work out" in four areas: worship, devotion, justice, and compassion. While maintaining what we excel in, we need to work to overcome our weaknesses to lead a healthy and balanced Christian life.

Victory takes enormous effort and constant preparation. But when we discipline ourselves for the race of faith, we receive a crown that lasts forever.

SUGGESTION FOR MEDITATION: What area of my life requires my attention and strengthening?

[‡]Vice president for Church Relations and Student Development, Wesley Theological Seminary, Washington, D.C.

The great games at Athens began an honored tradition in athletic competition that endures today—a tradition that the readers of Paul's letters to Corinth would have known. In Paul's time, people highly valued athletics. Every large city boasted an arena.

Consider yourself as part of Paul's metaphor of sports. Do you identify with the athletes, with the coaches, or with the trainers? It takes a lot of effort to train an athlete or coach a team. But on the athletic field the coach or trainer does not go through the same training or endure the same discipline as do the athletes. Though coaches and trainers participate in some training, they do not work at it with the same intensity.

But in the Christian life, we are all athletes. We are all runners. Some of us help train others, but everyone participates in the same race. No one is exempt. As Christian leaders we need not only to help others but also to discipline ourselves.

As a leader Paul talks about his own discipline. He uses strong terms to describe the intensity of the discipline. When Paul talks about being enslaved, he is talking about a self-imposed slavery. He counsels absolute self-discipline and self-control with no exceptions or excuses. Paul, who set a very high standard for himself, is still concerned that he not disqualify himself because he fails to live the code and life required by the gospel. The message here is to all athletes running in service of the gospel: Vigilance, discipline, and rigorous training are essential, day by day.

Paul set high standards. He exercised discipline "in all things": in a course of training focused on the final goal and in a commitment to honor the body as the temple of God. He did so in order to bear witness to Christ. We too must set standards for ourselves—standards that honor the rigors of the life of faith and that honor our bodies as temples of God.

Prayer: Make my body and my life a witness to your love and grace, O God. Amen.

Naaman, a great military commander, has won victory over Israel and by doing so has gained the king's favor. He seems to have everything anyone could desire: power, prestige, recognition. But he has a serious problem: he suffers from a skin disease (the text calls it leprosy), which carries with it a social stigma. This skin disease may keep Naaman from being in the company of persons he enjoys. Most folks work to keep their distance.

The story of Naaman's healing begins with a suggestion from a young servant girl, a captive from Israel. It is unusual for a powerful person like Naaman to pay attention to a captive slave's suggestion and to act on it. But he is desperate, so desperate that he not only carries the slave girl's suggestion to his king but willingly travels all the way from Damascus to a prophet in Syria.

When he comes before the ruler of Israel with his letter of introduction (after all, his country had recently defeated Israel), Naaman meets a panicky king. Despite Naaman's extravagant gifts, the king responds with despair. He takes the letter as a literal demand that he cure Naaman, and he knows he cannot. Naaman does find his way to the prophet's house and is healed (though through a different process than Naaman had imagined).

Naaman's story is full of colorful characters: Naaman, his country's chief military commander, desperate to find a cure; the captive Israelite slave girl—ever faithful to her God; the Israelite king—panicky and despairing, fearing the worst and failing to rely on God at all.

We too may find ourselves afflicted, socially stigmatized by some condition, behavior, mental attitude. Like Naaman, we may be desperate. We may be in difficult circumstances, like the captive slave girl. Will we remain faithful no matter what? Like the Israelite king, we may lose sight of our faith altogether in some hard situations. Will we panic? Where will we turn?

SUGGESTION FOR MEDITATION: **Remember Naaman, the captive slave girl, and the king. Ask God to be present with you no matter what circumstances you face.**

The healing of Naaman is a significant story—Jesus even mentions it: "There were many in Israel with leprosy in the time of Elisha the prophet, yet not one of them was cleansed—only Naaman the Syrian" (Luke 4:27, NIV). How does this important healing occur?

Naaman comes to Elisha, the prophet of his enemy's country. However, Elisha's response upsets him. He goes "off angry and [says], 'I thought that he would surely come out to me and stand and call on the name of the Lord his God, wave his hand over the spot and cure me of my leprosy.'" It seems that Naaman's willingness to listen and trust has vanished into thin air.

Naaman expects Elisha to do something about his disease; he isn't open to entertaining unconventional methods. Elisha asks Naaman to take action on his own behalf, which will bring about his own healing. Naaman has taken action and responsibility for his healing by coming to Israel. Now he seems unwilling to pursue some foolish notion.

Many times we look to others to heal our hurts or solve our problems. We wait for others to take action on our behalf, perhaps becoming angry with them for not doing what we expect. Naaman did that too. But he changed his mind and his attitude. He followed the prophet's easy instructions, and his skin disease disappeared. We, like Naaman, need to do what we can for ourselves before focusing on what others should do for us.

PRAYER: **Dear God, help us live a full life in the power that is ours rather than relying on others to do for us. Amen.**

Today's story about the leper and Jesus is as much about prayer as it is about healing. The leper approaches Jesus for healing but instead of making a request for healing, the leper makes a statement about what he believes. He knows Jesus' reputation as a healer, and he affirms that by saying, "If you are willing, you can make me clean" (NIV). The leper recognizes Jesus' power and understands it to be from God. He approaches his prayer with the sure knowledge that Jesus has the power to heal.

That's the way we must pray too. If we stand in the assurance of Jesus' power, we can kneel to pray as the leper does. This man's appeal reminds us of Jesus' prayer in Gethsemane, "Father, if you are willing, take this cup from me; yet not my will, but yours be done" (Luke 22:42, NIV). Jesus' prayer, like the leper's, came from a deep need. Jesus' prayer also came from a deep understanding of God's power and ability and the desire to follow God's will.

The leper had heard of Jesus' power, and he believed in it enough to begin his prayer with a testament to that power. Jesus, in one of his darkest moments, began his prayer with the same faith statement, the acknowledgment that God would hear his prayer and could deliver him from his suffering.

It's sometimes hard to pray with confidence in God's power, especially when our need is great. The leper willingly acknowledges Jesus' power, which has a dramatic impact on Jesus. The leper's prayer moves Jesus' heart. Though touching the leper is unnecessary, Jesus decides to violate the law by touching him. He reaches out his hand, touches the man, and says, "I am willing. Be clean" (NIV). Trust, and feel God's touch on your life. Pray with confidence. Even when it appears that God does not answer your prayer, remember the compassion that Jesus showed the leper. Remember the compassion that God showed Jesus. Remember the compassion that God shows us.

SUGGESTION FOR MEDITATION: What prevents us from praying to God, "If you're willing"?

After healing the man with leprosy, Jesus sternly warns him to tell no one about the healing. Why would Jesus do that?. The Bible doesn't say. Only one thing is clear: Jesus had a strong emotional response to the healing of the leper. The English words "sternly warned" don't begin to express the depth of Jesus' words to the man. The Greek word used here carries much more force and violence, meaning "to drive away" or "to cast out."

So why would Jesus do that? Faithful believers and Bible scholars through the years have guessed at reasons. Perhaps the culture's willingness to blame God for the man's leprosy angers him. Maybe the leper had been driven to ask Jesus for healing because a priest had already refused to declare the man clean. Or, perhaps Jesus didn't want miracles to divert people's attention from the message he preached.

Whatever the reason, the man who has initially asked about Jesus' willingness to heal him disobeys Jesus' will. He goes out and spreads the news. He does not hesitate; he feels he cannot be silent. He turns his back on the demands of the law and turns his face toward witnessing to Jesus' power. The man has experienced Jesus' compassion and healing touch.

The love we receive from Jesus goes far beyond mere touching and healing. Jesus gave us his life to save us and to free us. What shall we do with that freedom? With that freedom, let us go out and tell the world what Jesus has done for us.

SUGGESTION FOR MEDITATION: How has Jesus healed you? How are you witnessing to the work of Jesus in your life?

We all have found ourselves in difficult circumstances. Some of us might be experiencing adversity right now. When have you felt that you were going down to the Pit? What situation triggered that feeling?

The psalmist feels like he is in a grave. In great misery he cries for help, and God delivers him from desperation, bringing him joy and thanksgiving. How does that experience of salvation affect him?

Once the psalmist had thought that he would "never be moved." Now he learns that he has misunderstood. He has a new awareness that it is God who has "established me as a strong mountain"—that God gives life and preserves life. And he also learns that God responds when called upon. God can turn his sorrow to joy. It is God to whom he can turn in trust.

How much do we trust God? When we find ourselves in the pits, to whom do we turn, to whom do we call out for help? We cannot be completely insulated from misfortune, no matter how hard we try or how much we worry. What matters is not how much we have or how secure our life is, but how much trust we have in God. Only our deep trust in God's purposes for our lives can sustain our happiness and peace—even in trying situations.

This new awareness prompts the psalmist to say that he will give thanks and praise to God forever. He will still face difficulties, but his faith and trust in God allows him to navigate life more confidently. God has turned his mourning into dancing, clothing him in joy. May it be so with us.

PRAYER: Almighty God, free us from anxiety over what we cannot control. Restore our deep trust in you so that we can always rejoice and be thankful. Amen.

God's Yes!

February 13–19, 2006 • Gene Cotton[‡]

MONDAY, FEBRUARY 13 • Read Psalm 41:1-3

I am not a theologian or a professional minister. I am a pilgrim of the faith; one who looks for truth every day, one who stumbles, and one who rejoices when God's light shines through. Walk with me in this season of Lent as we look at who God is calling us to be and who we really are.

"How blessed is [the one] who considers the helpless"(RSV). Rosa, the driver of the minivan, her husband, Sergio, and their five children were unaware of the tragedy about to befall them. A woman, sound asleep, crossed the median and hit them head-on. Rosa's husband was killed and two of her five children were seriously injured. One of Rosa's children had been a student in my wife's third-grade class that year. The news of the accident traveled fast and hard. The family had no money; they were in the country illegally; no one was going to speak for them.

God calls us to consider the helpless. I cannot tell you that I heard God speak to me aloud, but I sensed an inward nudging to make a difference in that family's life. That was over two years ago. Through the generosity of friends, churches, and community organizations, Rosa has paid her rent each month; the phone and lights are still on; and they have food on their table.

Do we do these things to be blessed? Of course not. But I cannot tell you how much richer our lives have been since Rosa and her children have become a part of our extended family. We celebrate birthdays and holidays. We eat at their house; they eat at ours. We hug, we laugh, and we cry together. But most of all, we see God in one another, and we are blessed.

PRAYER: God, open our hearts to your celebration of considering the helpless. Amen.

[‡]Singer-songwriter, community activist, and environmentalist; member of Christ United Methodist Church, Franklin, Tennessee.

How many sermons have we heard about this paralytic and his four friends? We have made much of their camaraderie and how the four helped their paralyzed friend. But what if they weren't his friends? What if they didn't know him very well—or even at all? It is possible, even in a small town like Capernaum, for people not to know one another. What if one of those four just happened to see the paralyzed man, recruited three of his friends, and carried the man to see Jesus because they believed something good might happen?

A cafeteria worker in the school where my wife teaches told us about an eighty-three-year-old woman who lives near us, but whom we did not know. She had raised her grandson from infancy and, in his forties, he recently died of cancer. We learned that the grandmother was quite poor and was worried sick about being unable to pay the funeral bill.

I spoke with the funeral home and the staff agreed to reduce the balance by twenty-five percent if I could raise the rest within two weeks. I called some area churches and organizations and told the story to a few friends. I was amazed at how God brought people to me who said they would help. On Thanksgiving eve, I called the grandmother to tell her we had enough money to pay the bill. She could hardly speak. The day after Thanksgiving my wife and I went by the grandmother's trailer and gave her the "paid in full" receipt. What a Thanksgiving moment it was standing on her porch, all of us in tears, as she could hardly let go of us with her hugs.

God calls us to be present in this world, even to the stranger. Were these guys the paralytic's friends? I can't prove that they weren't. . . . but you can't prove that they were.

PRAYER: God, open our eyes to your needy world. Amen.

Paul had planned to visit the Corinthian congregation but changed his mind. Evidently, he is responding to some complaints and criticism because of his alleged indecision. Isn't this just like the church? I had to laugh when I read this passage. It reminded me a bit of that old *Saturday Night Live* skit with the "Whiners." They were a couple who would complain and whine about anything and everything. Their negative attitude was overwhelming. How destructive this can be. We can become so self-righteous in our finger-pointing, criticism, and whining that we miss opportunities for ministry that God is trying to reveal to us.

My friend Norman edited a magazine published by one of the denominations headquartered in Nashville, Tennessee. He had spent several years trying to make his marriage work. After months of counseling and therapy, it became clear that divorce was his only option. When he mentioned to his bosses that he was going to get a divorce, they told him that he would have two weeks from the date he filed to clear out his office. Just when he needed support from the church the most, he got the rug pulled out from under him. Why do we do that? Why is the church so willing to kick and stomp folks at the time of their greatest vulnerability? Instead, we should support them in love, whether their pain was self-inflicted or beyond their control.

Paul points to God's yes in Christ. In this season of Lent, let us find someone, some individual, some family—maybe someone in your family—who needs to be wrapped in the arms of God's yes. Let us embrace this person and stand firm with him or her as Christ stands firm with us. And in doing so, we will reveal the glory of God.

PRAYER: God, help us to be your yes in the world. Amen.

The Jews coming out of exile are headed back to Palestine. It was a time of uncertainty and confusion. Their world has been torn apart, and they are starting over with great pain and suffering. In the midst of this traumatic time, God reminds them of the divine presence and forgiveness. Ever had a time in your life when you experienced uncertainty and confusion? pain and suffering?

I was standing next to our car leaning over the fender, trying to fix my windshield wiper in the rain on the interstate, when a man dozed off and sideswiped the car going seventy-five miles per hour. My wife says I did this beautiful somersault down the interstate. I broke legs, ribs, hips, and just about everything else. I was able to prop myself up to see my wife trying to calm our two-year-old son. I looked back at her and shrugged my shoulders as if to say, "I need this like I need a hole in my head." I can't explain it, but I had this incredible sense of God's presence as I lay on the pavement waiting for the ambulance.

At the time of the accident, my wife and I were headed out on a two-month concert tour that would have provided our income. I didn't know what we were going to do. Several days later in the hospital while reading the paper, my wife burst into tears. She was feeling bad about our situation when she came across a story about a highway patrolman who had been killed instantly the day before while writing a ticket.

I am a "new thing" that God is doing. Every day is a "grace day" for me. It truly is amazing how God provides and "grows us" amidst the pain and confusion of our lives. I would not be the same person without having had that experience in my life.

PRAYER: God, help us to see the difficulties and uncertainties in our lives not as liabilities but as opportunities to learn more about who you want us to be. Amen.

"Sticks and stones may break my bones, but words will never hurt me." Not according to the psalmist. After acknowledging his sin and asking for mercy, he proceeds painfully to talk about those who speak evil about him and slander him. Even his trusted friend betrays him. While some people often interpret verse 9 as prophecy having to do with Judas's betrayal of Jesus, it serves as a reminder of the divisive world we live in today. Who among us cannot remember a heated discussion over recent political issues and elections with close friends or family members? Ever taken a stand for or against something and felt the sting of a friend's tongue? Our response can either throw fuel on the burning fire or suck the very life out of it. Unfortunately, most of us enjoy the heat.

I had never gotten along very well with my mother. A tension between us seemed to turn holiday visits into horror stories. A number of years ago we left her home after an Easter visit. Pulling away from the house I said to my wife, "I will never come back here again." However, my relationship with my mother was an area of my life where God was always "nudging" me. Finally, it dawned on me one day that all I ever did was respond and react to her words. I realized that the only meaning her critical, negative, or argumentative words could have was the meaning I would allow them to have. If I would quit allowing them to mean anything, they couldn't have an impact on me.

Did it happen overnight? No. However, over a period of several years I found myself wanting to visit my mother. She hadn't changed, but I found myself in a new relationship with her because of the way I perceived her words. *Integrity* and *presence* have new meanings for me.

PRAYER: God, bring new meanings to relationships with our adversaries. Amen.

Jesus has just healed the paralytic and forgiven his sins. This ticks off some scribes who want to know who he is to forgive sins. Jesus turns it back on them and says, "Which is easier, to say to the paralytic, 'Your sins are forgiven,' or to say, 'Rise, take up your pallet and walk'?" It's an interesting question. Which is easier: to forgive or to cause an action that brings about a tangible result? I think it's easier to forgive than to get into the business of healing. Maybe Jesus is telling us that we need to do a little of both.

I think it's easier to forgive people, then walk away or distance ourselves from them than it is to do the hard work of healing relationships. How many times have you heard, "I'll forgive him, but I can't forget"?

I'll never forget the night I came home after being on the road for several weeks. Sitting down at the kitchen table, my wife told me that our daughter, who was away at college, was pregnant. You could have stuck a knife in my gut, and it would not have hurt as much. I mean, how could she? Why? After all we had taught her! What about her future?

I went around for the next four days kicking doors and screaming at God. I'm glad I had that time before our daughter came home that weekend. When she arrived on the front porch, I was able to put my arms around her, kiss her cheek, and say, "I love you, I love you, I love you."

It's not easy, this business of healing. Sure, sometimes it is instant, but most of the time it's just plain hard work. I'm so glad God understands slamming doors and loud utterances.

PRAYER: God, teach us to forgive, and help us understand the importance of healing. Amen.

In a real sense, I think Jesus is saying that to all of us: Pick up your mat, take all of your junk, and just get out of here and go home. Go amaze someone! You're now forgiven! Most of us are so paralyzed by the trappings of our lives that we wouldn't recognize a miracle if it stared us in the face.

But it doesn't have to be that way. God is waiting to do miracles through us, to show us miracles, and to amaze us as well as those to whom we would minister. These miracles turn up in the simplest of things to the most profound.

The small rural town where I live sponsored a turkey shoot at Thanksgiving. Now they don't shoot real turkeys. They shoot targets, and the one with the most holes gets a voucher for a turkey at the local store. Floyd, a developmentally challenged middle-aged man from our community, was watching from the sidelines. Someone paid his fee so he could shoot too. That "someone" also got to all twelve of the other shooters to aim at Floyd's target instead of their own. Floyd could hardly contain himself when he found out he'd won! He was hopping and skipping and running around waving his voucher in the air. *Yes!*

Daily miracles bear witness to God's work in our lives. We can all recall times when we too have said, "We have never seen anything like this!" I drove the twenty-six-year-old young woman to the airport to meet her birth mother for the first time. She had been given up for adoption and was finally meeting her mother all these years later. As her birth mother walked into the concourse area from the plane, the two embraced; we were all full with tears of joy. The young woman finally turned to me and said, "I finally look like somebody." This is the miracle! This is what God is waiting for us to discover: who we really look like.

PRAYER: God, help us to discover that we can look like you. Amen.

Open Our Eyes; We Want to See!

February 20–26, 2006 • Linda H. Hollies‡

MONDAY, FEBRUARY 20 • Read 2 Corinthians 4:1-3

I'm an early morning prayer walker; during the daylight hours it's easy to see. But when I had to go out one night, I asked my spouse to "wander" with me. We were seeking a specific address, and it was almost impossible to view numbers in the dark. Finally, we decided to go up and knock on the door. Thank God! It was the right house, for we could not see the address in the night.

Few of us see well in the dark. However, the good news of this passage is that our personal relationship with God through Jesus Christ allows us to see! Regardless of our current situation or circumstances, we have the light of God's word to keep us focused and seeing clearly at all times.

Paul the apostle felt certain that false teachers were challenging his credentials and causing God's people to doubt and stumble, as in the night. The apostle affirms the bright glory of the new covenant of Jesus Christ. God desires that we allow our lights to shine in the nighttimes of our present world.

False teachers are continually present. Imitations continue to present themselves as truth. And "the god of this age has blinded the minds of unbelievers, to keep them from seeing the light." A light bulb exists solely to brighten areas of darkness. By the holy living of our lives we help to dispel the power of the "night."

We stand in the glorious presence of God as we live, breathe, and proclaim the good news through our lives. Wherever we might be, we are the lights of the world.

SUGGESTION FOR MEDITATION: Walk your prayer time and really see today!

---

‡Wife, mother, United Methodist pastor, author, lecturer, seminar designer, and spiritual director; living in Grand Rapids, Michigan.

When I was young, there was a stigma to being called "four-eyes." The choice of eyeglass wear was slim pickings; there was no glamorous variety of frames, tints, or contacts! I wanted to be pretty and hip; but to see to read, I had to wear glasses. Whenever possible, I would leave those ugly things behind, a habit that continued into adulthood and my early preaching years.

The apostle Paul wants to encourage this community of believers at Corinth in their life and witness to Jesus Christ. He tells them they have the very best type of "seeing glasses" as they look at the present world through the eyes of the gospel of the glory of Christ.

The community's responsibility upon seeing the light is to proclaim Jesus as Lord. Their lives are to bear witness to their "insight" into the way, the will, and the word of God. Paul wants the Corinthians to allow the light of God in their hearts to be visible in their associations with the outsiders for whom the gospel is still veiled.

We experience the glory, the brightness, and the fullness of God when we come to see Jesus as the Christ of our salvation. Our vision is corrected. Glasses are not necessary! We may leave them behind. Our authentic relationship with the expressed human glory of God allows us to become "Sonbeams," reflecting the Light!

SUGGESTION FOR MEDITATION: Through what kind of "glasses" do I view the world? Am I seeing through eyes of faith with eyes open to God's truth?

PRAYER: Dear God, help me focus on you and your word. Make my light shine so that people will know, honor, and glorify you. Amen.

We went to a wedding, and the bride was beautiful. For a few minutes, I could not figure out what was different about her appearance. Finally I realized that the bride was not wearing a veil. She wanted to see her beloved, and she wanted him to view the love shining in her eyes.

Elisha refuses to wear a veil over his eyes. The school of prophets at Bethel, Jericho, and those at the Jordan all tell him, "Surely, Elijah will be taken!" Yet Elisha alone walks with Elijah the prophet, steadfast and unmovable. He wants to see what will transpire with his mentor. They have a mutual love affair with God. Elisha will not walk away.

After crossing the Jordan, Elijah asks, "Tell me what I may do for you, before I am taken from you."

Elisha wants a double portion of the spiritual abilities that Elijah has displayed. He wants to work more diligently for God. Traditionally, the first son would receive a double portion of the father's inheritance. Elisha does not seek fame or fortune. He desires ministering abilities from a pure heart that loves God. In a time of spiritual decline, he wants to win souls.

Elijah tells Elisha that he has asked a difficult thing. "Yet, if you see me as I am being taken from you, it will be granted you; if not, it will not." Only God can grant the request that Elisha seeks as the new successor.

When the chariot of fire comes, Elisha sees them and witnesses the lifting up of Elijah into heaven. Elijah, like Enoch, became another forerunner of the Resurrection story.

Elisha asked; he kept his eyes open and received his request.

PRAYER: **Resurrecting God, help us to see afresh the needs of those around us. Open our eyes! Amen.**

I will never forget the day that my youngest adult son said, "Mom, the color just went out in my right eye!" The effects of glaucoma had robbed him of his sight. Despite many surgeries to retain the sight in his other eye, he continued to have difficulty with his vision. When my son Grelon Renard Everett died, he was legally blind.

However, Grelon had an inner sight that was acute, aware, and relatively well-adjusted. Despite his physical challenges with the ravaging effects of diabetes, his relationship with God remained steadfast and firm. He continued to see that God cared for him, and he offered God his best worship and his highest praise. The Sunday before his death, he was in worship, living in God's strength, God's beauty, and God's power. His life situation did not rob him of his high praise of God!

In this passage the Almighty calls us to consider our acts of worship. The Creator of heaven and earth summons us as believers to look into our hearts to see what actually prompts our actions. I have heard it stated that there are none so blind as those who refuse to see. Our motives for worship are in question. God calls us to have an inner-vision check!

At the time of the psalmist, people were bringing sacrifices without considering the meaning. The disciplines of gathering, hearing the scriptures read and interpreted were being practiced without any follow-through action. God calls, "Gather to me my faithful ones, who made a covenant with me by sacrifice!"

The Perfect One sees our imperfections: those we confess and those we attempt to hide. God will not remain silent although we pretend to be blind and to behave as if all is well. Spiritual blindness will bring God's sure judgment.

The good news is that we can change and offer our best praise in the worst of times. But first we have to see ourselves as God sees us.

PRAYER: Consecrating God, my heart is open before you. Help me to see myself. Amen.

There was a time in my life when we lived on the "other" side of the river, a distinct landmark in our city. We lived on one side and "they" lived on the other during the days of segregation. But civil rights and changed hearts came along, and those of us on the "other" side finally got the opportunity to cross the bridge and view life from a different perspective.

My first memory of integration was a holiday picnic in the park from which African Americans had formerly been denied access. My grandparents took my siblings and me, along with one of our uncles. Now Big Mama, my grandmother, was not big at all. We grandchildren had always experienced her as a petite woman with a soft and loving voice.

Big Mama took us all to get ice cream cones, lining us up like little soldiers. Standing in line, a tall, well-muscled man, who felt that we were yet out of place, pushed past us to get in front. This big, booming voice came from behind me, "Don't you see me and my children standing here."

There was a major transfiguration, transformation, and change that occurred in our presence! Big Mama's clothes did not become dazzling white like Jesus' did, but she assumed a new identity that day. She, like Jesus, asserted her understanding of herself as a child of God. The petite woman became a major force to be reckoned with. The man meekly apologized and moved out of the way. I kept watching for Big Mama to do it again. But, like the disciples, I never again experienced this amazing change.

Jesus' transfiguration was a pivotal moment in the lives of those three disciples. Yet, there was more suffering and even death to come on the other side of the event—glory doesn't last always! And glory and suffering cannot be separated from our Christian experience. Both form and transform our salvation story.

PRAYER: **Transforming Agent, change me today! Amen.**

Folks tell us to believe only what we see and one-half of what we hear. But today's passage tells us a story that was difficult to believe even while being seen.

The same Jesus that the men have been walking, talking, eating with, and watching has changed before their eyes. They see him in his fullness. They see him in a different light. They see him in the company of Elijah and Moses, great saints from ages gone. These witnesses stand there with their mouths wide open, bedazzled!

The disciples see the same Jesus in a new light. The same Jesus has transformed into "more" right before their eyes. These privileged three: Peter, the mouth, and James and John receive a preview of the Resurrection. These three become the first ones to experience the glory, identity, image, and full power of the Most High God. The same Jesus is no longer the same! All three are terrified! But Peter jumps right in, filling in the uncomfortable and fearful space with words. He wants to build three abiding places for these "special" men. Like us, perhaps he longs to preserve the moment.

Small moments of change fill our lives. In our world, even change is changing! Transforming opportunities come our way every day. Pregnant possibilities await us each new morning. The question becomes, Can we see them?

How often do we allow the opportunities for change to slip past while we hold to a time that is already gone? How often do we build a shrine and live there, allowing God's continuing revelations in our lives to go unnoticed. Jesus Christ continues to show up in our lives in startling, surprising, and mysterious people and events. We, like those three disciples, have to be fully alert and ready to see.

PRAYER: Change-maker God, don't allow my next transforming opportunity to pass me by unnoticed! Open my eyes. Amen.

TRANSFIGURATION SUNDAY

The words *once upon a time* indicate that a story is about to be told. These words raise the awareness of young and old alike. As Peter, James, and John watch the Transfiguration unfold, I'm sure that each of them hears these words afresh.

"Once upon a time" there was a great man of God whose name was Moses. He had been given the Law directly from the hand of God. Moses had seen God do great miracles: parting the Red Sea, feeding a multitude with manna, and providing water in the desert from a rock. Moses was a man of history with God.

"Once upon a time" there was a great prophet of God named Elijah. He was the first in a long line of prophets that God used to bring Israel to her spiritual senses. Elijah had seen God perform great miracles: causing fire to fall from heaven on water-drowned wood, confronting kings and queens, stopping rain, and healing foreigners. Elijah's history with God included Elijah's provision by a nasty raven and a Gentile woman.

When these two come to stand and to talk with Jesus, a new story makes its way into the visible world. Peter, James, and John are eyewitnesses to the Messiah's linking the covenants made with humankind by God. Old Testament Law and prophetic promises find fulfillment in Jesus.

Finally, the disciples understand that Jesus is not a reincarnated figure from the past. They recognize God's power at work in Jesus in this transforming moment. Their eyes are opened. At last they can see.

But just in case the three don't quite get the message, God speaks: "This is my Son, the beloved; listen to him!" The story continues! Praise be to God!

PRAYER: Storytelling God, help me to see the story that you are unfolding in my life. My eyes are open; I'm willing to change. Amen.

The Gift of Newness

February 27–March 5, 2006 • *Wendy M. Wright*[‡]

MONDAY, FEBRUARY 27 • **Read Genesis 9:8-17**

The back alley leading into the parking lot of my neighborhood supermarket is not a place I generally expect to experience an epiphany. But as I circled around the edge of the huge store, skirting the trash receptacles, I caught sight of a man leaning against the wall, his face turned upward with a rapturous look. Was he looking at something or carrying on some strange interior monologue? I glanced up quickly, but the angle of my windshield prohibited me from following his gaze.

I pulled into the lot to see a couple with their little girl standing by their parked auto, smiling and pointing upward. Following their outstretched arms, I found myself canopied by the soaring arch of a brilliant double rainbow. A light rain had just trailed off and left in its wake an astonishing multicolored, twinned ribbon of light. News quickly spread, and complete strangers smiled and greeted one another: "Have you seen it?" There we all stood on a dreary Tuesday afternoon in an oil-smeared parking lot, an inarticulate joy spreading among us.

We are fast approaching the most solemn season of the church year: Lent, that time when we are drawn with Jesus into the mystery of suffering and death. It can leave us, as does our encounter with our own and our world's suffering, mute. Yet we are promised at the culmination of the season that on the other side of suffering is a joy so deep that its presence will surpass our capacity for words. May the rainbow, with its resonance of the promised covenant, prepare us for the journey to come.

PRAYER: Prepare us, gracious God. Give us eager eyes. May we see the outstretched arms of the prophets who direct us to the mystery of your covenantal love. Amen.

[‡]Professor of Theology and holder of the John C. Kenefick Chair in the Humanities, Creighton University, Omaha, Nebraska.

Depending on the year, my birthday often falls just after Lent begins. So do I fast for a day then eat chocolate cake for the obligatory birthday week? Feast or fast? Celebrate or solemnize?

The Jerusalem Bible's heading for Psalm 25 is "Prayer in danger." While we may not personally be in situations of immediate peril (the potential overdose of chocolate aside), nevertheless there is a liminal quality to this liturgical time we enter together today. Lent calls for conversion, and true conversion involves pliable, flexible selves, selves ready for change. The unmaking and remaking of ourselves, the constant conversion to which the Christian life urges us, is felt keenly now. Any invitation to spiritual transition can be fraught with peril. We may fail to heed the invitation. We may hear it but, busy about the thousand things we are always busy about, we may fail to engage at all. We may confuse God's call to us, assuming that *our* Lent should look like someone else's. We may think that our unique challenge can be answered with a generic response.

The traditional name given to this threshold of Lent is Shrove Tuesday, a day named from the ritual of shriving, or confession of sin. But it is also Mardi Gras, "Fat Tuesday," the day observant Christians—not wishing to waste food—would eat up all the meat, fats, eggs, and milk products forbidden during Lenten observance. It is likewise the day popularly celebrated with abandon: the feast before the fast, the revelry before the discipline, the wildness before the asceticism. In its own way, Mardi Gras points to the liminal nature of the cresting season: the unmaking that precedes the remaking, the reversal of roles, and the suspension of rules. It is important to remember that this day is both for shriving and for celebration. To anticipate the season we need to be ready for change and be ready to be changed.

SUGGESTION FOR MEDITATION: **Practice your own "shriving." Also spend some time being mindful of the ways that God has been present during your life. Celebrate this. Let this sense of belovedness give you courage to enter the Lenten season.**

Ash Wednesday

The university campus on which I teach swarms with handsome young people. During the frigid winter months they bundle up in down and fleece or wrap in woolen hats and scarves—indistinguishable bodies protected against the cold. But when a hint of spring breezes through, to a person they strip off their heavy outerwear and emerge, chrysalislike, as colorful, summer-clad creatures. It is not only the love of warmth that prompts them to so display themselves but the instinct to show off the newest fashions, impress their peers, be admired by others. Graduation day, no matter what the weather, always brings out the filmiest fabrics, the prettiest frocks, the sleekest blazers.

Here we are, on this most reflective day of the church calendar, Ash Wednesday. And what do we hear proclaimed? Gather. Fast. Pray. Remember that from dust you came and to dust you will return. Repent and heed the gospel. And then, do this in secret. Do not parade your piety before others.

We can easily allow our faith to be a matter of convention, even a matter of self-promotion. But we observe the season not simply because it is expected of us. We pray not so we may be seen attending worship. We fast not so we may be admired for our devotion. We repent not so we may be perceived by ourselves and others as godly. We enter this day with deep humility as individuals and communities. The imposition of ashes reminds us of our mortality, fragility, and painful incapacity to live fully into the gospel life. We strip off all the figurative garments that cover us—our accomplishments, our pretenses, our excuses, our illusions. When we are seen as we appear before God, both unconditionally loved yet profoundly flawed, we are ready for this day.

Prayer: Dear Lord, may your example, as one who came to us naked in a manger and who died naked on the cross, accompany us today. May we begin to see ourselves as you see us. Amen.

Of the many memories I have of my father, our spur-of-the-moment walks in the rain is one of my favorites. Growing up in the desert climate of southern California, we did not have much experience of rain. When rain came it tended to come in the form of a downpour, flooding the city streets and washing the coastal hills of Malibu into the ocean. Inevitably, my father's response would be to wrest my mother and me out of bed or away from the living room sofa, wrap us in coats, cap us with headgear, and set out for a long walk in the rain. Thunderstorms do not accompany California rains as they do in the Midwest, so it was with impunity that we would trek around the hilly streets near our home, drenched and laughing, until the skies cleared. There was always something cathartic about these walks in the rain. The smog-clogged air would be refreshed; the parched home gardens, barely surviving on the meager ration of moisture allowed by civic water-use control, would drink in the welcome rain from heaven. And I would feel newly washed, cleansed, renewed both by the energized ions in the air and by the spontaneous adventure of our wet and wonderful family walks.

The season of the church year into which we enter this week calls both for solemnity and for a joyful, adventurous spirit. The psalmist who cries out to be washed white as snow also cries out for a clean heart in which joy is renewed and praise becomes possible. The psalmist implores God for tenderness, for mercy, for the gift of newness.

SUGGESTION FOR MEDITATION: **Each Lent is different. We may need to let go of something. Or we may need to expand our vision, taking into consciousness the searing needs of others, especially the marginalized. Or this Lent our preparation may be more subtle. We may need to ask for and seek a renewed capacity for joy, for hope, for the ability to continue the journey of fidelity. We may need to replenish our spirits in whatever way possible. May we be open to the surprise of God's gentle mercy that rains down and washes us each year anew.**

My husband arrived home from an archdiocesan social ministry commission meeting agitated. As an exercise in mutual understanding, commission members had played a game designed to raise awareness of ethnic and class issues. The culturally, ethnically, and economically diverse group started out on the same line. Then, as various statements were read, members stepped either backward or forward, according to the instructions given. "If you are white, take one step forward." "If you completed college, two steps forward." "If your family has an income of less than $20,000, three steps backward." "If you are a woman, one step backward." My husband, long engaged in social justice work, was not surprised by the implications. He alone of all the members never had to step backward. He, a white, middle-class, well-educated male, ended up far ahead of his compatriots on the scale of privilege. What agitated him was the later angry encounter with a new member, a woman of minority ethnicity, who railed against him, "How could you ever understand my experience?" He felt caught, knowing that he in fact could not claim to stand in her shoes but nevertheless pained by the hostile rebuff.

Later that week we attended our faith-sharing group. The topic was forgiveness, and my husband decided he should make an effort at reconciliation. The commission had actually instituted a practice of individual members getting together outside of the scheduled meetings. He nervously called and invited the woman to join him for lunch, and the next week returned home with a joy-filled tale: as she listened to his story and began to know something about him, whatever had separated them was dwarfed by the common ground they shared as Christians dedicated to the realization of a just world. The cleansing of the heart before God cannot take place unless the heart is right with one's neighbor.

SUGGESTION FOR MEDITATION: With whom do you need to reconcile? Begin the process of making your heart right with your neighbor today.

When little children are frightened of the dark or of being alone in a strange bedroom, they instinctively call for a parent to be with them. Somehow, the comforting presence of one who knows and loves them as no one else does is enough to calm even the most fearful of little ones.

There is something analogous but not at all childish about Peter's words in his letter to Christians in the diaspora. These words are also for us. Our immersion in the waters of Christian baptism has conjoined us to Christ's death and resurrection in a radical way. Even as we move into the season of dying, of letting go, of being un-made and re-made, we have the assurance that we do so in the presence of someone greater than ourselves. We are accompanied, comforted, held, known, and loved with unimaginable tenderness.

SUGGESTION FOR MEDITATION: Allow yourself to call up your deepest fears that surface in this season. What causes you to cower, tremble, and cry out? Bring the Lord into your fears. Recall the promises made from ages past. Remember too the more personal ways you have been accompanied through darkness over the years. Close with a prayer for trust and confidence in God's faithfulness to you.

SUNDAY, MARCH 5 • Read Mark 1:9–15

FIRST SUNDAY OF LENT

From childhood, the desert has held a lure for me. To the super-ficial gaze, the desert landscape is barren; but when you spend time there, its rich variety becomes evident. As the sun goes down, it comes alive with many kinds of creatures. The desert is a wonderful, complex ecosystem that yields its mysteries slowly over time.

Since the fourth century the church has observed forty days of preparation before the great feast of Easter. And on the first Sunday of those forty days, the church proclaims the story of Jesus' temptation in the desert. Set in high relief, with its spare, stark language, Mark's temptation scene strikes us with its auster-ity. Washed in the waters, Jesus hears himself addressed as beloved son; then, he is immediately driven out into the wilderness.

So it is with us. To be a Christian is to be incorporated into the body of Christ. We enter that mystery through baptism. As in the Gospel narrative, we are called to the fullness of our bap-tismal promise through a kenotic process: temptations, struggles, reevaluations, new and often painful learning and unlearning. To be a Christian is to be driven out into the desert. Yet the desert is not barren but full of life, a rich and complex environment that reveals itself as beautiful, healing, life-giving, and restorative. So too our Lent. We are called to sacrifice, to self-denial, to radical reorientation. But we are called thus because we are beloved sons and daughters, because we are infinitely loved and called to more than we can presently imagine.

SUGGESTION FOR MEDITATION: **Consider the struggles or temp-tations you bring into this Lenten season. Know that you are not only present to these struggles with the beasts but with the angels as well, as was Jesus. Into the barren loneliness of your desert, bring the knowledge that you are deeply loved because you are a child of God. Allow yourself to explore this desert place in its unexpected richness, its potential to bring you to insight, healing, and new life.**

All in the Family

March 6–12, 2006 • *Steve Harper*[‡]

MONDAY, MARCH 6 • **Read Genesis 17:1-7, 15-16**

People view the "end times" in two basic ways. Some emphasize those left behind, excluded from life in the new heaven and new earth. Others focus on those included in God's "forever family." This week's readings take the second approach.

The Lord tells Abram and Sarai they will be the parents of "many nations" (NIV). Their descendants will come until the end of time. God will make an everlasting covenant with this family. In fact, covenant-family imagery will dominate the biblical narrative. Stronger than biological relations, spiritual kinship will develop over the centuries among children of the covenant.

Abram cannot take it in. He laughs—even before Sarai does. Neither of them can imagine how it will happen, especially at their ages! But that's the point. If they could make it happen and figure it out, they wouldn't need God. God's family is more than they can create, and so God arranges things to insure there is no doubt as to who is bringing it to pass. Yet God does not bypass people in creating the covenant community. Abram and Sarai are part of the miracle through very natural means.

God still works that way, and it is still too much for us to take in. We still laugh with amazement. Clearly, we cannot create a covenant family; God must do it. But that does not relieve us of responsibility. Rather, God invites us to become cocreators with God who always has "many nations" in mind.

PRAYER: Dear God, what a vision! So large, I know I cannot create it—yet, so real, I know I must be part of it. Make me part of your family. Amen.

[‡]Vice President and Professor of Spiritual Formation at Asbury Theological Seminary, Orlando, Florida.

When I was a child, I pretended to be a famous cowboy star. It seemed logical to have this cowboy's name, so I asked my mother if it was possible to change my name. Even though she told me it was, nothing ever came of it. Deep down I knew I was just pretending.

However, God is not pretending. A new name is in order because Abram and Sarai constitute a new family. From then on, others will be given new names when they become children in the family of God. Names matter. Parents-to-be select a name with care. Sometimes it's drawn from the family tree. At other times, the name conveys a message. We tell our children, "This is your given name"—a name they did not choose; one chosen for them to wear gladly for the rest of their lives.

Names identify us. They connect us to a larger family. Some people spend years tracing their genealogy, and most of the time they come away with a richer and fuller sense of how they fit into the scheme of things—including links to heroes and outlaws! But, we're all in the family.

In today's passage, name change reflects life change. They will be Abram and Sarai no more, because their lives will never be the same again. Their new names signify a new nature, a new status, and a new place in the work of God. From now on, they are Abraham and Sarah.

God delights in giving you and me "new names"—names that signify new life and new participation in the covenant family. And unlike the pretend names of our childhood, our new names as God's children become our way of telling the world we can never be the same again.

SUGGESTION FOR MEDITATION: If God were to give you a new name to reflect your deepest participation in the covenant family, what would it be?

Family life is a mixture of joy and sorrow. Being in God's family is no different. We experience brilliant mountaintop days as well as dreadful dark-valley days. Our passage today is one of the down days—a day of suffering and sadness. Following two celebratory psalms, this one tells us to hold on even when things take a turn for the worst.

Jesus prayed the opening verse of Psalm 22 as he hung from the cross. But we too have used those words when bad things happen to us or to those we love. A quick look at today's newspaper will reveal who is using the words right now. In today's reading the psalmist exhorts Jacob's many descendants to persist in glorifying God. God has not despised their affliction or left them to face it alone. God's promises are not reserved for the prosperous; those who go down to the dust are benefactors of God's goodness as well.

Families make it through hard times. Somehow we survive. Members of God's family do too. We may cry out in anguish, but somehow we make it through. The pages of history confirm the story. We ourselves have cried out to God, and we have been heard. The psalmist reminds us that this is the story known all over the world by all the nations. We do not suffer alone; we suffer "in the family"—with countless others (past and present) who have clung to the name "God's child" and found the sufficiency of grace.

PRAYER: Ever-present God, thank you for the assurance that you never leave us or forsake us. Thank you that we do not suffer alone but always in the family. Amen.

When my father died in December of 2003, I became the heir of his estate. What had been his for eighty-seven years was now mine. The amount was insignificant; what gripped me was the realization that tangible dimensions of his life had passed to me. He had been the family patriarch, but now I was.

Thoughts like these swirled in Paul's mind and heart as he sought to connect Abraham and the Christians in Rome. And to do it, he used "heir" language. But what had the Roman Christians inherited? Paul did not mean a literal genealogy, because Abraham was a Jew and many of the Romans were Gentiles. No, they had become heirs of Abraham's best gift—his faith.

We come into God's family not by genetics but by belief. Abraham's descendants are like him—not racially but spiritually. Just as he was accounted righteous because of his faith, we become God's children as we profess faith in Jesus Christ. (See also John 1:12-13.) God could look down the corridors of time and see the centrality of faith for every person, and thus Abraham could be called the father of many nations.

Abraham is long gone, but the opportunity to believe remains. Faith is the determining factor for anyone, anytime, anywhere. Faith is multiracial, multicultural, and multidenominational. We may differ in many ways, but we are all in the family "by faith."

The greatest thing my dad left me was the legacy of who he was—not what he possessed. Similarly, the possessions of Abraham are lost to history, but "who he was" remains—a man of faith. In his day, Abraham's faith made him an heir of the promise. We become heirs of the promise in the same way.

PRAYER: Gracious God, thank you for the invitation to become an "heir." Like Abraham, I want to profess my faith in your promises—the best of which is that Jesus Christ is Savior and Lord. Amen.

Faith places us in the family of God. We are God's creations by nature; we are God's beloved sons and daughters by faith. But we must not think that having faith or expressing it comes easily, nor must we think that faith is only words.

The "righteousness of faith" does not come without struggle. The temptations not to believe are powerful, and Abraham embodied many of them. He wrestled with intellectual doubt. He knew how old he and Sarah were. The story simply did not make sense. He must surely have also wrestled with visionary doubt. The "father of many nations"? How could he have possibly seen that reality, given where and how he was living when God first spoke the promise?

Almost certainly Abraham wrestled with fulfillment doubt. Even when the story got underway with Isaac's birth, it must have seemed cruel and ludicrous to "put an end" to the promise the way God seemed to be asking him to do it. I believe Abraham must have thought he was losing his mind.

But the struggle and doubt had a point: that faith might rest on grace, not effort. Abraham would "father many nations" by invitation, not initiation. He had to believe God, not himself. Abraham had to be fully convinced that what God promised, God could deliver.

We come into the family the same way. Our profession of faith is not nearly as easy as some believe it is or make it appear. We struggle with our versions of doubt. We struggle to believe God rather than ourselves. When we meet other family members, we meet people with sweat on their brow, not teacups in their hands. Faith is always connected to struggle at some time and in some way.

PRAYER: Dear God, save us from the seduction of "easy believism." Let us look at Abraham until we realize that our faith will similarly arise and live in the midst of doubts and struggles. Amen.

Self-denial is a characteristic of life in the family—human or Christian. Without it, chaos results. With it, potential for purpose and resolve surface. Today's passage is Jesus' first prediction to the apostles concerning his pending suffering, death, and resurrection. His companions fail to grasp his words in all three dimensions. Because each of the areas Jesus describes can only be experienced by self-denial, the disciples fail to understand. Yet, it is impossible to be "in the family" without self-denial.

But we must realize that denial of self is not cancellation of self. That kind of self-denial is not Christian. Jesus never called for the annihilation of self but rather the abandonment of self. Dead people cannot "take up" anything, nor can they "follow" anyone. Only living people can.

I marvel at how this passage has been misunderstood and poorly proclaimed. Many have viewed it as a "death" passage, rather than as a "life" one. During the season of Lent, people often speak of what they are "giving up." But notice that today's reading centers more on what we are "taking up."

Of course, self-denial includes renunciation. Most of the time our lives are too full of stuff and sin to be able to take up much of anything else. Certain things have to go, but that is not the ending point for denial; it's the starting point. The aim is what we ultimately gain, not what we lose. We celebrate the season of Lent properly when we move beyond "giving up" to the life of "taking up" the work of ministry. God's ultimate concern is what we have in our hands, not what we have dropped from them.

PRAYER: Inviting God, we need to give up some things but not as an "end" of the journey. Show us what we can "take up" for Lent, in order to become the people you want us to be. Amen.

SECOND SUNDAY OF LENT

Life in God's family is vocational and missional. Christ invites us to take up *our* cross and follow him. The word *our* contains the message. Sometimes, people refer to a burden or a bother as *my* cross, which stems from the notion that a cross must be painful or unchosen. So, they reserve the phrase for those people or tasks that are thrust upon them and that hurt them in some way.

What does "our cross" really mean? Painful situations and frustrating relationships can sometimes be our cross, but Jesus surely had more in mind than that. Jesus' cross was his mission—the reason he came into the world. So, when he tells us to take up *our* cross, he is telling us to discover our mission and live it out.

So many people trade in their deepest selves for shallow images they hope will impress others. Some spend their lives trying to be like someone else. Still others perform their tasks without any sense of fulfilling a particular purpose. In these ways, we fail to take up our cross.

The season of Lent gives us sufficient time to ask, "God, why am I here? What am I supposed to do with my life? What is my cross?" We may find that, like Christ's cross, ours will contain painful aspects, but we will discover that more truly our cross is about purpose and calling.

We enter into the family of God when we willingly live our lives (not someone else's) for God's glory. Then we take up our cross and follow Christ. God has no greater joy than seeing beloved sons and daughters find and fulfill their reason for being through the ordinary days of their lives.

PRAYER: Cross-giving God, you have a purpose for me. Help me to find it, accept it, take it up, and follow Jesus. Amen.

Bearing Witness

March 13–19, 2006 • Barrett Renfro[‡]

MONDAY, MARCH 13 • Read Psalm 19:1-6

The witness of creation

This psalm declares that the physical world witnesses to the power and wonder of God. The heavens declare the glory of God. The skies proclaim the work of God's hands. The voices of nature never cease their praise of the divine.

Let me recount my first experience of God. My mother had secured a teaching job in Texas during the Second World War. My father was somewhere in the South Pacific. I was in the seventh grade. How lonely I was in this new east Texas town! My father was not there; my friends had been left behind. We were Cumberland Presbyterians; no such denomination existed anywhere in town. It was a desolate fall and winter of 1943.

In the spring the Methodist women came around and asked mother if I could attend Vacation Bible School. They came by the house each morning for two weeks and took me to Bible school. In the morning we studied the Bible, and in the afternoon we worked on a project.

The Vacation Bible School also had night sessions. At the end of the evening we all sat on the church steps and sang songs together. I looked into the heavens on those dark nights, and the heavens sang God's love back to me. The witness of God's great creation brought me close to God.

PRAYER: Dear Father, I thank you for the witness of your creation, for the way you spoke tenderly to a lost boy who needed your love. And most of all I thank you because you have never stopped that witness. Amen.

[‡]Retired United Methodist clergyman living in Austin, Texas.

The witness of the law

The law, statutes, precepts, commands, and ordinances of God are perfect, trustworthy, right, radiant, pure, sure, and precious. This law makes for good living. It revives the soul, makes the simple wise, gives joy to the heart, and lights the eyes. It endures forever and is like pure gold.

Psalm 19 eloquently testifies to the greatness of the law. C. S. Lewis, English scholar, novelist, and Christian apologist, considered Psalm 19 the greatest poem in the book of Psalms, as well as one of the most beautiful writings in the world.

God provides life-giving guidance and instruction. Living by God's law makes us whole. Inevitably we will make mistakes. But verses 12 and 13 ("But who can detect their errors? Clear me from hidden faults.") offer remarkable words of grace. They remind us that we can ask for forgiveness when we fail and that God will forgive us out of love. The familiar words at the end of the passage sum it up: God is our rock because all our strength comes from God. God is our redeemer because each of us experiences that strength personally.

The love that moved God to create us is the love that moved God to give us the law to live by. The Israelites experienced that love, as did the psalmist. It is the love we know through Jesus.

SUGGESTION FOR PRAYER: **Pray these words, "May the words of my mouth and the meditation of my heart be acceptable to you, O Lord, my rock and my redeemer." As you pray, give thanks for the strength and love of God in your life.**

The witness of the Ten Commandments

Nearly everybody knows something about the Ten Commandments. Because of the word structuring, many people think the commandments are negative; but they are intended to be positive. If we follow these commands, life will be good and significant—not easy, but good and significant.

If the Ten Commandments enable this true life, a reversal of the commands describes the false life. If you want to ruin your life you can do just that by following the list of the Ten Commandments reversed.

1. You can have all the gods you need to secure your future. You can be polytheistic because that is your nature.
2. You can make idols of anything that exists anywhere, and you can worship them as your gods.
3. You can curse God.
4. You can work seven days a week because economics is the meaning of life.
5. You cannot respect your parents or elders because they are old and know nothing about your life.
6. You can kill.
7. You can have sexual relations with anyone you please.
8. You can take as your own anything you want.
9. You can lie anytime you choose.
10. You can desire anything your neighbor has for your own.

The choice is ours. The Ten Commandments lead to holiness of heart, mind, and life.

PRAYER: Dear God, help me live a life that pleases you. It may be hard and difficult, but it is truly rewarding. May all I do be in the name of the Father, Son, and Holy Spirit. Amen.

The witness of God's power

God's "eternal power and divine nature" (Romans 1:19, NIV) have been clearly seen. This power and nature shows through in the things God has made. Interpreted broadly, that means not just the physical creation but also the events of life. So the message of the cross as a life event is foolishness to those who do not know God through God's divine power and nature.

For those who see behind the events of life and acknowledge the power and nature of God at work, all aspects of living offer direct experience of God. Paul indicates that in both Jesus' cross and ours, we stand in the presence of a power and nature that we do not manipulate but must come to terms with as the meaning of life.

My own experience of life events bears this out. In June of 1997 my youngest daughter was diagnosed with malignant melanoma. Over the next few months no treatment had any effect on that vicious and fast-growing cancer. In late December the doctors sent her home with hospice care. She died, and we buried her in February 1998.

Amy's death became a life event called "Glory Observed." In the death of my daughter I received the opportunity once again to stand before the passingness of all things. I experienced the power and nature, and, yes, the love of the Great One who is revealed in all creation.

What is foolishness? What is wisdom? This scripture from Corinthians turns wisdom on its head and tells us that things— good things, bad things—are not always as they seem. The power of God claims us in the midst of all the circumstances in our lives and sustains us in mysterious, sometimes unknowable ways.

PRAYER: O God, may we see you at work in the events of our life. Amen.

FRIDAY, MARCH 17 • Read 1 Corinthians 1:20–25

The witness of God's wisdom

God's wisdom is not a philosophy of life. In fact God's wisdom according to this reading is not about thinking or reason at all. Mental activity is the wisdom of the world, and the Holy One has made God's self known in another manner. Heady people want rational proof. At its best, life is unreasonable. Life presents us with puzzling situations that seem to defy our ability to reason out an answer. If we seek to live our life through human wisdom, we receive the promise of an impossible journey.

In the garden of Gethsemane Jesus realized that the answer lay in no answer. The answer comes in the utterance of, "Nevertheless." He prayed, "Father, if thou art willing, remove this cup from me; nevertheless not my will, but thine, be done" (Luke 22:42, RSV). That "nevertheless" represents the supreme act of obedience, totally disregarding self-sufficiency and human wisdom and placing the answer in the hands of God.

Paul says we preach the human answer crucified and God's answer accepted. The "nevertheless" as an act of faith says God knows more about me and my needs than I know.

I first experienced this "nevertheless" act of faith when I was five years old. My daddy parked the 1934 Ford in the backyard of the house. As he walked toward the house I would climb on the porch rail some six feet from the ground. When he came into range I jumped into his waiting arms. I never thought that he might move out of the way and that I would fall on the ground. I loved him and knew he loved me; I trusted him to catch me every time. That's the way of life: a never-ending series of jumps into the arms of God. Now, go ahead and jump.

PRAYER: Father God, we trust you to be there when we jump. Amen.

The witness of the clean Temple

From Capernaum on the north shore of the Sea of Galilee, Jesus comes south along the Jordan River, then up to the center of government and religion: Jerusalem. He goes to the Temple, the house of worship. What happens next is both chaotic and prophetic. The scene in John is dramatic. Jesus herds animals and people out of the Temple. He turns over tables and scatters money. This event wreaks havoc on worshipers at the Temple that day.

The story is familiar and it sounds straightforward: Jesus sees abuse, and he acts against it. But his action in this passage is a bit more complicated. Worship in the Temple involved the sacrifice of animals. Because people came from all over to worship, the sale of animals at the Temple was a necessity. There were, to be sure, abuses in the system. The system took advantage of the poor, and the exchange rate for currency favored the money changers. But Jesus confronts not just the abuses in the system; he confronts the system itself. In cleansing the Temple, Jesus throws everything into chaos. The scandal of this action, Gail O'Day writes, is "not Jesus' anger that proves his humanity, but the authority this human being claims for himself through his words and his actions."

So this is the radical truth: Jesus, the son of God, requires that we recognize his authority and power in our lives and in the life of the church. If habits in our lives or practices in our churches get in the way of following Christ, we must "turn the tables over" and focus again on Jesus.

PRAYER: Dear God, who enters our lives and makes them clean, help us rid our hearts of the clutter that hinders our love and action for you. Let your Holy Spirit live with and in us that we may truly serve you. Amen.

THIRD SUNDAY OF LENT

The witness of the holy life

After the witness of the clean Temple, the question arises about Jesus' authority to do such things. The sign he offers is his resurrection from the dead after three days. Yet he speaks in parables, "Destroy this temple, and in three days I will raise it up." Unknown and misunderstood by the questioners, Jesus is referring to the temple of his body. "But the temple he spoke of was his body" (John 2:21, NIV).

Yes, those in the Temple want a sign. They question Jesus' authority. But they are not seeking a sign of revelation or understanding. They want a sign from Jesus that proves his authority. Jesus answers, but the questioners gain no satisfaction.

Jesus has the authority to challenge the Temple system because he is God's revelation on earth. The last verse of this passage from John points clearly to what we, as believers, must now do: we must remember the stories of Jesus and claim them as our own so that we may witness to the world.

This challenge comes to us personally, but it also comes to our churches. We must be willing to discern where and when our churches have become overprotective, stubborn, or resistant to change. Maybe we need to renew our worship. Perhaps our religious leaders have become stubborn and require challenge. Maybe the structures of our churches have become a hindrance that stands in the way of seeing our mission in new ways.

The Fourth Gospel declares time and again that Jesus is the Word made flesh. We too bear witness to that truth in our prayer life, in our daily lives, and in our lives as members of our faith community.

PRAYER: Gracious God, you have shown me your power, your authority, and your love. Help me to live today as a witness to you. Amen.

Beacons of Light

March 20–26, 2006 • *Cristian De La Rosa*[‡]

MONDAY, MARCH 20 • **Read John 3:16-17**

These two verses summarize the relationship between God and us as people of faith. God loved us eternally and came to this world not to judge but to save us! God's grace toward us is so abundant that we cannot contain it.

During this month of March many communities of faith celebrate Central America Week and note the life and ministry of Oscar Arnulfo Romero of El Salvador. During the civil war in El Salvador, government forces killed him because he opposed injustice and violence against the marginalized. He died at the altar of a church, blessing the elements for Communion.

Archbishop Romero comes to mind at this time because of his incredible love for those who suffered. In spite of danger, he accompanied representatives of the church to proclaim God's grace. Terrorist tactics against religious leaders during that time were brutal. Many faith communities worldwide witness to the courage of people like Romero.

Romero made his decision in response to God's incredible gift of Jesus. He would proclaim to others God's grace in the face of danger and violence. That decision, made in response to the witness of Jesus, finally cost him his life.

God's love for us does not condemn us or judge us but saves us. That was the love Romero tried to live out. He offered God's grace, not judgment. Romero's self-giving showed itself as courage—even to his enemies.

SUGGESTION FOR MEDITATION: The kind of love Romero lived reflects the love and grace God has for each of us. How does God call you to respond to that love today?

[‡]United Methodist clergy; coordinator for The Hispanic Youth Leadership Academy at the Mexican American Program, Perkins School of Theology; teacher at the Hispanic Institute of Ministry, Dallas, Texas.

TUESDAY, MARCH 21 • Read Ephesians 2:4-10

The writer of Ephesians packed the letter with densely worded notes of thanksgiving, praise, and spiritual counsel. Today's reading offers exuberant words. They praise God even as they direct us in the history of God's revelation. We may find ourselves striving to analyze these sentences to gain a deeper understanding of the author's passion for Christ. Here we find words that attract us to the light of Christ.

Phrase upon phrase move us toward Christ. The word *grace* shows up at least three times, and this passage reminds us that God is "rich in mercy." Indeed, these few verses define grace by speaking of the gift of salvation. Nothing else matters.

The image of a vase with three red roses came unsummoned to mind as I pondered the passage. How did this image connect with the passage? In prayerfulness I began to recognize that the gift of flowers indicated beauty, which begins to reveal the deep love of God. Like the image of the vase with flowers, I know that the love of God comes unmerited and certainly unearned. One rose reminded me of God the creator. A second rose represented Jesus Christ. The third rose reminded me of the presence of God at all times and in all circumstances. I confess that I sometimes need that reminder.

This beautiful image took me in turn back to Ephesians: "In the ages to come [God] might show the immeasurable riches of his grace." When I read this passage, I hear voices singing in praise. I want to sing praise to God who is rich in mercy, and I want even more for others to come to the light of Christ and to join in this chorus of grace. The creative power that brought beautiful roses to life is also my Creator and Savior.

SUGGESTION FOR MEDITATION: Give thanks to God for the many roses you have experienced. Free yourself to receive images of grace that this passage generates. After reflection time, join in a song or hymn of praise to God for the wealth of mercy that we inherit.

This reading seems to be an Old Testament version of the expression used by many congregations to express the goodness of God. The preacher might say "God is good," and the congregation responds, "All the time." Then the preacher repeats, "All the time," and the congregation affirms, "God is good."

Psalm 107 begins with a similar call-and-response. Pilgrims traveling to Jerusalem for the holy festivals probably sang this psalm as they journeyed. They traveled through desert and wilderness. They came from many different places and lived among strangers, and yet they traveled to their spiritual home on earth. Imagine the thoughts of these pilgrims as they cross the wild places in which their ancestors also sojourned. Hear the priestly call to the company of travelers and notice the way in which the psalmist speaks of those "gathered in from the lands." The pilgrims who join in this psalm are scattered people, people who have experienced exile in one form or another. The psalmist invokes the traditional understanding of the four corners of the earth: east and west, north and south. While we may find ourselves too modern to think of the "four corners of the earth," worshiping traditions as distinct as Native American and Eastern Orthodox refer to gathering the people from these four corners. These directional signs point to a longing for home by those who have experienced oppression and exile—whether the oppressive memory of Egypt for the Hebrew people or other times for other peoples.

The psalmist draws us to the light of God. We find strength in gathering together. We recognize, as did those ancient pilgrims, the encouragement of community and the ways in which we experience grace in community. We remember the ways in which God redeemed and redeems us.

SUGGESTION FOR PRAYER: **Pray for those who feel unable to experience the goodness of God, especially those who are in exile. Give testimony today to the goodness that comes from God to each of us.**

THURSDAY, MARCH 23 • Read Psalm 107:17-22

The psalmist sets a scene before us. The message of God seems distant; humanity does not listen to its creator. Yet the psalmist smiles because the people cry out, and the Lord saves. He bears witness to the presence of a faithful God, who promises redemption and announces a new reality for the people of God.

The psalmist captures the prophetic essence of redemption rooted in God's faithfulness toward humanity. In our deepest affliction, often caused by our own doing, we can call on God with the assurance that God will deliver us.

Always we are tempted to rely upon ourselves, our strength, our might. We may rely upon our medicinal power or our financial power. We may think that our security rests in military power or the power of a strong fence surrounding property or nation. Take time to think about the greater context of these few verses from Psalm 107. They are set within the context of pilgrims who have a collective memory of exile. The psalm is set among people who live and breathe the stories of the Pentateuch. They know the stories of Creation and Fall; of Babel; and of Abraham, Isaac, and Jacob.

Walk with the pilgrims toward the holy city. As you walk, remember those who trusted God, those who were sick and cried out to the Lord. Remember how God saved, healed, and delivered. Let these people stand as beacons of light who mirror the grace and mercy of God.

SUGGESTION FOR MEDITATION: **Consider your experiences of healing and deliverance. Thank God for the mercy and grace that you know.**

These verses stir up questions. We may wonder whether our complaints will bring on worse problems in the way that the complaints from the Hebrew people brought on poisonous serpents. We wonder whether this story gives us insight into God. Maybe this passage teaches us more than we know about humanity and about ourselves.

It is all too normal for us to fear something new, even if the something new is better than the old. In Numbers 21 the people show their fear of freedom and perhaps fear of the responsibility that accompanies freedom. They demonstrate a collective amnesia because they have forgotten the harshness of life in Egypt. They do not remember the brutality of Egyptian overseers and the repetitive burden of making bricks without straw. They do not remember the infanticide or Pharaoh's army. They do not remember God's liberation of them. All they seem to remember is yesterday or perhaps a moment earlier this day.

It takes a harsh sign to point the people toward God. Poisonous serpents bite them. In despair, they seek God just as Psalm 107 describes. Healing occurs, and the people move on in faith.

How might this passage connect with your life story? How does it connect with my story? Do I need such a harsh reminder to seek God's grace? I pray not. Better that I wake each day with the words of praise: "This is the day that the LORD has made; let [me] rejoice and be glad in it!" (Ps. 118:24). Better that I take time throughout the day to remember God's mercy and grace for all people and that I offer intercessory prayers. Better that I remember that God's mercy endures in my sickness and in my health. Better that I end each day with prayer and reflection on discipleship. Better that I open myself to the embrace of God's love.

PRAYER: Loving God, help me reflect the light of your love throughout this day. Amen.

SATURDAY, MARCH 25 • Read Ephesians 2:1-10

Have you ever accomplished something you never believed you could? Many times I have walked out of a meeting, an event, a presentation, or a difficult situation praising God and giving thanks with the statement, "It had to be you, God!" In such situations God's grace becomes tangible, reminding me anew of the reality of my unity with Jesus Christ. I acknowledge that from circumstances of brokenness, fear, and imperfection God makes me shine in the light of Jesus the Christ.

God brings us back to life and renews us through the process of formation and transformation when we accomplish things beyond our own strength and capability. The letter to the Ephesians invites us to join in praise and in witness! As Christian disciples, we witness to God's grace as we share with others our relationship with God. We share that relationship as we bind the wounds of broken people and give water to those who thirst. We remember that every encounter with another person invites us to witness to our relationship with God. We witness in silence and in speech, in action and in word. By grace we have been saved—and by grace the world is saved!

Each of us has a purpose in life. Ephesians 2:10 says that we are "created in Christ Jesus for good works, which God prepared beforehand to be our way of life." We sometimes think that life's divine purpose applies only to famous people, to great heroes of the faith. But Ephesians is adamant that all of us—every one of us—is destined for a life of love and good works and that what we do with our lives matters. By grace we have been saved through faith. By grace we have been saved to live lives that glorify God.

SUGGESTION FOR MEDITATION: You, God, are rich in mercy and love. You made us in your image and called us to live in Christ. May your grace reflect through my life this day. Amen.

FOURTH SUNDAY OF LENT

God always finds a way of redemption. John 3 reminds me of a favorite song of students at the Hispanic Ministry Institute. The song names us as the people of God, redeemed and called to proclaim the good news of the one who came to save us. When we sing this song, faces shine and convey the meaning of these words about God's incredible grace.

As we read this Gospel passage, we remember also Numbers 21. There Moses raised a pole with an image of a serpent on it, and the people were healed from serpent bites. Now we read that Jesus, the Son of Man, must be lifted up for the healing salvation of the world. As we read both Numbers 21 and John 3, we know that we are *Un pueblo de Dios redimido* (God's people redeemed by grace).

At sporting events people hold up signs bearing the reference *John 3:16*. That is a form of witness, but unless a person already knows the verse, simply putting the reference on paper does little good. I wonder if our witness could become more specific than that one. Would we not speak a word of grace to a broken world if we were to quote the entirety of verse 17? Would it help people to know that God desires to save the world and not to condemn it? Would people gain a better sense of God's deep love?

The God of life, who is great in mercy and grace, invites us to enjoy life's fullness as a redeemed people. God loves us, became one like us, lived among us, taught and healed, died and was resurrected. You and I and the world are redeemed by God's grace, and we live in the riches of God's mercy.

SUGGESTION FOR MEDITATION: Remember that God did not send the Son into the world to condemn the world. How does this truth inspire your ministry?

Our Covenant with God

March 27–April 2, 2006 • E. Glenn Hinson[‡]

MONDAY, MARCH 27 • Read Jeremiah 31:31-34

A God-initiated covenant is the heart of the Jewish-Christian revelation. You and I would be presumptuous to claim a relationship with God had God not sought us out and forged a relationship as intimate as a human marriage. Indeed, it is not at all surprising that Jews and Christians drew on the analogy of the wedding tryst of the Song of Songs to depict the relationship of God both with the church and with individual believers. What analogy more aptly describes the intimacy we mortals covet with this God who has sought us even before we thought to seek God? And how awesome to think that the Creator of this vast universe of 150 billion galaxies would love and seek us, mere grains of sand on an endless seashore, with such infinite care!

The eighth-century BCE prophet Jeremiah shocks us by adding to this profound word of hope a promise of a new, unbreakable covenant that we Christians have placed at the center of our tradition. We reiterate it each time we observe our central covenant rite, the Lord's Supper or Eucharist. "This is my blood of the new covenant" (Matt 26:28; Mark 14:24) or "This . . . is the new covenant in my blood" (Luke 22:20; 1 Cor. 11:25). Since so often broken, how now "unbreakable"? Jeremiah has the answer: tattooing on the heart! The living God will inscribe God's revealed will "not on stone tablets but on the fleshly tablets of the heart" (2 Cor 3:3, AT). Knowing God with intimacy will depend not on catechesis but on the Spirit, God with us.

PRAYER: Thank you, O God, for this new covenant promise. In response to your assurance, I renew this day the "I do" I spoke in baptism and repeat in your sacred meal. Amen.

[‡]Professor Emeritus of Baptist Theological Seminary, Richmond, Virginia; teacher at Baptist Seminary of Louisville and Louisville Presbyterian Seminary.

At the seminary in Finkenwalde where he prepared ministers for the Confessing Church between 1935 and 1937, Dietrich Bonhoeffer suggested that students might meditate on the same passage of scripture for thirty minutes every morning for a week. Though I won't spend the whole week with these verses, the richness of Jeremiah 31:31-34 merits more than one day's meditation. In his word for each of us the great prophet will not let us glide past the inescapable fact that our relationship with God must find its center in the heart. We will "know" God, he assures us, not through head knowledge, valuable as that may be, but through heart knowledge. As the precocious seventeenth-century mathematician and philosopher Blaise Pascal put it, "The heart has its reasons, of which reason knows nothing."

In an era in which one scientist declared, "We scientists have a right to play God," we may have trouble understanding Jeremiah's perspective. Saints through the ages have not had the same difficulty. An anonymous fourteenth-century saint penned a work titled *The Cloud of Unknowing*. In it he asserted that God will remain ever unknowable to our "knowing" faculty. Not so, however, to our "loving" faculty. We can penetrate the cloud of unknowing with "a sharp dart of longing love."

We know it works this way in human relationships. No matter how brilliant, you will never unravel the mystery of another person by intellectual analysis. The more you analyze, the more you may paralyze the friendship. The heart, though, may open another to deep and authentic disclosure so that you transcend the mystery by love. Jeremiah gives us God's assurance that without exception "from the least to the greatest" (AT) we shall all know God.

PRAYER: Thank you, O God, for your love that pours into my heart. I open my heart that you may teach me to know you. Amen.

WEDNESDAY, MARCH 29 • **Read Psalm 51:1-12**
Jeremiah 31:31-34

A healthy, vital relationship with God depends on confession on our part and forgiveness and forgetting on God's part. Jeremiah gives voice to God's assurance in the new covenant: "I will forgive their iniquity, and remember their sin no more." Openhearted, whole-souled confession is the doorway toward restoring a broken relationship.

The psalmist, identified traditionally as David after his affair with Bathsheba, suffered from some physical ailment but, far more, from the disablement of sin. Are physical illness and sin interdependent? Not necessarily. Jesus, for instance, repudiated the direct equation of physical suffering with sin (John 9:2-3) when he healed the blind man. But you and I know that they can and sometimes do have a connection. Professing to be "born guilty" and a sinner from conception, the psalmist poured out his heart to God to claim the kind of mercy only God can supply.

Whatever its connection with physical health, confession is powerful. Søren Kierkegaard, the great Danish philosopher, called remorse, repentance, and confession "eternity's emissaries" to humankind. He made them the first step toward purity of heart. Our psalmist evidently would have agreed. Only God could offer a remedy for this guilt-wracked soul. The besmirched covenant needed a complete overhaul, renovation from top to bottom. When it comes to guilt, priestly absolution isn't enough. God, full of compassion, has to remove all traces of guilt from the stained and blot-marked soul—wash away the evil, scrub out the sin, purge with hyssop. God, divine love, recreates truth in the inward being, wisdom in the heart of hearts, purity of heart, a new and right spirit within, the joy of salvation, and a willing spirit.

PRAYER: Forgive me, O God of mercy, for sins both known and unknown. Enable me to realize that you accept me and to accept myself just as I am. Amen.

The astonishing aspect of this covenant with God is its restorability dependent on only one gesture—repentance. However badly Israel violated the covenant, God still went after an errant people and brought them back, just as Hosea went after an unfaithful Gomer. However much David mangled the covenant, God still listened to pleas of a penitent to restore the ruptured relationship. However rebellious and riotous a prodigal, the parent raced down the road to greet his return, threw his arms around his neck and kissed him, and ordered the best robe, a ring for his finger, shoes for his feet, and a celebration symbolic of his acceptance as son.

Some Christian groups, like the ancient Novatians, have had trouble spreading the net of divine mercy so widely. They accentuate God's holiness rather than God's compassion. If we follow our psalmist, God weights this covenant overwhelmingly on the side of mercy and love. And however extensively you've damaged your relationship with God and however far you've strayed from your vows, still there is hope.

You realize, of course, that God has to do the restoring, just as God had to establish a relationship in the beginning. Our psalmist states it in the right way. Clean heart . . . right spirit . . . joy of salvation . . . willing spirit—all are God's doing. No amount of good deeds, penances, sacrifices, almsgiving can do it. At best we, like the tax collector of Jesus' parable (Luke 18:13), can beat our breast and say, "God, be merciful to me, a sinner." By that simple gesture, Jesus added, the tax collector went home okayed by God not even on the basis of that small act but on that of God's incredible loving-kindness.

PRAYER: On the basis of your mercy, O God of infinite compassion, restore to me the sense of your presence and the joy of fellowship with you and my fellow believers. Amen.

In our meditations we've been looking at the covenant chiefly from God's side. A God of infinite love has sought us out to forge an intimate bond with us. What does the covenant require from the human side? In a word, *faithfulness*. Steadfast adherence to an "I do." Sadly, as Jeremiah, Isaiah, and others of Israel's prophets declared, the people of the covenant have not always remained faithful. The prophets looked for a remnant. Finally, in Christian understanding, that remnant narrowed to one: Jesus of Nazareth. Through him God effected the new covenant.

How could one person be the instrument for restoration of the covenant relationship with God? Early Christians sought to explain with diverse analogies. The author of Hebrews drew an analogy from Israel's temple worship. The Son, high priest not by human but by divine appointment, yielded to God's will unreservedly. Learning obedience through suffering in the garden of Gethsemane and on the cross, "he became the cause of eternal salvation for all who obey with him" (Heb 5:9, AT). Note, please, my translation. In this writing Jesus did not take our place as a sufferer for sin. Rather, through his faithfulness in suffering to the point of death he started a company of the committed.

"Community of fellow sufferers" is one way to think about the church. Entrance into suffering, Thomas Kelly has said in the classic *A Testament of Devotion*, is one of the gateways to holy obedience. Persons who join this company do not walk through the world with eyes averted. Quite the contrary, they develop "excruciatingly sensitive eyesight." Still more, Kelly said, "the heart is stretched through suffering, and enlarged." Indeed, out of God's own suffering, God "has planted the Cross along the road of holy obedience." That's costly grace!

PRAYER: Remind me, O God, not to forget the costly way you have entered into covenant with me, and inspire me to more observant faithfulness. Amen.

You would think crucifixion of the founder of Christianity would have repelled and driven people away. The Romans reserved the savage method of execution for punishment of the worst criminals. Yet Jesus, according to John's extraordinary portrayal, looked to it as the "hour" he had pointed to throughout his ministry (John 2:4; 4:21-23, 53; 5:25, 28; 7:30; 8:20). In what sense? It was the time at which he would be lifted up on the cross, his hour of glorification when he would draw all persons to himself. Even before he spoke these words, Greeks (Gentiles) approached the two disciples with Greek names—Philip and Andrew—demanding to see Jesus. As a seed that dies when it falls into the ground bears much fruit, so too would Jesus' death. So too would his followers' suffering and death.

What is amazing is how prophetic these words proved! By the time John penned his Gospel, Christians could not have substantiated the point. But by the time Constantine halted the persecution of them in the Roman Empire, Christians had won over about ten percent of the population. In some areas such as Asia Minor (modern Turkey) they claimed a fourth to a half of the population. Not only had they survived sometimes severe persecution, they had thrived.

How do we explain the drawing power of the cross? We can't. But in John's Gospel the "lifting up" is at the same time an exaltation. In the Suffering Servant, God discloses what God's tabernacling in human life (John 1:14) is all about. God became human in order that we might participate in God's own life, the life of the "I AM." In Jesus' "hour" he brought to its apex the greatest story ever told.

PRAYER: Open the eyes of my mind and heart, O Living Christ, to see you and to serve you everywhere in every day. Amen.

FIFTH SUNDAY OF LENT

Under the old covenant God did not call a people just to shower them with blessings. God called them that they might bless others (Gen. 12:2), live in a certain way (Exod. 20:1-17), and serve God in effecting God's purpose for the world (Deut. 6:13). Our covenant obligation did not change under the new covenant. Indeed, knowing God with a new sense of intimacy should heighten the desire to love like God loves and to give our lives in selfless service even as Jesus gave his life.

Jesus snaps us to attention with faith's sure paradox. To follow Jesus requires us to deny ourselves and take up our own cross. Saying no to self, to ego, of course, entails suffering. Self-denial gets right in the face of a natural tendency to please and gratify our own desires and to grasp for the artificial and contrived needs the world around us creates. So Jesus puts it in stark terms for people who at the time John wrote faced certain persecution and death. "Follow my example. Do as I am doing. Put yourself completely and unreservedly in God's hands. You may lose your life, but you will have eternal life" (AP).

Most of our lives you and I don't come up against such overwhelming demands in discipleship, though believers in many parts of the world today do. Yet doesn't covenanting with God require the same—self-denial and cross-bearing? To live as if our covenant did not require us to live in a different way would mean denial of the covenant itself. If you cling to your life with all your might, Jesus says, you will lose it; if you give up your tight grip on it in your present time and circumstances, you will have it forever. Putting yourself in God's hands is worth it!

PRAYER: Dear God, bring life to me and through me this day. Amen.

Having the Mind of Christ

April 3–9, 2006 • Larry R. Kalajainen[‡]

MONDAY, APRIL 3 • Read Mark 11:1-11

The Jesus movement arose from the strain of prophetic Jewish religion. Mark's story of Jesus' entry into Jerusalem just before his arrest and trial bears the marks of his own encounter with the prophets and the psalms. The structure of his story appears to have been influenced by Zechariah's proclamation (Zech. 9:9-10) of a king on an embassy of peace, riding on a donkey rather than a war horse, a text that had already begun to be interpreted messianically. The hymnlike ascription of praise that the people speak as Jesus rides by is partially drawn from Psalm 118, one of the "Hallel" psalms typically recited during the Passover celebration.

The use of these two Old Testament texts gives us clues to Mark's understanding of the story of Jesus' entry into Jerusalem: Jesus enters the holy city offering himself as the Messiah but does so in humility as a bringer of peace. The connection to Passover with the citation from Psalm 118 evokes images of God's deliverance of his people from slavery in the Exodus, a deliverance preceded by the sacrificial death of the Passover lamb.

This evocative use of older texts and stories raises some interesting questions for us. If Jesus is the Messiah, God's anointed deliverer, as Christians have always claimed, what does that mean for the way we actively follow Christ today? Is Mark's image compatible with the variety of triumphalist Christianity so prevalent today? And what is implied by the evocation of the Exodus story, which celebrates deliverance from bondage but only after the sacrifice of an innocent lamb?

SUGGESTION FOR MEDITATION: If Jesus presented himself as a humble bringer of peace, how should I present myself, as Christ's disciple, to those around me?

[‡]Senior pastor, First Parish Church, Brunswick, Maine; dual standing in The United Methodist and United Church of Christ Churches.

Psalm 118 is the last of the "Egyptian Hallel" psalms (Pss. 113–118), which were used liturgically during the annual Passover celebration. The individual psalms might have been composed for a variety of occasions; but liturgically, they were most often used together. They celebrate God's deliverance; and naturally in Israel's religious life, they were associated with Israel's deliverance from slavery in Egypt in the Exodus.

Two things stand out prominently in this psalm. The first is that in each of the first four verses, the line "His steadfast love endures forever," is an affirmation the people themselves are urged to repeat. Many modern worship services might call this form a "litany." The term *steadfast love* translates a Hebrew term *chesed*, for which we have no exact English equivalent. It combines elements of our words *compassion, mercy, steadfastness,* and *faithfulness.* It describes God's disposition toward God's people. Unlike us, God is not fickle, self-interested, wavering, or faithless to promises made. God's disposition is to love us with *chesed*— with steadfast love and kindness, despite what our disposition toward God may be!

The second standout theme in this psalm appears in verses 22-23. God accomplishes our deliverance in a manner that makes little sense to most of the world. A stone rejected as useless by worldly builders becomes the chief cornerstone. Such a reversal of value and worth can only be "the Lord's doing"; human minds can scarcely imagine such upside-down assessments.

SUGGESTION FOR MEDITATION: **The notion of God's steadfast love is cause for both celebration and repentance: celebration because we are loved! And repentance because our own love for others is so little like God's love for us.**

Within the text of Isaiah 42–52, four shorter oracles are embedded (42:1-4; 49:1-6; 50:4-11; 52:13–53:12), known collectively as the Servant Songs. Interpreters (both Jewish and Christian) have variously understood the Servant as the whole nation of biblical Israel, the faithful remnant within Israel, or the prophet himself. Early Christian interpreters insisted that Isaiah was (consciously or unconsciously) predicting the rejection, vicarious death, and vindication of the Messiah, Jesus. More recent interpreters suggest the influence ran the other way—that the Gospel passion narratives derived their structure and some details from the Servant Songs.

In this third Servant Song, the Servant speaks of both his vocation and the popular rejection that results. His vocation has two complementary parts: listening and speaking. "Morning by morning he wakens—wakens my ear to listen as those who are taught." This listening results in his being able to fulfill his mission: "to sustain the weary with a word."

If the church today saw itself, not in triumphalist terms of growth in power and prestige and influence, but as the Servant of God whose mission is be still and silent enough to hear a word that when spoken would sustain the weary, bind up the brokenhearted, and encourage the fainting, what a difference we could make in the world!

Such a vocation might not build megachurches; it might very well, as it did the Servant, bring us opposition and abuse. But if, like the Servant, we trust in God for our vindication, what a force for healing and salvation we can be!

SUGGESTION FOR MEDITATION: **How well developed are my listening skills, both as an individual and as a member of a congregation? What would have to change in my (our faith community's) life in order for me to hear and speak a sustaining word?**

Psalm 31 is one of eight "Passion Psalms," so named because they are the source of images or phrases that recur in the Passion narratives of the Gospels. While some Christian interpreters believe that these passages actually foreshadowed the events of Jesus' passion, others believe that the Gospel writers (or someone before them) constructed the Passion narrative on the basis of their reading of these psalms.

Psalm 31 itself takes the literary form of a lament. The psalmist cries for help and deliverance from personal enemies. As such, it speaks to a common human experience—the feeling that everyone is against us. Which of us hasn't experienced a feeling of having our back to the wall, surrounded by hostile people or circumstances? As an old quip goes, "Even paranoid people have real enemies."

Sometimes our own stress or warped perspective produce these feelings of being alone against a hostile world. Circumstances are not really as grim as we imagine them to be, but our imagination powerfully convinces us that they are. At other times, we do face real adversaries and situations in which we feel hemmed in on every side by enemies, whether personal or circumstantial. Real or imagined as the enemies may be, the feelings of isolation, loneliness, and fear are real enough to defeat us and cause us anguish of spirit or depression.

Yet the enemies do not have the last word. "But I trust in you, O LORD; I say, 'You are my God.' My times are in your hand." The last (as well as the first) word belongs to God. Trust in God makes the difference between defeat and victory.

SUGGESTION FOR MEDITATION: **How do I discern which of my enemies are real or imagined? What will trust in God entail for me in my situation?**

Most New Testament scholars agree that this well-known text is an early Christian hymn that Paul has cited to ground his exhortations regarding the way Christians are to live. We need to read it in the context of the verses that immediately precede it, which give these exhortations. Humility, self-giving, servant-hood, and sacrifice are the hallmarks of genuine Christian discipleship and genuine human community.

Yet we do not have to look far to recognize how foreign those characteristics appear in modern culture. Our culture teaches self-promotion, self-aggrandizement, self-fulfillment, and self-enrichment, often at the expense of others. Competition rather than cooperation, individual gratification rather than the common good, hard-nosed self-reliance rather than sympathetic compassion dictate our actions much of the time. Little wonder that so many are lonely and alienated.

Someone, commenting on this text, said that being a Christian means losing our minds . . . and gaining the mind of Christ. This may be why G. K. Chesterton once said that the problem with Christianity is not that it has been tried and found wanting, but that it has been found difficult and left untried. Difficult, yes. Impossible? Thankfully no. We have the examples of many great Christians through the centuries who have lost their minds and gained the mind of Christ and who have shown us by their examples what is possible for us. But it will take courage to stoop as low as Christ. Yet both Christ's exaltation and ours is the consequence of such courageous "stooping to conquer."

SUGGESTION FOR MEDITATION: **Where in my life do I see the need to "lose my mind" and gain the mind of Christ? What specifically would have to change in my attitudes, behavior, and values?**

Many scholars have noted that in Mark's Gospel the disciples of Jesus don't come off very well; they are antiheroes rather than heroes of faith. This Gospel almost always portrays them as thick-headed, unable to comprehend anything at all about the significance of Jesus' words and teachings. Peter confesses Jesus as Messiah (8:28-30), and, at long last, it appears that he's finally gotten it. But his next words betray his total lack of true understanding of what his affirmation means, and Jesus soundly rebukes him.

The theme reappears here in the story of Jesus' agonizing struggle in the garden of Gethsemane and in the story of his arrest. In Gethsemane, Jesus' sweat becomes like great drops of blood (Luke 22:44) as he wrestles with his destiny and contemplates his imminent death at the hands of his enemies. He begs his disciples repeatedly, "Remain here, and keep awake"; but as usual, they're "out of it." Jesus prays and agonizes; the disciples catch forty winks. At his arrest, they readily take up the sword in Jesus' defense, but Jesus' surrender unnerves them. Mark's scathing ending to the story, and the last we hear of the disciples in this Gospel, is "All of them deserted him and fled."

What should we make of this harsh assessment of Jesus' closest followers? William Stringfellow once referred to this portrayal of the disciples as "exemplary disbelief." If even those closest to Jesus could get it so wrong again and again and yet follow, then perhaps there's hope for us who also get it wrong, who misunderstand, who go to sleep when we should be watching and praying, who bluster but turn tail and run in the crunch.

SUGGESTION FOR MEDITATION: **How does my following of Jesus connect with that of the disciples as Mark portrays them? Why am I so dense, so indifferent, or unfaithful?**

Palm/Passion Sunday

Mark's literary artistry continues to amaze the careful reader. This Gospel begins with an inscription: "The beginning of the good news of Jesus Christ, the Son of God" (1:1). Yet none of his followers ever recognize his identity. Only the demons (5:1-13) whom Jesus' exorcises confess him as "the Holy One of God." Now, here at the end of his story, as a broken, tortured Jesus breathes his agonizing final breath on a Roman cross, another witness to his identity enters the picture. Is it one of his closest disciples? No, Mark's version of the crucifixion makes no mention of the disciples. None of Jesus' friends seem to be there; he dies surrounded by the jeering crowds of spectators who always turn out for public executions. Even Mary Magdalene and Mary the mother of James and Joses, and Salome, three faithful women, are "looking on from a distance."

No, this witness is none other than the Roman centurion responsible for seeing the execution carried out. This pagan soldier, brutalized by war and the rough duties of his trade, becomes the final human witness to Jesus' identity. "Now when the centurion, who stood facing him, saw that in this way he breathed his last, he said, 'Truly this man was God's Son!'" Strange Gospel! Demons and pagan soldiers recognize Jesus' identity, but his friends and followers do not. And the real kicker is that the manner of Jesus' death—death on a cross—elicits the centurion's confession.

SUGGESTION FOR MEDITATION: Why do Jesus' friends resist the direction toward which his life heads, while his enemies recognize God's presence in him? What does this Gospel's story tell me about where to find God in my life and my world?

Sharing the Last Journey

April 10–16, 2006 • J. Philip Wogaman[‡]

MONDAY, APRIL 10 • **Read John 12:1-11**

This is the beginning of Holy Week, the dramatic last days of Jesus before Easter. Think of this as a journey we are invited to share with our Lord. What do we observe? The stage is set with a dinner in Bethany a couple of days before Jesus' entry into Jerusalem, hosted by Martha, Mary, and Lazarus. Incredibly, Mary pours costly perfume all over Jesus' feet. What! Wasting all that money on a transient moment, a fleeting gift borne out of loyalty and love?

John's Gospel relates this story as an anticipation of Jesus' death. But we might also pause over this as a more joyful moment, friends gathered for a meal, climaxed by the giving of a gift from the heart. Perhaps as we share this last journey of Jesus, we are also invited into that circle of friendship.

Sometimes Christians feel they must relate to Jesus only through the lens of their own guilt. Jesus is so perfect; we are so sinful. That's true enough, but Jesus invites us to share real friendship. The story emphasizes that point by the accusation of Judas of all people, that Mary should feel guilty for not selling the perfume and giving the money to the poor. But Jesus doesn't allow this part of his journey to be a guilt trip. The gift and the circle of friendship in which it is generated is intrinsically good. Does this mean we should neglect the poor? Of course not! As we share the fellowship we are drawn into greater caring about all of the world's neglected people, inviting all into that same great circle of friendship.

PRAYER: Thank you, God, for the gift of friendship, into which we are drawn by our Lord. Help us extend that gift to others. Amen.

[‡]Professor of Christian Ethics, Emeritus, Wesley Theological Seminary; author; former pastor, Foundry United Methodist Church, Washington D. C.

TUESDAY, APRIL 11 • **Read 1 Corinthians 1:18–31; John 12:25**

Has not God made foolish the wisdom of the world?

Continuing the last journey, we are invited to share the wisdom of Christ. Paul puts it bluntly: "In the wisdom of God, the world did not know God through wisdom." This passage comes through as a real put-down of the life of the mind, until we read later in First Corinthians that "I would rather speak five words with my mind, in order to instruct others also, than ten thousand words in a tongue." Wisdom isn't in the rejection of our minds but how we use them. Paul's point is that God's wisdom conveyed through the cross of Christ—through the painful execution of Christ, rejected and disgraced—surely defies more conventional wisdom.

What kind of divine wisdom could that awful event disclose? Perhaps it discloses how love, supremely expressed by Christ on the cross, is central to the meaning of life. And how self-righteous sin, as illustrated by those who put him there, is exactly contrary to what we are created to be. And how easily we drift into such sin. And how we are invited into that deeper reality of love. Yes, divine wisdom is about these things and runs so contrary to the common, conventional wisdom of a broken, materialistic world.

The verse in John reminds us of another aspect of divine wisdom: "Those who love their life in this world lose it, and those who hate their life in this world will keep it for eternal life." We are here on this earth but for a moment. True wisdom entails the use of this precious, fleeting gift of life on earth as a lasting investment in eternal good.

PRAYER: Help us, O God, not to be so distracted by the false pretenses of worldly wisdom that we miss the deep truths. Amen.

Let us run with perseverance the race that is set before us, looking to Jesus the pioneer and perfecter of our faith.

The journey of Christ required perseverance. Can we also share in that? We may unconsciously discount the importance of Jesus' perseverance because we know how it all turned out. Mentally we place ourselves in the company of the heroes of our faith as they faced persecution, kept the faith, endured to the end. Surely, had we been alive then, we would have been among them! We would have seen beyond the narrow horizon and petty prejudices of the times. We would have been enlightened and courageous, even if our stands made us unpopular or forced us to risk our lives.

I'm not so sure! Most of our great spiritual forebears, the heroes of our faith tradition, had at least this in common: they didn't know how it was all going to turn out. They could not have imagined their being venerated by later generations for their prophetic insight, courage, and perseverance. But, convinced of the truth and justice for which they witnessed and acted, they stayed the course.

The passage from John illustrates the depth of Jesus' perseverance. Here, gathered with that intimate band of disciples with whom he has shared so much, he comes face-to-face with the betrayal of Judas, an intimate companion on the journey. What is Jesus to do? He faces the issue squarely but shares the broken bread even with his betrayer. Jesus' perseverance goes far beyond physical endurance to maintaining the spirit of love despite the cruelest kind of disappointment.

We too face disappointments and reversals, and we may not know how everything will turn out. But, like Jesus, our confidence in God can assure us that in the end God will take our faithfulness and use it for a good beyond our imagining.

PRAYER: God, grant us the wisdom and courage to face frustrations and disappointments in the assurance that we belong to you, the one who is ultimately in charge. Amen.

MAUNDY THURSDAY

Then [Jesus] poured water into a basin and began to wash the disciples' feet.

The Gospel of John does not recount the Last Supper in the same way that we read the story in the other Gospels, with the bread and wine symbolizing the body and blood of Jesus. Instead, we have this extraordinary account of Jesus washing the disciples' feet! Given the appearance and odor of the feet, it serves as an unimaginable act of humility—and not a pleasant one! Thus did Jesus express the humility of one who had come to serve, not to be served. Can we share that humility as we continue the journey with Christ?

It's not easy. We always observed Maundy Thursday with a moving Communion service at the church I served for ten years in Washington, D.C. Most participants could relate to the drama of that service at a deep spiritual level. But we also offered a foot-washing service in the church's fellowship hall, preceding Communion. You can imagine which service was better attended!

At first the foot-washing aspect made me hesitate, but, as the pastor, I felt duty-bound to participate; so I did. It didn't turn out to be so unpleasant, since most participants, unlike the disciples, made sure to clean their feet in advance. But more basically, the unpleasantness dissipated because of the subtle bonding that occurred as we took turns around the tables to serve one another in this way. In this act of service, all pride and pretensions, all status and privileges dissolve. We are God's family drawn together by the humility of the One who came to serve and in whose service we come to see the presence of God with us.

PRAYER: **Holy God, empty us of every vanity and pretension, and grant us the gift of humility that we may be brought together with you through Christ. Amen.**

FRIDAY, APRIL 14 • **Read Psalm 22:1-8; Isaiah 53:3-9; John 18–19**

GOOD FRIDAY

As one from whom others hide their faces
he was despised, and we held him of no account.

Now comes the hard part. To share the journey with Christ is to share the rejection, so well anticipated in the readings from Psalm 22 and Isaiah 53 and described in the passages from John. Sharing the journey doesn't mean we desire rejection—Jesus himself didn't want that to happen. But he did not turn aside when it came to that.

Why was Jesus rejected? For several reasons, some of them out-and-out political. But I am also struck by Jesus' constant affirmation of and association with the outcasts of his society: Samaritans, tax collectors, lepers, poor people, and (while they were not exactly "outcasts") the marginalized women. Jesus treated them as equals. In other words, he willingly identified with people who were stigmatized in one way or another. And when you make friends with stigmatized people, you acquire the stigma yourself. That stigma may have played a major role in the readiness of the power structure of his day to have him crucified.

As a pastor, I recall how people often asked me why Christians call this "Good" Friday, this day on which an unspeakably evil deed was done. Surely it is good because of the immeasurable love of Jesus on the cross, which we understand to be the love of God for all of us.

An appropriate spiritual exercise for Good Friday involves thinking about people in our time who bear particular stigmas; ponder quietly what it would mean to make friends with them. Then go do it!

PRAYER: Gracious God, help us, like Jesus, to see those who have been rejected in our time as equally beloved in your sight; free us from the fear of rejection. Amen.

HOLY SATURDAY

But mortals die, and are laid low; humans expire, and where are they?

A passage in Charles Dickens's *A Christmas Carol* emphasizes the death of the skinflint Ebenezer Scrooge's late partner, Jacob Marley. Marley was really dead, absolutely dead. Dickens writes that unless we grasp that point, we will be unable to grasp the goodness in what is about to transpire. That is also the point in what is sometimes called Holy Saturday. Jesus has died. He is really dead. If that was not so, then nothing that follows would matter.

Can we share that part of the journey too? We surely will, at least in the basic physical sense, for every single one of us is destined to die sooner or later. But to share the death of Jesus is to share his acceptance of the prospect. It was not that he wanted to die at his young age and in a painful and disgraceful execution. He had prayed to God that, if possible, this cup would be removed, but nevertheless "not what I want, but what you want." To share the death of Jesus is to place a higher value on the purposes of God than even our own continued physical existence. People not dominated by the fear of death are free to live life to its fullest.

Perhaps you thought of this aspect in the aftermath of that terrible event we call 9/11. But even in the face of such an awful act of terrorism, we do not have to be immobilized by fear. We can recognize in faith that in death, as in life, we are in God's hands. We can share the death of Jesus as a part of our own journey if, like Jesus, we can trust God.

PRAYER: Loving God, calm our anxious hearts as we face the reality of death, and grant us the grace to be faithful in our journey of life. Amen.

EASTER SUNDAY

*Now I would remind you, brothers and sisters, of the
good news.*

Is this the good news about the end of our journey with Christ
or its beginning? Perhaps it is both, for the beginning we proclaim on Easter is linked to all that has gone before. Paul's words
in First Corinthians bespeak his wonderment at what has happened. He is especially touched by the appearance of Christ to
him, for he had persecuted the church and even thought he was
"unfit to be called an apostle." But now, he continues, "By the
grace of God I am what I am."

So it can be with us by the grace of God. We, like Paul, are
scarcely worthy of the unfathomable gift expressed by the Resurrection. But, like Paul, we can respond to that gift of grace by
living it out faithfully and joyfully.

Living the faith can mean different things to different ones
of us. But one thing we all have in common: our response to the
Resurrection cannot be self-centered. We cannot allow preoccupation with personal immortality to obscure regard to God's loving intentions for the whole creation. The Resurrection invites
us into a wonderful new life in a divine, eternal community
formed by grace and in purposes beyond our comprehension.

This day can be a hard one for people who have recently lost
loved ones and for all of us when we struggle with doubts about
what lies beyond the mystery of death. And yet, the day can be
celebrated as the centerpiece in the hopeful love that draws us
closer to God.

**PRAYER: Dear God, help us share the wonder of the Resurrec-
tion as we have shared the last journey of Christ on earth. And
through your grace, help us to be all that we have been created
and redeemed to be. Amen.**

Healing from the Inside Out

April 17–23, 2006 • Nancy Fester[†]

MONDAY, APRIL 17 • Read 1 John 1:1-4

We are writing these things [to you] so that our joy may be complete.

Sharing good news really does make me feel good. It's a warming from within, a thawing of a cold knot of fear, sorrow, and aloneness. I'm sure you have experienced this too.

The writer of First John takes hold of a wonderful opportunity, a tremendous chance; boldly and unselfishly sharing or "declaring" what he and his friends have experienced. The author uses all the senses as he relates the experience of Jesus' life, death, and resurrection: "We declare . . . what we have heard, what we have seen with our eyes, . . . looked at and touched with our hands." Not what he has read in a book. Not what someone else has suggested. Not what his brilliant mind conceives as truth but his very real, sensory experience of Jesus. And the writer declares it for his own good, his own joy, as well as ours, using the resource at his disposal: writing a letter.

Recently, a thorough and wise discharging nurse talked to me about the steps needed once I left the hospital to recover from surgery. She reminded me that the healing inside had already begun—in fact, was progressing rapidly; that healing always takes place "from the inside out."

This writer is well along the way of his own healing. Only then can true sharing begin by taking the deep truth revealed, sharing it in fellowship, then declaring it onward and outward.

PRAYER: Lord, help us discover anew the joy and healing that is shared with us through those who unselfishly declare your good news. Amen.

[†]United Methodist layperson; hotel manager; member, Westlake United Methodist Church, Westlake, Ohio.

The doors of the house where the disciples had met were locked for fear of the Jews.

While I'd like to hope that the disciples are meeting to pray, to commune, to gather strength in their unity, I'm guessing that they've gathered primarily out of fear. Here they are in the room where they'd met just days prior to observe the Passover with Jesus. Now even this house is not exempt from their fear. Jesus had washed their feet here, reassured them of his love and commitment, reminded them of the coming of the Holy Spirit. Jesus knew his friends, and knowing that they would be filled with sorrow he had promised peace: "Peace I leave with you; my peace I give to you" (John 14:27). And then he had promised to be with them always.

So why all this fear? The disciples are no different from you and me. Don't we have locked doors that keep us inside for fear's sake? I think Jesus knew full well what that nurse told me: we heal from the inside out. Jesus made these promises to people he knew really well. He knew their fears as well as ours: fears of inadequacy, commitment, disappointment, even fear itself. Only by coming into the locked rooms of our souls and declaring his presence does the risen Christ get our attention.

In Naomi Nye's poem "Stone House," she says, "It was a hard place to be if you were staying." Jesus knew that his disciples wouldn't stay forever in that hard place, behind those locked doors. Instead they would take their newfound resurrection strength to the frightened world outside. "Peace be with you" were his words of greeting and reassurance.

"Peace be with you." Indeed. The healing peace of Christ begins inside our own seemingly locked doors.

SUGGESTION FOR MEDITATION: What fears lock the doors to Christ's peace and healing?

How very good and pleasant it is when kindred live together in unity!

When I hung up the phone from the unexpected call, I wasn't sure whether to rejoice or lament. When discord rips through familial relationships and lies unattended over time, that disharmony accumulates and desensitizes. Neglect of the relationship becomes the norm, rather than attending to the means of healing. Neglect replaces familiarity and becomes the routine. Inside, you grow content with the lack of contact. You convince yourself that you don't care one way or another, that it just doesn't matter.

Truth to tell, it's lonely living apart from someone you love. You can convince yourself that the wounds you feel inside aren't your fault, that you can't do a thing to fix things. And you discover that, as a friend of mine likes to say, "Wounded people wound." It's a vicious cycle.

The psalmist eloquently weaves his way metaphorically into the mystery of reconciliation—choosing to speak of God's touch upon the physical person, upon the earth in the form of anointing oil and morning dew. From my own experience, I might reweave the metaphor in this way:

How lovely is the day when relationships reconcile in love. It is like the healing touch of a nurse, maternal in its gentleness. It is like the voice of a distant sibling on the phone, familiar as the sound of waves on the shore, allowing a departure from alienation, a going out toward unity.

How lonely it was before that phone call. How glad I am to have begun to experience the healing of this woundedness upon my spirit, deep inside.

SUGGESTION FOR MEDITATION: "Kindred" souls may be found in family and in friendships. Consider a relationship that has been damaged. How could its healing renew your own spirit?

Thomas answered him, "My Lord and my God!"

Perhaps doubt has gotten a bad rap. It's unlikely that faith can reach any level of maturity without having grown through (and beyond!) some healthy doses of doubt. And it's unlikely that Jesus would have appeared specifically to Thomas without the rest of the community present—for their sake as much as for Thomas's sake. In truth, witnessing the experience of others who overcome doubt bolsters our faith. Thomas had to see for himself—see and touch and hear—but not in isolation. Instead, revelation comes in the company of those who know Thomas best, who have already seen for themselves.

In *To Kill a Mockingbird*, young Scout Finch meets the man whom she and her older brother, Jem, had for years feared but longed to see. They had schemed to lure the mysterious Arthur "Boo" Radley outside in the daylight, simply to catch sight of him. While the badly wounded Jem sleeps, Scout has the opportunity to sit with Boo, to talk to him, and to escort the shy man to his house. She knows that Jem will disbelieve her story in the morning. "As I made my way home, I thought what a thing to tell Jem tomorrow. He'd be so mad he missed it he wouldn't speak to me for days."

John's Gospel speaks of being "written so that you may come to believe" (John 20:31). In community we share the stories again and again, just as young children clamor to hear and repeat the same book, the same story, over and over. I never tire of this "story" of Thomas, of seeing and believing for himself, of overcoming his inner doubts and fears in the glad company of close companions—and of his Lord and God!

SUGGESTION FOR MEDITATION: In whose good company do you tell stories? What reassurance do the friends and stories offer?

PRAYER: Lord, I long to hear the old stories anew and rejoice in seeing therein the presence of "my Lord and my God!" Amen.

There was not a needy person among them, for as many as owned lands or houses sold them and brought the proceeds. . . . and it was distributed to each as any had need.

Jesus formed the core of this community of believers, and their healing began with his victory over the cross. The early believers, led by Jesus' apostles, were privy to a truth that has sustained our church throughout history: you must build your strength and commitment, your faith, from within—in the safety of community—before you carry it out to a world that wants to deny the Resurrection and any hope of a better situation.

I participated in The Upper Room Academy for Spiritual Formation #17. For two years, members came together in San Antonio for five days and nights, four times annually, dubbing our community the "Salsa Academy." Each session drew us together more intimately in our faith formation. Each session evoked deeper longing when we parted. At each session's conclusion, my covenant group debated whether we were returning home *to* the real world or returning home *from* the real world.

Each week spent together strengthened our lives in both worlds. We shared Christ at the Oblate Center in San Antonio. We returned home to share Christ in our families, congregations, at work, and among neighbors.

The early church took its sharing to a degree unimaginable in today's material world. They found freedom in giving all they had received. How delightful to live in such simplicity of possessions sold and given as needed. Perhaps with Jesus as the core of their lives and community, they no longer feared going without. Perhaps, faith heals poverty, replacing it with freedom and joy in sharing unselfishly.

SUGGESTION FOR MEDITATION: **Where do you go to receive the richness of companionship through sharing God with others?**

There the LORD ordained his blessing, life forevermore.

Keep in mind, this psalm begins with a specific mention of unity, of the goodness of living together in unity. All the stories I enjoy—the books, the movies, the classic tragedies—seem to revolve around a family united or divided, a family or a neighborhood or a nation. Relationships and bonds rely upon the individuals therein; each person contributes to the strength of the bond or the intent toward dissension and division.

Now the psalmist tells us that in unity God's blessing of life is available. How can we proclaim this unity unless we have lived it? How can we proclaim the Resurrection without its imprint upon our souls?

We travel from single-mindedness to comprehension of a greater strength, a spirituality born of a greater spirit: from the ancient psalms to the life and death of Jesus, from his death to this blessing ordained by God of "life forevermore." Our woundedness within leads to dependence. Are we willing to follow and depend on Christ? on others who appear to us in his stead? on what appears as weakness in this world—woundedness—which is, in fact, deliverance?

I think of my dad standing at Mom's grave on the day we interred her ashes. After sixty-three years of marriage, he appeared so lost. The joy and time we shared was, on that day, simply emptiness and loss. Still, we stood with him, family and friends. We stood to pray together, to sing and mourn and celebrate life in harmony and unity.

One of my Spanish Bibles has an annotation on Psalm 133 that translates as "where there is harmony, certainly there." Certainly there lies God's blessing!

PRAYER: Lord, give us the certain power of your blessing as we journey together in the light of your glorious life. Amen.

But if we walk in the light as he himself is in the light, we have fellowship with one another, and the blood of Jesus his Son cleanses us from all sin.

So the writer of First John bears witness from his personal walk with Christ. Thomas experiences the resurrected Jesus in a roomful of close companions. The psalmist states unequivocally that goodness and unity are the blessings of life God gives to those who would be reconciled with others. And the early church lived together in a body of sharing, bound in a faith that had to be taken outside to a world in need of healing grace.

The writer of First John examines the matters of sin—and restoration. We are to "walk in the light as he himself is in the light." That "right" walking leads to fellowship, both with God and with one another. God does not expect us to lead sinless lives, but only our acknowledgment of sin will lead to forgiveness and restoration. Our denial of sin also denies the truth of God within us. Yet the writer affirms Jesus Christ as our Advocate before God, even when we do sin. Hard to believe!

Like Thomas, I simply can't see or believe—until I see and believe! At that moment Jesus becomes very real, a moment from which we never want to go backward again. From seeing and believing we can journey outward in the fullness of life.

Our relationship with Jesus is inside out. We recognize the resurrected Christ in the depth of our being. Only then can we learn to love fully within the core community of believers. And we can go into the world with the certainty of faith when we have known our own spirit healed by God's Spirit—from the inside out!

PRAYER: Christ has died; Christ is risen; Christ will come again! God, give us eyes to see this coming, ears to hear your word, arms to embrace your healing presence—then encourage us to move outside to share the faith. Amen.

Hope in Our Luggage

April 24–30, 2006 • Stephanie A. Ford[‡]

MONDAY, APRIL 24 • Read Acts 3:12-19

Peter's speech here at Solomon's Portico sounds harsh in places. Indeed, he speaks with fiery passion about the powerful name of Jesus, the name Peter called upon for the healing of the disabled man described in the verses just before. Yet, as Peter reminds his hearers, this is same name as the one who was sentenced to death before them. Despite that hard fact, if we listen closely, we can hear the deep concern in Peter's voice. It's as if he pleads with his friends, "Now you know."

Members of the Religious Society of Friends (Quakers) talk about the importance of being faithful to the light that one is given, trusting that more light will follow. There is something spiritually freeing about this belief. We do not have to hold on to past failures, even grievous sins or tragic ignorance. (What could be more grievous to a new believer's heart than to realize he or she had been part of the crowd that jeered Jesus?) Rather, we can start anew this day, being obedient to the words we read in scripture and being faithful to the testimony of Christ in our hearts and lives. Later in Acts, we read how the apostle Paul made such a turnaround. The energy he put into persecuting the followers of Jesus was transformed into passionate church-planting!

Living in the name of Jesus Christ of Nazareth, we are called to trust the amazing grace that changes hearts; the past no longer has power to condemn us. Alleluia!

PRAYER: Again, dear Lord, we are reminded of the incredible gift of your salvation. Like Peter and Paul, help us to forget what lies behind, and "press on toward the goal for the prize of the heavenly call of God in Christ Jesus" (Phil. 3:14). Amen.

[‡]Ordained Baptist minister, professor of Christian spirituality at Earlham School of Religion, a Quaker seminary, Richmond, Indiana.

We all carry stories of hope. In 1984 a friend and I packed up our hopes and journeyed to Beijing, China, to teach English for six months. The first day, nauseated by new smells and foods, I tried to smile amid the sea of unfamiliar faces, many of them children staring at our round-eyed foreign faces. When we finally registered at the American Embassy, I burst into tears at the sight of a large photo of Ronald Reagan. The next day, I felt worse; I found the prospect of six months away from home overwhelming. I prayed anxiously. My friend then suggested I call her father, a man with a lot of experience living overseas. I'll never forget what he said to me in my desperation, "Give it two weeks; and if you don't feel better, then you can go home." His words, short and simple, were like a miracle cure; hope welled up in my heart. I could imagine two weeks! Of course, I ended up staying and had the experience of a lifetime. The "two-week" story of hope became precious luggage in my closet of memories.

Here the psalmist, facing feelings of despair, recalls times of trust in the God who has heard his prayer before. The memory fills him with a gladness that is deeper than the joy of feasting at a generous table! The Psalms are full of such retellings, recitals of hope like the Exodus from Egypt. We too can call to mind stories in our lives where God's grace has been manifest. Perhaps a friend called you when you had just received terrible news, or you felt Christ's presence in the midst of terrible fear or stress. Opening these memories can renew your faith and hope!

PRAYER: O Lord, remind my heart of your steadfast presence, and call to mind the memories of your surprising and miraculous touches in my life. In a fresh way, may I live with trust in the unexpected grace of this new day. Amen.

In this era of uncertainty around the globe, issues of peace and security are utmost in our minds and hearts. We fear for the safety of our children and grandchildren; we fear for ourselves! The *Oxford English Dictionary* gives one definition of "security" as "well-founded confidence, certainty." In fact, the psalmist could not have put it better.

As a child and even well into adulthood, I rarely went to sleep without a light on in the hall. Besides illuminating the benign objects behind the mysterious shadows in my room, the light reassured me that Someone was indeed keeping watch. This was my hope and my prayer.

Still, as believers, when we talk about our hope in the Lord, we do not consider physical safety to be ultimate. We also recognize that our security is grounded in a heavenly reality—and that we can only find true peace as we release our spirits to the One who secures us forever. Of course, this truth is more easily said than lived, but if we honestly acknowledge how little control we have over a myriad of factors in being human, we realize how much surrender and trust are part of our daily lives.

The surrender we make to God in falling asleep is a kind of spiritual discipline. We let go for a number of hours and rest in joyful expectation of sunrise. In a small way, we get to practice our own death and resurrection—having well-founded confidence in the One who created and redeemed us, our Lord who sustains us always.

PRAYER: It is hard, dear Lord, to keep our hearts from the fearful outlook that permeates the news and has become common conversation at the marketplace. Help us remember the gift of Christ's resurrection and the promise we carry of heavenly security. Amen.

I have a friend whose father was a famous college basketball player in the state where he grew up. Everywhere my friend went, when folks discovered the relationship to his popular dad, doors would magically open. Unfortunately, my family name doesn't give me special perks when I try to buy a car at the Ford dealership. Henry is not my dad's first name.

In this passage, the epistle writer reminds us of the amazing heritage of being sons and daughters of a Parent more remarkable than any father or mother on this earth. Moreover, we read that the full realization of the spiritual genetics of being God's children has yet to be revealed! Yet, as the author of First John explains, when our eyes are fixed on God's son, Jesus, we find ourselves naturally growing into this divine purity. And therefore, we become more and more like our beloved Parent.

Sometimes we easily forget that through Jesus Christ we are no longer limited to the genetics of our human egos or by our earthly life cycle. When we surrender to the transforming power of the Holy Spirit, our true sonship and daughterhood begin to be revealed.

For example, Christians around the world are rediscovering the powerful gift of healing prayer, and, indeed, Christ invites us to be his brothers and sisters in this ministry. As children of God we are called to tell others joyfully who their Parent is and to watch as doors of grace open.

PRAYER: Lord, we belong to a precious family tree, and yet we often forget our eternal lineage and the wonders of growing into our genetic possibilities. Help us fix our eyes on your son Jesus whom we get to know through scripture. May we grow to be more and more like him! Amen.

While meditating on this passage, my eyes were drawn to two words: *children* and *righteous*. Then came the memory of an incident that happened just as I moved from childhood to adolescence, an experience in which I learned the true meaning of the word *righteous*—that is, conforming to the way of God.

That summer, my sister and I took the bus to stay with my aunt and her family for a week. My aunt's home was a magnet for the neighborhood children, who found in her a person who expressed genuine interest in them. One girl, about my age, who came around was someone I really didn't like. Outwardly during the day, I said and did the "right" things, but inwardly and then later whispering to my sister, I voiced my disdain.

One morning, my aunt brought up this sticky subject; it became obvious that she had overheard my belittling gossip. She told me that I needed to understand the hard story of this child's life, how she lived with relatives because her parents were unable to care for her. I was shocked, both because I had showed such an ugly face to my beloved aunt and because I had judged this poor girl with such meanness.

I could no longer deceive myself, nor would my aunt allow me to do so. Whether we label our actions and behaviors as mean, inappropriate, or offensive to God, we run a grave risk when we refuse to acknowledge our sin as sin. "Everyone who does what is right is righteous." Being truly righteous as a child of God is to see the other through God's eyes, to consider the other with a broad-minded mercy, to be righteous, "just as [God] is righteous." We will never fully know the story of another; our task is to be faithful in Christlike compassion, both without and within.

SUGGESTION FOR MEDITATION: **Reflect thoughtfully on the people in your life. To whom have you closed your eyes in secret disdain while masking it with superficial righteousness? Invite God to soften your heart so that you might see this child of God with divine eyes.**

Did you know that one square inch of skin contains 4 yards of nerve fibers, 1300 nerve cells, 100 sweat glands, 3 million cells, and 3 yards of blood vessels? The body is a creation that God declared "good," and a vessel of God's most amazing gift of all, Jesus Christ. Here, at the end of Luke, the disciples are startled by the sight of the resurrected body of their beloved teacher. Jesus seems to speak gently to his bewildered friends and invites them to touch and see for themselves that he does indeed have "flesh."

In the history of the church, we encounter a mixed record on the ways Christians have treated the gift of the body. Certainly, we believe there is more to us than our bodies; but if we are not careful to remember the incarnation and resurrection, we may forget how the very body of Jesus testifies to God's esteem of earthly life.

As Luke reminds us, the physical body of the resurrected Christ reveals to the disciples the fullness of God's plan. With Jesus no longer physically present with us, then our hands and feet carry on God's work, bearing witness to the resurrection of the Lord.

Seeing Jesus left the disciples forever changed. Believing in the risen Christ leaves us changed forever too. Luke's message is simply this: believers who affirm that the Lord is risen must ready themselves for what God has in store. We open ourselves to God's will, God's mission, God's call.

As Luke promises, the peace of God will be with us—now and wherever our faith in God takes us.

PRAYER: Creator God, we give you thanks that we are fearfully and wonderfully made! Remind us to celebrate the gift of eternal life by beginning here as earthly vessels for your Spirit to work. Amen.

SUNDAY, APRIL 30 • Read Luke 24:44-48

It is a breathtaking moment in scripture. The bewildered disciples have seen Jesus in the flesh, eating before them. The cloud of grief and confusion evaporates before their eyes, for Jesus opens their minds to the meaning of his life, death, and resurrection, which has eluded them. This moment would have an impact on generations to follow. Jesus commands the disciples to translate their newfound joy into evangelism, to witness to this miraculous testimony of forgiveness of sin, the Gospel message of reconciliation and new life.

As young teenagers, my sister and I witnessed door-to-door with our church youth group. Later on in our teens, we handed out tracts at a popular vacation spot. I look back on these worthy endeavors thoughtfully; were we the kind of witnesses that Jesus calls his disciples to be in this passage? Consider the meaning of "witness" in verse 48. Jesus refers to the kind of witness brought to speak before the court, someone who can witness to a personal experience of certain events!

It is important to witness to the principal beliefs of our Christian faith but equally important is our testifying to our encounters with Christ and sharing our ongoing spiritual experiences. Such witnessing can feel countercultural, and some times and places are more appropriate than others. But such timidity is not in keeping with the way of Jesus, who defied cultural taboos regularly by speaking with women and other social outcasts.

Perhaps on a plane trip for several hours, you strike up a conversation with the person next to you. Or you have a regular lunch group at work, and you find yourself wanting to tell them about a recent answer to prayer. In these typical, daily encounters, let us remember that witnessing goes far beyond passing out tracts.

PRAYER: Lord, sometimes it is easy to "fall asleep" around the daily witness to our faith. Nudge our hearts and help us take advantage of the regular opportunities to tell others of our faith experiences. May we be stirred even this day! Amen.

Demonstrating Holy Courage

May 1–7, 2006 • Steven J. Christopher[‡]

MONDAY, MAY 1 • Read Acts 4:5-12

Peter's willingness to speak the truth about Jesus demonstrates boldness and courage. Peter states that a recently executed Jewish peasant was actually the savior for whom the Jews yearned. His claim of Jesus as the "cornerstone" of the Temple, the hub of Jewish religious life, challenges the authority of the Jewish religious leaders.

Peter knows that his speech also endangers his life. The Roman leaders, preoccupied with maintaining order, have probably forgotten about Jesus by the time Peter delivers his speech. But now another Jewish troublemaker talking nonsense about the Messiah confronts their assumption that things are back to normal. If passed along to the Roman authorities, Peter's comments would give them reason to execute him.

Peter's willingness to speak the truth about Jesus provides a model for the church's witness today. Peter spoke the truth, no matter how dangerous or politically incorrect the truth sounded to the political and religious authorities of his day. Christ calls us to speak the truth like Peter, even if our proclamation violates social norms and established standards of reason. Sometimes the word of God will sound comprehensible, sometimes incredulous and silly. Our concern as the church is not whether the proclamation receives a favorable response but whether we proclaim the word with boldness and courage.

PRAYER: God of mercy, may your Spirit enter our hearts to motivate us to live with holy boldness, following in the way of the Christ, who voluntarily confronted the principalities and powers of this world. Amen.

[‡]Staff attorney, Legal Aid Society of Middle Tennessee and the Cumberlands; pastor, Douglass Chapel and Liberty United Methodist Church, Gallatin, Tennessee.

The psalmist's comparison of God to a shepherd reveals God's guidance and direction. The analogy also suggests that the role of the believer is to be under the shepherd's authority and protection. The role of the ancient shepherd was to lead the sheep through the wilderness and, when necessary, return the sheep to the right path. The sheep did not exercise the same freedom that they would have had if the shepherd abandoned the sheep and left them alone. But such freedom would have come at the price of losing the shepherd's guidance and protection.

One of the central principles of the Jewish faith is "salvation history"—the notion that God has acted in Israel's history and has blessed and punished Israel in accordance with Israel's adherence to its covenant with God. Whether good or bad, the political welfare of Israel rested in God. Israel even believed that God worked in guiding the hands of those who did not know God. After the Babylonian exile, the biblical writers portrayed God as using Cyrus, the Persian emperor, as an instrument to facilitate the rebuilding of the Temple and the restoration of Israel's military strength.

Just as a shepherd leads a flock of sheep, God led, guided, and directed the nation of Israel throughout history. Israel attributed its periods of prosperity to God's grace; its time of slavery in Babylon reflected God's judgment and condemnation of Israel for its failure to abide by the terms of its covenant with God.

Like ancient Israel, we believe that God guides our lives. Being God's people does not mean that our lives will be easy—God is a God of judgment as well as grace as the Israelites experienced in their Babylonian exile. But the good news of salvation history is the assurance that God's intentions for the world will ultimately prevail.

PRAYER: O God, give us the wisdom to discern your guiding hand in our lives, and give us the steadfastness to follow your directive action, so that your kingdom may be revealed on earth as it is in heaven. Amen.

The image of walking through the valley of the shadow of death would have been evocative to an ancient reader. Imagine the terror of walking through dark valleys in the evening in the ancient Israelite wilderness without the benefit of flashlights or other modern technology. Those trapped in the wilderness after dark risked becoming lost and dying of thirst. The darkness also rendered travelers helpless and defenseless against wild animals and thieves. It is no coincidence that the psalmist refers to this experience as the "shadow of death" (RSV).

The psalmist indicates that God freely and voluntarily chooses to walk beside us in those moments when we find ourselves trapped in the darkest valley. We are there because we have inadvertently lost our way. People contemplating being stuck in the darkness of the wilderness would have pitied those caught in this situation and would have thanked God that they were not caught in the valley themselves. Out of love and concern for the psalmist, God chooses to be in the dark valley of human suffering where others would choose not to go in order to provide guidance, direction, and comfort.

As followers of the Christ, we believe that the Christ chose to go to the darkest of valleys, the cross, and die for our sins to reconcile us to God. And the risen Christ walks with us during our occasions of suffering and despair. The Christ is there with us freely out of grace and love, providing guidance and direction. We believe that as disciples called to follow in the way of the Christ, we must seek out places where persons suffer and be present in those places to mirror the love and compassion of Christ. Through God's grace, those places of darkness will be transformed from places of terror and despair to places of peace and light.

PRAYER: **Almighty God, give us the desire to go voluntarily where persons walk in the shadow of death, to places of oppression, sickness, and suffering. May we be Christ for others in those places. Amen.**

The author of First John defines love for one another as the central hallmark of the Johannine community. We can best translate the Greek word for love chosen by the author, *agape*, into contemporary English as "active goodwill." The author associates love with taking action to meet physical need. As the author suggests in verse 17, it is inconceivable that persons with an abundance of physical possessions could claim to manifest love for those less fortunate without sharing their possessions.

The author also associates love with a willingness to sacrifice for the object of love. The ultimate model of love is the love of Christ who willingly humbled himself as a servant and sacrificed himself for our sins. The author expects that the true believers in his community will sacrifice themselves for the good of the world, even being willing to die for the faith as Christ did.

The author calls his community to manifest *agape* love to the whole world. The writer tells the reader to love others without placing any limitations on those the reader is called to love. Nothing indicates that the community should limit its love to those within the community, those who are righteous, or those who otherwise merit love.

As the church, we are called to demonstrate *agape* love by acting to meet the physical and spiritual needs of others. As Jesus sacrificed himself for the world, we have the responsibility to sacrifice ourselves for the good of others. And we are called to manifest *agape* love to everyone, not just those who share our nationality, skin color, or religion. We must manifest love if we seek to live in accordance with the new covenant established through Christ's sacrifice. If we claim to live as disciples and do not manifest *agape* love, we live a lie.

PRAYER: Loving God, as the Christ laid down his life that all humanity might live eternally in your presence, mercifully grant that we may lay down our lives for others and live as servant people. Amen.

Christians often behave differently in church than they do during the week in the workplace and at home. When Christians gather to worship, they tend to talk differently, dress differently, and behave differently. Christians tend to act in a manner that they consider more pious and sanctimonious when they are in God's house.

Perhaps our belief that who we *really* are is unacceptable to God accounts for the distinction between our behavior on Sunday morning and our behavior throughout the week. Even if we have genuinely professed our faith in Christ and have accepted Christ as our savior, we still feel the nagging sensation that we are not reconciled to God and God does not accept us as we are. On this basis, we feel that we have to be someone other than our true selves when we enter God's house.

The author of First John tells us that if we have truly turned to God and accepted the redemption offered in Christ, we have been reconciled to God and are accepted by God as we are. When we turn to God in worship and prayer, we may approach God's presence with boldness, and we have the privilege of feeling comfortable in God's presence. The Greek word *parrhesia,* translated as "boldness," also suggests "speaking freely and openly."

Through Christ, we are no longer strangers to God; we feel at home in God's presence. Like the prodigal son who is welcomed home, God welcomes us with the warmth and excitement that a father welcomes home a son who was lost. Our welcome home and ability to approach God with boldness is not due to our own merit. Our status as God's children is due only to the gracious love of God that accepts us as we are and calls us to enter into relationship.

PRAYER: O God, in the resurrection of your son you have welcomed us as children and entered into a covenantal relationship with us. Through your Spirit, may we obey your commandments and live as your covenant people. Amen.

SATURDAY, MAY 6 • Read John 10:11-13

Jesus identifies himself as the good shepherd who willingly goes to any lengths to save us, even to the extent of laying down his own life. The image of a shepherd going to great lengths to protect his flock would have resonated with Jesus' ancient listeners. Shepherds in ancient Israel were known for their willingness to sacrifice themselves for the flock's welfare.

Many shepherds endangered themselves for the flocks out of economic self-interest. If a shepherd owns the sheep, they might be his only asset and source of livelihood. If the sheep wander off or are eaten by wild animals, the shepherd would be left penniless. Alternatively, if the shepherd safeguards the sheep for an owner, the loss of the sheep would indebt the shepherd to the owner. Paying such a debt would create an enormous financial burden for a shepherd. Faced with the prospect of economic ruin, shepherds understandably would go to extreme lengths to ensure the flock's protection.

Jesus manifests this same energy and diligence in nurturing and protecting the life of the world as a shepherd who protects his flock. But where ancient shepherds' primary motivation was that of survival, Jesus' sole motivation is love for the world and a desire that the world be reconciled to God. God's survival and welfare does not require the world's survival or redemption. And yet in Jesus, the Divine chose to voluntarily lay down his life for us to ensure our capacity to experience eternal life.

PRAYER: O God, your will is that someday every knee shall bow and every tongue confess that Jesus Christ is Lord and Shepherd of our lives. Grant that your people, illumined by your Spirit, may accept the salvation you offer and live as your people. Amen.

Jesus uses the image of a shepherd protecting a flock of sheep to describe the relationship between him and the world. Shepherds in the ancient Near East were regarded as physically strong, courageous, and resilient. They had the responsibility of caring for a flock in the middle of a desolate wilderness. The image of the shepherd was so revered that many ancient Near Eastern cultures favorably associated their rulers with shepherds. The authors of Second Samuel focused upon David's former life as a shepherd in portraying him as an ideal king.

The image of human beings as sheep suggests the necessity of the church's reliance upon Christ's leadership and strength. Without the leadership of a shepherd, sheep are prone to wander off the path and end up scattered and disorganized. Without the shepherd's strength, sheep fall prey to the attacks of thieves and wild animals. The only hope for the sheep's survival and direction lies in the hands of the shepherd.

The church is strong when it submits to Christ's leadership and is guided by the hand of Christ. When the church orders its life without the direction of Christ, the church is as helpless as a flock of sheep without a shepherd. The world that the church exists in is a dangerous place filled with temptations and trials. The world is also a confusing place that makes it easy for the church to lose its direction. The church's only hope lies in discerning the guiding voice of Christ through diligence in Bible study, worship, and good works.

PRAYER: O Lord our God, you sought us and offered us redemption before we could speak your name. You manifest yourself to us as a shepherd who watches over his flock—one flock, one shepherd. We give you thanks and praise your name for your mercy and grace. Amen.

Love from the One for All

May 8–14, 2006 • Ron Barham[‡]

MONDAY, MAY 8 • Read 1 John 4:7–21

No fear in love

The stranger had appeared at Sunday school after a long weekend of drinking at a local festival. A large man, he broadcast hangover breath and an unchanged-clothes "fragrance." Nonetheless, the Sunday school class had invited him to stay for worship. Their small membership church practiced "open hearts, open minds, open doors."

The man, not quite housebroken to church customs, heartily joined in the Palm Sunday service. The largely older congregation joyfully paraded with palms and hallelujahs. Processing with uncertain step, the visitor caught on quickly and waved his palm branches without reservation.

Just before the sermon, the congregation passed the peace. The visitor seemed genuinely blessed as each person, taking his hands, looked into his eyes, and said, "The peace of God be with you." But when others sat down, he did not. He restlessly ambled around the edge of the sanctuary. No one knew what to do. Trying to start the sermon, the pastor felt rattled and quite uncertain as to what would happen next.

After several minutes a woman rose from her seat and, taking the imposing man by the hand, asked, "Would you like to come sit with me?" He complied with her gentleness and sat quietly and attentively through the remainder of the service.

Only weeks before, that kind woman had told her pastor of her inordinate fear of strangers. They had prayed that God would help her overcome her phobia. Fears are real, but the kind of love God gives nudges out, expels, and conquers fear.

SUGGESTION FOR MEDITATION: cast out

---

‡Executive Director, Wood Institute, Mathiston, Massachusetts; pastor of Sturgis and Big Creek United Methodist Churches.

The essence of God

This passage uses some form of the word *love* no less than twenty-nine times. For the writer, love for one another characterizes the Christian community.

Clearly the writer has been bathed in the love of God for all. He bears witness to the singular, saving act of God wherein God's very essence is conferred: "His Spirit. . . . his Son as the Savior of the world." All are the intended recipients.

Saying the same thing about six different ways, the writer tells of the divine intention of multiplied love and the sign of belonging to God: "Beloved, since God loved us so much, we also ought to love one another." Love defines a relationship marked by trust, hope, acceptance, goodwill, mutuality, and concern for the other.

The story from yesterday continues. When it came time for the offering during worship, the you-could-hardly-miss-him stranger fumbled about earnestly for something to give. He literally emptied every pocket somewhat noisily, dropping their contents. Turning each pocket inside out, he put all that he had into the offering plate: one penny and two Mardi Gras doubloons (fake money).

The treasurer gave the "coins" to the pastor who has placed them on the pulpit to remind her that the church must welcome the next person God wants in God's family, especially "strangers" (3 John 5). These coins also remind her that on a particular occasion, one child of God gave all that he had. Perhaps his giving was in response to the accepting love extended to him from the One for all through God's children in a small village church.

SUGGESTION FOR MEDITATION: the next stranger

A song everybody sings sooner or later

This last part of Psalm 22 echoes many of the other psalms of praise. The psalmist catalogs a list of those to whom witness of the praiseworthiness of the Lord will be given: kindred and worship gatherings (22), all the descendants of Jacob (23), great festal gatherings (25), the poor and seekers (26), all the families of the nations (27), even the dead (29), plus future generations (30). God's deliverance knows no bounds of geography or time.

We could paste this passage into many other psalms, and it would blend quite well. However, the praise is all the more significant because of what comes before. Having begun with words that echo the abandonment many have felt in dark nights of the soul ("Why have you forsaken me?"), the psalmist recalls God's help (9-10), prays for deliverance (19-21a), and claims rescue as God's answer (21b). It is precisely over against the experience of forsakenness that this praise is profoundly magnified. Jesus, at the zenith of his suffering on the cross, called up this psalm to give voice to his hour of agony (Mark 15:34). Surely he embraced the entire psalm, which affirms that God does not hide God's face but rather hears each cry for help.

I asked some adults at church to share in groups of three a time they felt farthest from God and a time they felt closest to God. When the small groups reconvened, one group reported that each member had shared that the season closest to God was the same time as the experience of feeling farthest from God. Incredibly, each group, meeting separately, reported the same peculiarity for twenty-three of the twenty-four participants.

Although each psalm can stand alone on its own poetic and spiritual expression, it is probably no accident that Psalm 22 is immediately followed by arguably the most universally comforting and affirming psalm of all.

SUGGESTION FOR MEDITATION: **farthest and closest**

Good news without borders

Luke, having given an orderly account of the Jesus event in the Gospel, recounts in the Acts of the Apostles the spread of the good news about Jesus. Luke speaks of a Jesus not confined to the limited time and place spanned by the Savior's brief ministry. Luke, himself a Gentile, records Jesus' encounters with Samaritans, lepers, women, a Roman military officer, children, down-and-outers, demon-possessed persons, all sorts.

Acts chronicles the expansion of the proclamation and the beginnings of "the church" as it blossomed beyond the tiny region where Jesus' ministry took place. Acts 1:8 could properly be called Luke's outline of the book of Acts. The story line moves from the coming of the Holy Spirit in Jerusalem just days after Easter, to the surrounding region (Judea), to Samaria, and finally to Paul's arrival in Rome, doorway "to the ends of the earth." The book of Acts gathers up first the Jews, then Gentiles, and proceeds in widening circles of inclusivity.

The Ethiopian is an important officer in the court of his queen. On a religious pilgrimage to the holy place in Jerusalem, he perhaps picks up a religious tract or scripture left by the Gideons of his time in his hotel room. On his return trip he encounters Philip, whom the Spirit dispatches to the desert-road meeting. Reading scripture aloud, as was the custom, the eunuch does not understand its meaning. Yet he exhibits a receptivity to learning: he invites Philip to sit beside him and then raises the pivotal question, "About whom, may I ask you, does the prophet say this?" Philip then begins interpreting the scripture about Jesus in such a way that the eunuch receives it with conviction as good news.

The spread of the good news of the gospel depends upon receptivity and Spirit-led mentors. With the eunuch's baptism Luke clearly affirms that Jesus is Christ for all people.

SUGGESTION FOR MEDITATION: disciples from different cultures

FRIDAY, MAY 12 • Read Acts 8:26-40

A guide to the essence of God

Philip is the lead actor in the drama of Acts 8. Following the stoning death of Stephen (7:54-60), a great persecution arose against the church in Jerusalem. Philip went to proclaim the good news of Christ in the hill country north of Jerusalem. The Samaritans there were a mixed culture with a muddied ancestral connection with the Jews (Judeans) but despised by their southern cousins.

Luke records Philip's considerable success in Samaria: multitudes respond and "there was great joy in that city" (8:8). His powerful work draws the services of Peter and John from Jerusalem to add to Philip's successes (8:14–17). The great news spreads among the Samaritans, and they receive the Holy Spirit.

Then an angel of the Lord directs Philip to go in the opposite direction to a nowhere place away from both the northern villages and the responsive crowds. On a deserted wilderness road he spots the only person around, sitting in a chariot (the convertible sports car or humvee of that day) reading something, perhaps resting his horses.

This guy is an official in the court of the Queen of Ethiopia. He is also a foreigner; but Philip has been warming up on Samaritans, so he feels at ease in conversation. He inquires, "Do you understand what you are reading?" and the Ethiopian replies, "How can I, unless someone guides me?"

This passage is a paradigm for the ministry of teachers. Philip has done well as a preacher before the crowds, but here he chats about the gospel in the give-and-take of an individual conversation. The man's question is the voice of every student, seeker, and inquirer after the ways of God. A disciple is a learner. Serving as a guide is the blessing and honor, as well as the task, of all good teachers.

SUGGESTION FOR MEDITATION: guide

A broken connection

A muscadine and scuppernong vineyard grows at our mission institute. Volunteers carefully prune the runners (branches) away from the main vine during the dormant season in winter. Such pruning stimulates the spring and summer growth of new runners on the vine. Grapes emerge only on the new growth. The volunteer vine growers appreciate the necessity of cutting away the old in order to bring on the new. And, yes, to insure destruction of any possible disease carry over, they even build a fire for the vines and branches that produce no fruit.

Every few days in late summer last year, I stopped by to observe the grapes' steady growth toward maturity. On the fourth row one particularly large cluster of grapes drew my interest. I checked it with each visit as the fruit swelled and began to ripen.

One evening I stopped by just in time to see a raccoon dragging away that very branch, heavy with the largest bunch of grapes in the entire vineyard. The masked bandit ran for the woods and left the branch on the ground. With each subsequent visit I observed the withering and waste of the unripened grapes on that separated branch even as the rest of the vineyard matured.

During my stopovers in the vineyard, I noted the difference in productivity between the pruned branches and those that are separated from the vine. John's presentation of the allegory of Jesus as the vine, the consequences of not staying connected, and the bearing of fruit became evident in our vineyard (and to the people of Jesus' day) in a simple and clear way.

SUGGESTION FOR MEDITATION: **attached**

A continuing connection

Especially in the Old Testament, grapes (fruit) and a productive vineyard symbolize both God's blessing/favor/goodness, as well as God's chosen people and their work on earth. The New Testament also presumes that same symbolism. Vines, vineyards, cultivation, and wine are part of the culture of everyday life. Metaphors, festivals, religious practices, scripture, and art spring from the Creator's life-giving gift.

This passage from John is reminiscent of "the song of the unfruitful vineyard" in Isaiah 5. Both passages affirm that the type of fruit produced becomes the basis for determining faithfulness. Obedience to God's covenantal expectations and commandments is the criterion for continued existence of the mutually fulfilling relationship (Isa. 5:8-24; John 15:10).

"Abide" is the key verb and activity emphasized in John. It means "continuing," "remaining." Addressing believers, Jesus declares them already cleansed (from the same Greek root word for pruning). Having established the relationship of faith, the concern becomes maintaining the relationship or abiding in the Father's love. Followers of Jesus Christ stay connected to the Creator, Redeemer, Sustainer; that connection determines who they are and who they become.

John Wesley, the accidental founder of the Methodist movement, labored over this matter of abiding. Briefly stated, his "General Rules" for the Methodist people are these: 1) doing no harm; 2) doing good; and 3) attending upon all the ordinances of God, which include public worship, ministry of the word, the Lord's Supper, family and private prayer, searching scriptures, fasting or abstinence. These disciplines put a person in a position to experience the grace of the One for all. They help develop spiritual health for all who know God's love and desire not only to stay connected but to abide.

SUGGESTION FOR MEDITATION: **staying attached**

Love First, Always

May 15–21, 2006 • *Jean M. Blomquist*[‡]

MONDAY, MAY 15 • **Read Acts 10:44-46a**

It's easy for me to read this passage quickly, smile at the quaintness of the "circumcised" believers' astonishment, and pass over its implications for my life today.[*] A closer look, however, makes me stop and think: *Whom do I consider the most unlikely to receive the Holy Spirit's touch?* Although I tell myself I believe that God holds all humanity in the divine embrace, who (even among those who call themselves Christian) do I believe lacks the capacity, openness, or humility to hear and receive the word of God? Wouldn't I be astounded (not to mention bewildered and perhaps a bit envious) if God poured out the Holy Spirit on that person or group in a concrete, visible way?

Earlier in Acts 10 Peter states, "I truly understand that God shows no partiality" (v. 34). The Holy Spirit fell on new and seemingly unlikely believers because they "heard the word," the gospel message. Key to that message is the centrality of love—love of God, self, and others. If God shows no partiality in embracing, loving, and bestowing the gifts of the Spirit, can I then love some and not others? If the answer is no, as Jesus teaches, how can I—how can we—learn to live out the inclusiveness of the Holy? How do we share the extravagance and even outrageousness of God's love? Perhaps we begin by acknowledging who we have excluded from our own love.

SUGGESTION FOR MEDITATION: Whom do you consider least likely to be touched by the Holy Spirit? Imagine the Holy Spirit being poured out upon this person (or people). How might the Spirit transform them—and you?

---

[*]Here "circumcised believers" means Jewish believers in Christ, including women.

[‡]Writer; attends St. Michael and All Angels Episcopal Church, Albuquerque, New Mexico.

"Club rules"—that's how a friend once explained much church behavior. His comment seemed flip and irreverent, but later I saw truth in his words. We people of faith sometimes misplace our priorities in the guise of being faithful, protecting the sacred, and keeping order in the church. Love takes a backseat to guarding long-established religious mores. But even Jesus, when attacked by the Pharisees for not observing the law when his disciples plucked heads of grain as they walked through a grainfield on the sabbath, said, "The sabbath was made for humankind, and not humankind for the sabbath (Mark 2:27). Perhaps Peter has this in mind when he speaks to the circumcised believers concerning the Gentiles upon whom the Spirit has just been poured out.

By this time baptism has become the standard ritual for acknowledging one's assent to the Christian message and acceptance into the Christian community, but the ritual has, up to then, been available only to Jewish, or circumcised (which, as we noted yesterday, in *practice* included women), Christians. Peter, citing the work of the Spirit, challenges the Jewish believers to open their hearts and minds by asking, "Can anyone withhold the water for baptizing these people who have received the Holy Spirit just as we have?" Though I imagine some may have grumbled, no one seems to have protested because Peter immediately orders that these Gentiles be baptized.

Clearly the Spirit can circumvent what we think is right and proper. Our challenge is to recognize when our once life-giving customs and rituals have calcified into unbreakable or unloving "club rules" that not only shut out the Gentiles but also the very Spirit of God.

PRAYER: Gracious God, help me to love first, always. Open my heart to those I prefer to shut out. Move freely in and through us all. Amen.

Whom would you invite to stay with you "for several days"? Most of us hesitate before we extend such an invitation because we're busy, don't have a guest room, or are just too tired to entertain. But when someone special comes along—someone who nourishes us deeply—our excuses often evaporate, and we welcome that special someone into our hearts and homes.

Cornelius, along with his friends and relatives, clearly recognized Peter as one of those special people. Peter brought them the good news of Jesus Christ. Now, we assume, they wanted Peter to teach them how to live the Christian life on a daily basis, including how to love as Jesus had taught. Although (or perhaps because) they were new in the faith, they invited Peter to stay with them.

In many ways, including the practice and practicalities of hospitality, life today is very different than it was for Peter and Cornelius. But in other ways, life—especially life in the Spirit—is much the same. When the Spirit comes upon us as it did Cornelius and his friends and family, our lives are transformed. We mark that transformation—sometimes in our community of faith, sometimes in the stillness of our own hearts—in some tangible way, just as their transformation was marked by baptism. And because we, as they did, continually need to develop and cultivate the reality and expression of the Spirit's presence in our daily lives, we seek over and over to open our hearts to those who teach and nourish us in the life of faith.

SUGGESTION FOR MEDITATION: **Invite someone who will nourish and teach you to stay with you for several days. That someone may be a friend you long to see, a book you want to read, a scripture passage that challenges or comforts you, or a favorite trail that, when hiked, quiets you and helps you hear the voice of the Holy.**

THURSDAY, MAY 18 • Read 1 John 5:1-5

A simple message permeates the Johannine epistles: God is love. Our capacity to love—and to forgive—is both the test and the testimony of our faith.

I once attended an interdenominational conference where tensions over theology, tradition, and liturgical practice flared; cultural differences strained discussion. I had particular difficulty with one man who, to me, seemed racist and judgmental. My stomach knotted up whenever he spoke.

Because of the tensions at the conference, plans for a closing service foundered until someone introduced us to a ritual from the Orthodox tradition. Just before Ash Wednesday, the community gathers, and each person asks forgiveness of every other person for anything said or done in the past year that caused offense or hurt. Then they share the kiss of peace. We were invited to do the same. I looked for, and dreaded seeing, that "difficult" man. He found me first, and without hesitation said, "If I have said or done, . . . forgive me." I responded in the same way. At the end, we laughed and hugged, our animosity gone.

But forgiving and loving is much easier when you don't expect to see someone again. Loving in a community can be much harder. The Johannine community, like many of our faith communities today, was divided. The elder confronted them (and us as well) with a challenging reality: those who believe that Jesus is the Christ have been born of God, and those who love the parent (God) love the child. That "child" is both Christ and other people of faith.

We cannot love in the abstract. Real loving can be messy, uncomfortable, even discouraging at times; but we are still called, always, to love.

PRAYER: Tender God, when I resist loving, draw me so deeply into your love that my resistance is washed away and love flows through me to all whose lives touch mine. Amen.

"Would you like ice cream or brownies?" I asked. Greg, my then-new husband, answered with a grin, "Yes!" Over the years, I've learned to phrase my questions more carefully, but occasionally I forget and get a resounding "Yes!" that doesn't really give me the answer I want.

Maybe the members of the Johannine community weren't getting the answer they wanted either. The question "Is Jesus human or divine?" (or, more accurately, the answer to it) is probably what divided their community. The elder answered their question with a resounding and perhaps annoying "Yes! Jesus is both human and divine."

What does that mean for us? It may, for one thing, help us understand the nature of faithful love more fully—that love is human and divine. When we embrace only the humanity of Jesus, we quickly find ourselves trapped in a messiah complex, feeling we must do all that needs doing in the world. When we embrace only the divinity of Jesus, we may separate ourselves from the world and fail to respond to the needs of those around us.

The truth to which the Spirit testifies—that Jesus is both human and divine—draws us into a deeper, fuller, and more balanced loving of God, self, and others that benefits and graces both others and ourselves. Balanced loving guides us toward living and loving as Jesus did: doing the hard work of the Holy while trusting always that God not only works through us but also far beyond what we have the capacity, vision, or wisdom to do.

SUGGESTION FOR MEDITATION: Reflect on the old adage, "Pray as if all depends on God, act as if all depends on you." Where in your life do you need to depend more fully on God, trusting that God holds all of life in holy hands? Where do you need to work more actively, knowing that you are God's hands in the world?

I grew up on a ranch in the Central Valley of California, a rich agricultural area. Almonds, apricots, peaches, and grapes, among many other crops, flourished there. But behind those flourishing crops lay a lot of hard work and a great deal of love.

In today's passage, spoken as he nears the end of his life and ministry on earth, Jesus once again reminds his disciples—and us—of the primacy of love. We are to "abide" in his love. But when we "abide" in Jesus' love, we don't simply sit there enjoying that love any more than a rancher sits in the middle of a peach orchard admiring the fruit without making any attempt to harvest it. That beautiful and nourishing fruit must be made available to the world.

Abiding in Jesus' love helps make holy fruit available to all, including the world within us and the world around us. Inwardly we experience a deep assurance of the Holy's love for and presence with us. Outwardly we are strengthened and given courage to do those things we otherwise could not do. Holy abiding helps us to love the unlovable and thus transform love from ideal into real. In both the inward and outward movements of abiding in the Holy, we begin to "bear fruit."

Jesus, I'm sure, had no illusions about the hard work involved in bearing fruit, the hard work involved in loving oneself, others, and God. But he did know that living and loving as God commanded—abiding in holy love—results in deep joy. That joy, which frees and completes us, cannot be taken away because it is the very joy of the Holy living within and through us.

SUGGESTION FOR MEDITATION: **Choose one of these phrases: "abide in my love," "I chose you," or "bear fruit." Pray quietly, abiding in Jesus' love and letting his words permeate both your being and your doing.**

Psalm 98 has long been one of my favorites. Even as a child, the wonderful, lilting cadences and images of roaring seas and floods clapping their hands captured my imagination and my heart. I understood the joyousness of the psalm even without fully understanding its prophetic message. I still have much to learn from this psalm, yet the wonder of the psalms is that they always speak to us. Even when we may not fully understand, our hearts and spirits are often touched. And when our hearts and spirits are not touched, our minds may understand.

Like the psalms, love often touches and transforms us—or prepares us for later transformation and deeper understanding—often without our knowing it. Perhaps that is why as a child I sensed without knowing that joy is linked to justice and vice versa and that both joy and justice are rooted in the reality that God is love. Holy love is not wimpy or sentimental love. It grows out of the heart of a compassionate God who seeks what is good for all creation. It carries us beyond the confines of our tight communities, closed minds, and hard hearts. The complete joy of which Jesus spoke (John 15:11) is linked to complete love—love of God, self, and others—and both love and joy are linked to the fullness of justice. In Psalm 98, the psalmist reminds us that God, who is love, not only has acted in the past but is present now and will come in the future. Love, carrying joy and justice with it, is a holy stream that flows through time. Perhaps that is why the "floods" clap their hands, and we sing new songs!

SUGGESTION FOR MEDITATION: **What new song do you need or desire to sing to the Lord? Pray that you may be given what you most deeply need to sing this song freely and joyfully.**

No Witness, No Joy But This

May 22–28, 2006 • *Don E. Saliers*[‡]

MONDAY, MAY 22 • **Read Acts 1:15-17, 21-26**

It is no accident that we are reading the book of Acts throughout the Easter season. The story of the newborn church in Jerusalem witnesses to the resurrected, Spirit-giving life of Christ in the world. Acts offers an astonishingly honest and detailed picture of the followers of the Way as they come to terms with their mission and ministries in time and history.

Peter has emerged as a transformed leader of the company of persons (numbering 120) in Jerusalem. They face the choice of a replacement for Judas: someone must "become a witness with us" to the resurrection of Jesus. Of two worthy persons, Matthias is chosen. We know little about the two except their presence with the disciples during Jesus' ministry. Surely both of them continued in ministry together in that company. What is clear, however, is how the ministry and apostleship of this earliest community must be continued following Christ's ascension.

So the church must be the ongoing prayer, word, and deeds of Jesus Christ in this same world in which the incarnate One of God came. Pentecost is yet to come, but here we already see the church making provisions to testify and to serve the Way of Christ. So we too must understand ourselves to be called to the mission begun in those immediate post-Resurrection days.

PRAYER: O God, grant us grace to see ourselves in the company of the apostles and to bring our best gifts to the work of Christ in the world. Amen.

[‡]William R. Cannon Distinguished Professor of Theology and Worship, Candler School of Theology, Emory University, Atlanta, Georgia.

Have you ever been called for jury duty? Recently I was called as a character witness in a court case. Sitting in the chair facing the prosecuting attorney after having sworn to "tell the truth, so help me God," I experienced an initial wave of self-doubt. Suppose I really didn't know the person whose character I was about to defend as well as I thought? Suppose he really had been living a double life? Or, what if my words simply were not convincing?

I experienced firsthand what the text refers to as "human testimony" and its limitations. I did regain some composure and simply told the truth as best I knew it. My testimony was, after all, only one part of a complicated process aimed at justice.

But now I think I understand even more clearly how much greater the "testimony of God" is than human testimony. In the letter of First John we read strong lines about God's testimony to Jesus Christ. There are three witnesses: the Holy Spirit, the water (of his baptism as well), and the blood that flowed from his side. These name specific details of Jesus' life by which the Spirit of Truth reveals who Jesus really is.

These witnesses point to one overwhelming gift that goes beyond any human telling: God's gift of eternal life in Christ. This gift is the shared life of God poured out into the world. This lavish life is God's most intimate witness to the world in the character of Christ. Human testimony is necessary—but God's own self-witness through incarnate love bears the final truth.

PRAYER: Holy Three-in-One, show us yet again signs of Christ who comes to us with the gift of eternal life for all who will receive him. Amen.

"Like a tree planted by the water, we shall not be moved." Those gathered for worship sang that old African American spiritual with gusto. We were toward the end of a two-day retreat on the meaning of baptism. "Where did that image come from, anyway?" someone asked. "It's a phrase from an old civil rights song," another replied. "I think it really comes from the psalms," another voice answered. Yes, many agreed that they had sung that psalm in church. Opening the scripture, we spontaneously spent some time reading and praying Psalm 1:

> They are like trees
>> planted by streams of water,
>> which yield their fruit in its season,
>> and their leaves do not wither.
> In all that they do, they prosper.

"Who are the ones like trees by the water?" someone asked. The replies were many: "The blessed ones don't follow the advice of wicked people." "They are blessed because they choose not to be sarcastic. They do not scoff at God's wisdom but delight in it." Finally a young girl said, "It's like the blessed ones really take God's words to heart." We agreed that she had captured the wisdom of this first psalm.

The "happy" ones meditate on God's law day and night. They bear witness to the truth God offers by walking the way of wisdom and living out scripture's life-giving words. Following Jesus is like being planted near streams of living water, and the church has been called to put down deep roots in the grace of Christ and to bear fruit in community.

PRAYER: Root us by your life-giving waters, merciful God, and cause us to delight with joy in your word and be fruitful. Amen.

Many Christian churches celebrate Christ's ascension on this day. Luke, who wrote the Gospel that bears his name, also wrote the book of Acts. He takes up the story of the early Christian community with the resurrection appearances of Jesus, which prepare them for the power of the Holy Spirit to make them all witnesses "in Jerusalem, in all Judea and Samaria and to the ends of the earth." To the astonished eyes of those gathered, Jesus ascends from their sight. They stand gazing upward, only to have messengers of God tell them that he will return to them in the same mysterious way he has departed.

Here a great mystery confronts us. Christ ascends from his life on earth, returning to the fullness of God from whom he came. But he leaves behind a community of those who hear his words and take them to heart. Now he is no longer confined to ancient Palestine and thirty-three years of a single lifetime.

With his return to the fullness of God, Christ promises the Holy Spirit and tells all who follow him that they will indeed be his witnesses to the ends of the earth. We cannot understand the Ascension if we think of it only as a dramatic levitation into the clouds. It is about who Christ is in this world, a story about how the saving grace of God is now permanently in the world. The story requires both Incarnation and Pentecost, just as the early church included the story of Christ's ascending in its celebration of the feast of Pentecost. This is why we read in Ephesians 4:10, "He who descended is the same one who ascended far above all the heavens, so that he might fill all things."

This is the mystery of our life in continuity with the disciples. We follow Christ now where he leads us. As then, so now, we bear witness to God's radical incarnate grace in this world, empowered by the Spirit his resurrected life bestows.

PRAYER: Gracious God, send anew your Spirit of wisdom and revelation upon your people, making our lives a joyful witness to all the earth. Amen.

Still echoing the story of the Ascension, we meditate today on the way in which Luke concludes his Gospel account. Following the beautiful and astounding story of the Emmaus appearance of the risen Jesus to Cleopas and the other disciple, we overhear Jesus again as he opens the meaning of the scriptures. Now he appears to the eleven others, showing himself to be fully alive, which fills them with a kind of disbelieving joy. Once again he speaks to them of the law of Moses and the words of the prophets and psalms that have been fulfilled in his life, death, and resurrection.

We may have difficulty imagining the startled disciples' initial experience of the risen Christ. In one sense, we already know the story of the emerging church. We already know the consequences that the Resurrection and the Spirit-giving had on the lives of the first followers. Yet I wonder. Perhaps we need the same bewildering joy now. The same commission and blessing that Jesus gave then, he gives now!

Does the world we know not need an arising from the dead? Do you and I not need the same shocking reality of repentance and forgiveness? Do not the nations still stand in need of a life-giving witness?

Sometimes I realize the superficiality of my grasp of what it means to be a "witness" to these things. Often I acknowledge how trivial my little round of human joys has become and how dull I am to the mystery of the gospel. Then it is, as of old, that Christ comes—breaking bread, breathing Spirit, and opening up the word in scripture. Then my life is broken open to the radical presence of Christ in this world.

PRAYER: Lord Christ, you are our Bread, our Word, our Way, our Life. All that we are and all that we have is a gift. We offer ourselves to you in return. Amen.

Have you ever been told, "I am praying for you"? Sometimes this statement expresses genuine concern for your well-being. Sometimes it expresses the speaker's wish that you could experience what he or she has experienced. Sometimes the phrase simply means, "I'll be thinking about you." In any case, I find it startling to realize that Jesus prays for us—in fact, he is the great intercessor on behalf of all humanity.

So we overhear ourselves being prayed for in John's Gospel. Scholars refer to this as the great "high priestly prayer" of Jesus for the church. What a remarkable prayer this is! Jesus is saying farewell to those whom he loves. In the prayer we hear echoes of the opening verses of John's Gospel: "In the beginning was the Word, and the Word was with God, and the Word was God." So Jesus pleads with the Father that those who follow him "may be one, as we are one." Since that time this prayer has empowered Christian unity. In this prayer we learn that we belong to Christ, and hence we belong to the full love of God: "all mine are yours, and yours are mine; and I have been glorified in them." He has given to the company of his disciples the very name of God and the words that speak the love of God for all humanity.

Shockingly enough, we may also realize that Jesus is praying before his arrest, before his trial and crucifixion. He prays knowing full well that he is heading for the death the disciples do not yet understand. Who has ever said to you, "I am praying for you," as they themselves face death and farewell? This is the love of God outpoured; God desires that we be united in this love made visible in Christ. So our visible disunity should cause sorrow but also a yearning to be in deeper communion with one another.

PRAYER: God of love and unity, take my life and faith and make me an instrument of your peace, your love, your reconciling unity in Jesus Christ. Amen.

We are to be witnesses to the One who prays for us. Among the last things Jesus does before giving himself over to suffering and death on behalf of the whole world is to pray for the community he calls out. This prayer reveals three things: the faithfulness of Jesus to the love that is God, his desire for our joy, and his sending us to be witnesses to all he said and did. There is no joy, no love, and no comparable human witness like this. We are prayed for, and that makes all the difference.

Each time I read this prayer in the context of John's Gospel, I am again reminded that Jesus prays for us in our life in this world: "I am not asking you to take them out of the world, but I ask you to protect them from the evil one." Here—in this time and this place—we are to love as God loves; we are to bear Christ's name and follow his way of life.

So we can take heart again, even when the hatred of the world seems so real, and the church itself seems to suffer such unhappy divisions. As Christ was sent from God to save us from the forces of death and evil, so we are sent to be signs of the unifying and reconciling love of God that is stronger than death and greater than our plans.

The fact that Jesus Christ, crucified and risen, remembers us in God allows us to sing with Charles Wesley: "Love divine, all loves excelling, joy of heaven, to earth come down; fix in us thy humble dwelling; all thy faithful mercies crown!"

PRAYER: God of lavish love, give us joy in our witness, that your joy may be complete as it was in Jesus our Savior. Amen.

Contemplation through Creation

May 29–June 4, 2006 • *Timothy W. Whitaker*[‡]

MONDAY, MAY 29 • **Read Psalm 104:24-34, 35b**

The distinctive Christian knowledge of God is that God is triune: Father, Son, and Holy Spirit. This knowledge represents the mind of the church as a result of its reflection upon the revelation of God to Israel and in Jesus Christ. Christians base the knowledge of God as triune not only upon the apostolic tradition in the New Testament but also upon the prophetic tradition in the Old Testament. Psalm 104 reflects a knowledge of God as Creator, the source of all, who makes everything in divine wisdom by the power of breath or spirit. Already in Israel's worship we can identify the Christian affirmation of God as Father (source), Son (wisdom), and Holy Spirit (breath).

To the Spirit of God is assigned the power of being: "When you send forth your spirit, they are created; and you renew the face of the ground." Because everything exists by the power of God's Spirit, there is an unfathomable depth in every creature. We assume that we comprehend a creature, for example a tree, because we possess the analytical knowledge supplied by botany. Yet a tree is a mystery. A tree has a presence that communicates itself to us through what we perceive in its noble trunk, its swaying branches, and its bright leaves.

By being attentive to the goodness of every creature, we can contemplate the glory of God the Creator. Every day we move through a world of marvels. To believe in the Holy Spirit, "the Lord, the giver of life, who proceeds from the Father and the Son" (The Nicene Creed) is to live in gratitude and joy.

PRAYER: Eternal God, by the same Spirit in whose power everything is created, enable us to see your glory through all of your creation until we are lost in wonder, love, and praise. Amen.

[‡]Resident bishop of the Florida area, The United Methodist Church; living in Lakeland, Florida.

According to the Gospel of John, Jesus offers a long discourse to his disciples at the Last Supper before his Passion. During this discourse Jesus promises to send the Spirit to them.

The Spirit does not first come into the world following the work of Jesus. It is by the power of the Spirit that everything exists. The Spirit had inspired the prophets of Israel and worked through the ministry of Jesus. However, after Jesus has completed his work of laying down his life so that all may have eternal life, he sends the Spirit on a new mission into the world.

The mission of the Spirit is nothing less than to illumine, inspire, guide, and empower the disciples of Jesus who are drawn to him from every nation throughout the history of the world in order that they may continue Jesus' ministry on earth. In the Gospel of John, the Spirit that Jesus promises to send from the Father is called the Paraclete. We usually translate the name Paraclete as Advocate or Helper.

This promise of the Paraclete enables the disciples to bear the news that Jesus is going to leave them. He assures them that they will not be deserted, for they will be given a Spiritual Helper. Indeed, it will be to their advantage that he go away because until he has completed his work and returned to the Father, they will not receive this Paraclete who is not limited by time and space as is the incarnate Son of God.

We who are disciples cannot accomplish our mission to continue Jesus' ministry throughout the whole world until the end of history without the Helper who is sent to us. What a mission the Spirit has! What a mission we have! With the help of this Spirit together we will do "greater works" than the Son did (John 14:12), and we shall receive anything we ask of the Father (John 16:23).

PRAYER: Eternal God, by the power of your Spirit send us into the world to do the ministry of your Son so that others might know and obey you whose nature and name is love. Through Jesus Christ our Lord. Amen.

The church is the community that confesses that Jesus Christ is the supreme revelation of God, for he is the Word of God who "became flesh and lived among us" (John 1:14). The disclosure of God's nature and purpose in Jesus Christ is a superabundant and inexhaustible source of knowledge for the world. Yet this revelation could not begin to be fully comprehended by the apostolic church or by the church in any subsequent period of history. Over time the Holy Spirit sent by Jesus from God the Father to his disciples illumines the mind of the church to perceive the depths of the wisdom of God in the revelation of Jesus Christ. The Spirit also guides the church to live more truthfully in accordance with this wisdom. If the revelation of God in the Son is final, then the illumination of that revelation by the Spirit continues.

In his discourse at the Last Supper, Jesus told his disciples, "I still have many things to say to you, but you cannot bear them now. When the Spirit of truth comes, he will guide you into all the truth." Even today the contemporary church needs the illumination of the Spirit to discern the meaning and implications of God's revelation in Jesus Christ.

The church and the Christian cannot live without the Spirit's help. This is the truth of the appeal for all of us to be Spirit-filled. Yet the Spirit who inspires, guides and empowers us is always the same Spirit who connects us to Jesus Christ and his ministry. Jesus told his disciples that the Spirit "will glorify me because he will take what is mine and declare it to you." To be Spirit-filled is to be Christ-centered. The Son and the Spirit are inseparably joined. The Spirit illumines our minds for the purpose of knowing Jesus Christ and following him in the way of service to the world.

PRAYER: Eternal God, by the illumination of your Spirit grant us the ability to see and to walk in the light of Jesus Christ, your Son our Lord. Amen.

THURSDAY, JUNE 1 • Read Romans 8:22-25

The apostles who were sent into the world following the death and resurrection of Jesus Christ lived by the power of the Holy Spirit, the first human beings to participate in the new mission of the Spirit of God. Their life in the Spirit filled them with hope because they experienced the power of the Spirit to make all things new. The apostles recognized that the emergence of the church as a missionary community and the changed lives of people were only down payments on the final purchase of the Holy Spirit, which is to transform the whole creation into a new creation.

The apostle Paul places the work of the Spirit in a cosmic context. He writes, "We know that the whole creation has been groaning in labor pains until now." The apostle views the entire cosmos as laboring in anticipation of a new birth, of a "new creation" (2 Cor. 5:17). Those of us who receive the Holy Spirit through faith in Jesus Christ enter into the life and mission of the church on earth with hope for the coming new creation. This new creation is the coming transformation in which the creation will become what God intends it to be. This is no pipe dream because God has already given us the sign of the new creation in the resurrection of Jesus Christ.

The purpose of the Spirit is not to destroy the world but to transform it. Therefore, everything we do now in the body and in history matters and may contribute to the coming new creation. The church and Christians know that it matters how we live our lives, when we offer hospitality to strangers and service to the poor, whether we witness to justice and peace, and that we cherish the creation. Through the power of the Holy Spirit our little lives are taken up into the great drama of the birth of God's new creation.

PRAYER: Eternal God, by the power of your Holy Spirit enable us to be born anew to a living hope through the resurrection of Jesus Christ and to be witnesses now to your coming new creation. Amen.

There is no Christian existence without prayer. Through the mystery of prayer we experience life in the Spirit and communion with God. It is more a gift than a task: the God within us enables us to commune with the God above us.

While a constant practice in the Christian life, prayer is especially needed in what the apostle Paul calls our "weakness." Christians know weakness as well as splendor in their lives. Yes, we know the joy of contemplating divine glory, the adventure of participating in God's mission in the world through the church, and the hope of a new creation. Yet we also know weakness: physical ailments, mental depression, emotional estrangements, spiritual apathies, griefs, disappointments, and persecutions. In times of weakness we need the help of the Spirit.

The irony is that we cannot pray when we need help the most. In acute crises when we cannot pray, we ask for the prayers of others. The church is a community in which we intercede for one another. Through intercession our spirits are touched at the center of their freedom to strengthen us in ways not possible through any other means.

Even though we need the intercession of others, we should continue to try to pray in our weakness. When our spiritual sensibility is numb, "we do not know how to pray." Yet we can ask for the Spirit's help in trust that "that very Spirit intercedes with sighs too deep for words." We may simply wait in silence. With quiet breathing we rest in solitude with an openness of spirit, trusting in the promise that the Spirit is our intercessor. Through the mystery of prayer as expectant receptivity, we experience the renewing energy of the Spirit of God in our innermost being. Often in our weakness we discover the greatest splendor of the Christian life through the intercession of the Spirit.

PRAYER: Eternal God, by the power of your Holy Spirit teach us how to pray. And when we do not know how to pray, grant that your Spirit may intercede for us with sighs too deep for words; through Jesus Christ our Lord. Amen.

According to the book of Acts, the day of Pentecost is the beginning of the church. Pentecost was a Jewish festival to give thanks for the spring harvest. During Pentecost the disciples of Jesus receive the outpouring of the Holy Spirit following the death and resurrection of the Lord. On Pentecost the Spirit comes to constitute a new community that witnesses to Jesus Christ and to transform the world into a new creation.

Acts describes the outpouring of the Holy Spirit with the metaphors of the rush of a violent wind, divided tongues as of fire appearing over the heads of the disciples, and speaking in other languages and hearing what is spoken. Has the experience of the presence of the Holy Spirit ever been described more aptly? The manifestation of the Spirit's presence brings an overwhelming sense of energy, spiritual warmth, and burning desire to communicate the reality of God's power and purpose.

The significance of what happened on the day of Pentecost did not lie in the unusual phenomena, however we may perceive them or even in the spiritual energy the disciples experienced. The significance lay in the ability of the disciples to speak and the people from many nations to hear "about God's deeds of power." In other words, the church was born in a miracle of communication to begin its mission of communicating the good news of Jesus Christ. On Pentecost the disciples became apostles sent into the world. On Pentecost we pray for power to be the apostolic church that exists to offer Christ to all peoples and to invite them to continue his ministry on earth.

PRAYER: Eternal God, by the power of your Holy Spirit enable your church to be faithful and fruitful in witnessing to others about the good news of Jesus Christ. Amen.

PENTECOST

Today Christians everywhere celebrate the day of Pentecost. By returning to the origin of the church as the community empowered by the outpouring of the Spirit to communicate the good news of Jesus Christ, Christians reclaim their purpose in history.

On the day of Pentecost, Simon Peter preached his first sermon. He began by telling the people who had come to the temple in Jerusalem from many nations that this outpouring of the Spirit of God fulfilled the prophecy of Joel who had promised that a time would come when God would inaugurate a new creation by pouring out the Spirit "upon all flesh."

The preacher on the day of Pentecost had an inspired choice for an inspired text. By choosing this text Peter showed that God is doing a new thing in human history. Now for the first time everyone can be a prophet! The gift of the Holy Spirit is offered not only to a few but to everyone. Everyone can receive power to tell the truth of God.

On the day of Pentecost the gift of the Spirit is universalized. What the writer described as the priesthood of all believers (1 Peter 2:9-10), as it was later called, is described in the book of Acts as the prophecy of all believers. On this day the church is reminded that the mission of the church is delegated to the laity. No layperson, not even the most socially marginalized, is to be denied her or his dignity as a member of God's people or role as a participant in God's mission to the world through the church. The majesty and the mission of the people of God in Jesus Christ had its beginning on the day of Pentecost.

PRAYER: Eternal God, by the power of your Holy Spirit grant that your church may fulfill its destiny to be a community in which everyone discovers his or her place in your divine love and mission to the world. Through Jesus Christ our Lord. Amen.

Transformation

June 5–11, 2006 • Heidi Schlumpf[‡]

MONDAY, JUNE 5 • Read John 3:1-7

As a coworker's due date approached, a group of employees were discussing her choice for childbirth without pain medication. We all hoped this first-time mom would have a relatively painless delivery. Then a younger woman posed a curious question: "I wonder if the baby feels pain when it's being born?" We were all struck silent as we pondered the process of being pushed by contractions, squeezed down the birth canal, and thrust into the outside world. We finally agreed that it must be painful, although gratefully the child doesn't seem to remember it.

In the Gospel of John, Jesus tells Nicodemus that no one can see the kingdom of God without being "born from above." Nicodemus finds this terminology so confusing that he asks for clarification. Jesus repeats, "Very truly, I tell you, no one can enter the kingdom of God without being born of water and Spirit." Being born again is no slight alteration; it implies a radical transformation in life that comes from accepting Christ and embracing the path of Christian discipleship.

What's often forgotten or downplayed is the fact that such transformation seldom comes easily. We do not wake up on a perfectly fine day and decide to change our lives radically. No, such life-altering change usually follows painful loss, alienation, or searching. The birth metaphor is apt. We do not get to choose the timing of our new birth; we are not in control of the process. It hurts but, thankfully, over time the memory of the pain fades, leaving only the new life to be lived.

SUGGESTION FOR MEDITATION: When have I been "born again"? Has it happened more than once? What initiated the birthing? What experience of pain do I associate with that new birth?

[‡]Managing editor, *U.S. Catholic* magazine; member, St. Gertrude's Catholic Church, Chicago, Illinois.

We had the perfect marriage. Until it ended, that is. Maybe that expectation of perfection—not only from others but from ourselves as well—explains why things fell apart. Only five years into forever, my ex-husband proclaimed he was no longer "in love" with me and left. It was, hands down, the most painful thing I've ever lived through.

But I did live through it, even though many days I swore I wouldn't. I met new friends whose enthusiasm helped numb the sting of rejection. I picked up old hobbies I had abandoned. I asked for help, not only from close friends and family but from new friends and coworkers.

I prayed, and listened in the silence for answers. And I witnessed the Spirit's movement in new places—in the board member who told me how she got through her own divorce, in the coworker who listened *ad nauseam* to my need to vent, in the women at the spirituality center who helped me see that God might have a new plan for my life. The wind was blowing, and I could hear it.

Jesus promises that "whoever believes in him may have eternal life." We often assume "eternal life" refers to life after death, but I think he also promises us life after the many smaller deaths we experience here on earth. A part of me died when my marriage ended, but a new me was given birth through the unending presence of God.

Though it's understandable to question "Why?" or "Why me?" when bad things happen to us, living a life of faith means trusting in God even when we don't understand or recognize God at work in our lives. "The wind blows where it chooses, and you hear the sound of it, but you do not know where it comes from or where it goes," John writes. Trusting the blowing of the Spirit means eternal life can begin now.

SUGGESTION FOR MEDITATION: What smaller deaths have I experienced throughout my life? When has new life been birthed out of those deaths?

I lived in southern California for three years, but I couldn't wait to get back to the Midwest. It wasn't the bumper-to-bumper traffic that did me in—it was the constant sunny, 80-degree days! I found I craved a crisp fall day, a thunderstorm, and even that four-letter word *snow*. The seasonal cycle reminded me of a basic spiritual lesson: out of death comes new life

Nature abounds with examples of new growth emerging from devastation, of life's being "born again." The ashes from a forest fire provide the fertile soil for new saplings to sprout. Falling leaves become mulch for spring's green grass. The trees' bare branches in winter remind us of the loss of fall's leaves, while anxiously awaiting spring's new buds.

"God so loved the world that he gave his only Son, so that everyone who believes in him may not perish but may have eternal life." This is the only verse in the book of John where God *gives* Jesus for the world's redemption; in the other references God *sends* Jesus. This is an important distinction. To send is to talk about God's will for the world—salvation. To give is stronger. It talks about God's love for the world.

Nature's cycles of life and death, death and renewal point toward an important truth: God can bring life out of death. But it doesn't reveal the deepest truth in this scripture: God's great love and Jesus' very presence in the world are important because they confront us with one life-or-death decision. God and Jesus confront us with the decision to believe or not to believe.

The changes of season show clearly God's work in the world and life's cycles of being born, living and dying. The gift of Jesus in our world shows the work of a promise more lasting: life lived from this day on in the unending presence of God.

SUGGESTION FOR MEDITATION: When have you felt Jesus' presence as a call to decide how you will live your life? Ask God, no matter what your season of life, to help you respond to the gift of Jesus with faithfulness.

In the movie *Eternal Sunshine of the Spotless Mind*, the characters played by Jim Carrey and Kate Winslet undergo a new procedure that erases all memory of the other after their romantic relationship goes sour. In selling the procedure to prospective clients, the doctor promises suffering people release from the pain caused by memories of an ex-boyfriend or ex-girlfriend, deceased child or pet.

It's tempting to avoid pain and suffering, but as the couple in *Eternal Sunshine* learn, sometimes the shortcut to healing isn't the wisest choice. The movie made me wonder: *If such a procedure were available, would I take advantage of it?* Thinking back to some of the worst losses I've suffered, I realized that in the middle of the most acute pain, the offer to make the suffering go away would sound very attractive.

Although the movie's technology doesn't exist, people can and do try to "erase" their memories with alcohol, drugs, or other unhealthy behaviors. But the avoidance of grief doesn't really work. As anyone who's suffered loss learns, you have to go *through* the pain in order to move past it. And, with the perspective of time, you see that although suffering is not a good thing, some good can come out of it.

In his letter to the Romans, Paul promises us that if we suffer with Christ, we may also be glorified with him. Jesus' death on the cross endows suffering with meaning; it has redemptive value. The pain of the losses in my life prompted massive emotional and spiritual growth that has made me not only a healthier but also perhaps a more compassionate person. Real life is better than illusory "eternal sunshine."

SUGGESTION FOR MEDITATION: Think back to a painful loss in your life. Would you choose to erase all the memories associated with that person or event to lessen the pain? What good has come from your suffering?

On election day, my sister and I volunteered to work for one of the presidential candidates. After several hours of knocking on doors, we returned to the central meeting hall where hundreds of other volunteers were grabbing a quick bite of pizza between assignments. Every couple of minutes an organizer with a clipboard would shout out, "I need ten people willing to go canvass a neighborhood" or "I need six people to make phone calls." Within seconds of the request, people would raise their hands, shout, "I'll go!" and gather around the clipboard guy to get their latest task.

"Whom shall I send?" God asks, and Isaiah responds, "Here am I; send me!" You don't see exclamation points too often in scripture, but I think the punctuation here is essential in conveying the sense of enthusiasm with which Isaiah answers God's call. This is no begrudging, "OK, I'll go if I have to." Isaiah experienced transformation beyond the area of personal growth. And being "born again" isn't just about securing our own salvation. After we are "born from above" and transformed by the Spirit, we are called to go into the world and be agents of transformation in the lives of other people. Our own experiences of life, death, and rebirth uniquely equip us to see the needs of others, to be more compassionate and caring toward those who suffer.

How do we know the task to which God is calling us? That in itself isn't always easy or straightforward. We might yearn for the sound of God's voice, for a clear sign, for a transparent word. But remember that even for Isaiah, the call did not come that way. God did not speak directly to Isaiah. Instead, Isaiah overhears God speaking to someone else, lamenting to the heavenly court about who might be sent on God's behalf. Isaiah, cleansed and purified, can respond with a resounding, "Here am I; send me!" Perhaps we need a readiness to overhear our call no matter how it comes and to respond.

Suggestion for meditation: Sit quietly and ask God to prepare you to hear—or overhear—your call to discipleship.

Arriving home from school one day, my sister ran ahead, slipped inside, and locked me out of the house. I pounded and screamed, but she continued to taunt me from behind the screen door and wouldn't let me in. Finally, enraged, I kicked the aluminum door until it was good and bent. Boy, was I in trouble. My parents punished me, not only for destroying a perfectly good door (I had to sell my bike to pay for it), but because I had lost my temper over a relatively benign thing.

Many of us have been taught that anger is a bad emotion, one of the seven deadly sins, in fact. Anger or wrath that leads to vengeful action disproportionate to the injury suffered is immoral. Our culture socializes women to avoid expressing anger at all costs. Better to keep quiet, even when an injustice has been done.

Many Christians who grew up with an image of God as an angry old man dishing out punishment on sinners have since decided they have little use for a deity whose voice "flashes forth flames of fire," "shakes the wilderness" and "strips the forest bare." It sounds like that kind of God needs to take an anger management course!

But sometimes anger can be a good thing—when it's righteous anger. Even Jesus was less than peaceful when he drove the money changers out of the Temple. A Christian conscience should become angry over injustice, violence, and poverty. The question is what do we do with our anger? Become bitter and cynical? Lash out at those we perceive to be our enemies? Or channel all that energy by working to fight injustice, denounce violence, and eliminate poverty?

SUGGESTION FOR MEDITATION: What injustice makes me angry? How can I channel my anger into making a positive change in the world?

One of my friends has undertaken a personal-growth program. Its underlying belief is that you can make anything happen in your life. That's a great message for people who need a kick in the seat of the pants to make some changes in their lives. But some situations and behaviors we can't change all by ourselves.

I once faced a difficult work situation. The company hired a new boss who was clearly unqualified for the job. Everyone in the department realized the mistake—everyone except upper management. When competent, long-term employees began to leave, the remaining employees begged that the problem be rectified but to no avail. My friend's personal-growth program would have told me to change the only aspect I could change: my reaction to the situation. True, but I couldn't do it alone.

This kind of self-sufficiency is dangerous. Belief in the absolute power of self-sufficiency is what got the followers of Baal in trouble. The belief that we are in control and that our efforts can secure our safety is not just a problem in the ancient Near East; it's also a problem for us now. When we act as though we are in control of our lives, Psalm 29 tells us the truth: the peace and security we seek don't begin with our efforts but with the Lord's unmistakable claim on us.

People in 12-Step programs recognize this dependence too. That's why the first three steps involve admitting your own powerlessness; acknowledging a Higher Power; and turning your problem, indeed your whole life, over to that Power. To overcome an addiction takes hard work on the part of the individual, but it also requires an admission that we can't do it alone. We need a supportive community, and we need God.

The universe is the sphere of God's reign. Our place is to trust God. Psalm 29 witnesses to the strength and peace that come from God and God's claim on us.

SUGGESTION FOR MEDITATION: What places of unrest in your life do you want to turn over to God? How can you work alongside God to help you find understanding and peace?

Ordinary People and the Spirit of God

June 12–18, 2006 • Rick L. Miller[‡]

MONDAY, JUNE 12 • Read 1 Samuel 15:34–16:13

Many of us find the thought of being considered ordinary insulting. We have built our lives, our reputations, our careers, our ambitions—by and large—on being extraordinary. We find most offensive a teacher's statement that our child is ordinary. A letter of recommendation that describes us as ordinary would likely make us angry. Nobody wants to be ordinary.

Yet the Christian faith is founded upon the experiences and expectations of ordinary people. The Bible is full of men and women who do not shake or shape the world on the world's terms. The greatest acts of God can be seen in and through the lives of people who are not all that philosophically wise, intellectually sophisticated, or even morally perfect. Nor do the greatest acts of God in scripture begin with those who wield political power and influence. David is but one of a long list of those persons involved in doing the ordinary when God calls them to do something extraordinary—and the Spirit of God accomplishes great works through them.

Paul Tillich once noted that saints are saints not because of goodness but because they are transparent for something that is more than themselves. Being a window of opportunity, a means of grace, a place in which the Holy Spirit makes its dwelling is the vocation of ordinary people. Through God's Spirit extraordinary things happen through those of us who are, well, ordinary.

SUGGESTION FOR MEDITATION: Consider for a moment the one thing that excites your passion. Invite the Spirit of God into your passion. As ordinary as you might be, God can use this moment to make a dynamic difference in the world.

[‡]Senior pastor, First United Methodist Church, Shelbyville, Indiana.

Who are you? This is not a question asked in passing. When persons ask this question, they expect an answer. Who are you? This question might simply be a friendly inquiry about our identity. Yet few of us find ourselves unchallenged by this question. It calls for explanation; perhaps it calls for a defense or apology.

Who are you? Some would answer with a description of what they do. Yet the question might be asking something more. We know who we are; this question might challenge us because others also know who we really are. We might have to admit that we are ordinary—maybe even imperfect.

Jesse Jackson often speaks about the greatest cause of social decay. He says it is not racism, poverty, drugs, war, or violence, for these are symptoms of some deeper problem. That deeper problem is lack of self-worth and self-dignity; people may not know who they really are.

Who are you? The Christian faith gives some remarkable answers to that question. God forms each one of us, nourishes us by God's love, preserves us by God's mercy, opens us to God's promise, and waits expectantly for God's future—the human expression of divine hope and love, God's best and last chance for the world, and the means for hope and love in the world. God in Christ has revealed that we are all of this and more through the Spirit that dwells in us mightily. Ordinary? Yes. But God has declared us to be much more!

Who are you? Who are we? As Christians, we are so much more than we could ever imagine before. We are new creations. *New creations.* Simple words, powerful words. Called to be disciples, we find out we have become new creations in Christ.

SUGGESTION FOR MEDITATION: "I am a new creation in Christ." **Listen for how God might be using you as a new creation in this world.**

We know God through divine actions as recorded in scripture. God's actions commanded the loyalty of the children of Israel, and, by indirection, ourselves. Scripture bears witness to a God of activity who enters history and makes events happen, a God who confronts and confuses nature. Supremely, though, through the gospel of Christ, we know God as the world's lover.

Terrible things happen in the world, for it is not perfect; it is not without pain. We must learn to cope with a world of ambiguity, danger, and pain. Yet, even through these experiences, God relates to us out of divine love. Through the incarnation of Christ we know that God's action, the act that truly counts, is motivated by love.

Because of God's love, we become not simply the objects of a benevolent, wrathful, or indifferent God. Rather, God commissions ordinary people to carry out the activity of God in the world. Through us—through our patience, labor, and love in a world content without God—the world can come to know and serve God. Indeed, the actions of God in the world around us become the actions of ordinary men and women who, through God's Spirit, know God and seek to serve the God who acts through their own actions.

While we know much about God through actions and incarnation in Christ, much about God remains a mystery. The seed lies hidden beneath the earth; only the appearance of ripe fruit gives evidence of God's action. The only response to what we know about God comes through our acting as we know God has acted: in love. The seed of love is all that we know to scatter. God continues to act and will take care of the sprouting and growth of God's love if only we scatter the seed.

SUGGESTION FOR MEDITATION: **In what way in recent days have you experienced an absence of God's love? What seed can you scatter to allow God's love to sprout and grow?**

A question from my Methodist tradition is not often asked anymore: "Are you going on to perfection?" What an unsettling proposition: ordinary people striving for perfection. The proposition did not originate with the early Methodists. The Bible speaks about perfection. Even Jesus, toward the end of his Sermon on the Mount, challenges us to be as perfect as God!

Jesus taught a summary of the morality of Israel, the counsels of perfection, as it were, from Moses onward. The keeping of these laws is what made a person good, but Jesus teaches us to go beyond being good. He teaches the ways of perfection—love of God and neighbor—and suggests that this represents the will of God and the reign of God.

It has been said that any fool can live in paradise. Paradise is easy: no right or wrong, no sin, no error, no mixed motives, no compromising opportunities. But we do not live in paradise, and we ordinary people are called to make the most out of where we are by the Spirit of God.

There are men and women today who are discouraged because peace is not yet achievable as an item of national policy. There are people who are upset because their vision of a just society with peace is not upheld in countries around the world—including ours. It could lead the most conscientious among us to despair. We are so far away from perfection.

However, Jesus' challenge to be perfect is not followed by an assurance that there will emerge a perfect world through our efforts. The virtue found in seeking perfection is making complete the will and work of God. The smallest seed can become the greatest of all shrubs. The work of going on to perfection is never done, which is the reason we must ever be about doing it.

SUGGESTION FOR MEDITATION: In what way can I be about "going on to perfection" today?

"The LORD answer you in the day of trouble!" Psalm 20 is quick to remind us that sometimes faithful people are driven to despair. Is there any justice? Will I be able to make a living, raise a family, love, work, play? Ordinary people realize there is trouble throughout the world—and at home. We often respond to this reality by expecting less rather than more of life's good things.

The world is not all rosy and bright, a land of wishful thinking and positive attitudes. However, faith and trust in God teach us that the world is a land of opportunity for the ordinary person filled with the Spirit of God. The Spirit goes before us preparing the way and bidding us to join in the pilgrimage that takes us from where we are to where we are to be. What we see in the world is not necessarily what we get, but what we get is the opportunity to see. Yet the future in God is so extraordinary that it exceeds our ability to see, even imagine.

The nature of faith comes in living life expectantly even when the immediate future offers little promise of celebration. Faith calls us to a life lived in its incompleteness, always expecting more. Faith calls us to a life of joyful hope even in the midst of despair.

Each ordinary person has the opportunity to join the holy pilgrimage, to take a journey with God's Spirit to the perfection of God. Our journey may not be perfect, nor will it always be easy and filled with joy. Yet God will be with us in times of trouble; God will support us from the depths of unfathomable mystery. Then we can affirm with the psalmist: "May [God] grant you your heart's desire and fulfill all your plans."

SUGGESTION FOR MEDITATION: **Look at the troubles of the world today. In what way can you place your biggest concern into the hands of God? Do it.**

Psalm 20 was written "for the king"—the anointed of God. Communities of faith have always prayed for their leaders—both church leaders and political leaders. That practice and this psalm remind us that, while we depend on our leaders, our leaders must depend on God.

Yet the psalm's words also speak a message to the subjects of the king. The subjects of a righteous king shall expect God's justice. The words of Psalm 20 appropriately become a prayer for king and subject alike.

The psalm urges us to pray for leaders. But it also cautions against pride in any power except God. Those who rely on "horses and chariots" will "collapse and fall." Only those who rely on the power of the name of God will "rise and stand upright." The psalmist prays for both the weak and the powerful who understand and work for the fulfillment of that witness.

The weak will pray for and look for the fruits of justice. Those who seek justice will have at their disposal the resources of love, faith, and hope. They will be informed by a longing for justice to prevail.

God's justice calls for a victory that overcomes the world with the interests of God. To allow for justice that empowers the weak and overcomes the oppression of the unjust powerful, the powerful will need a well-developed sense of sin. The weak will need an understanding of the often-used rhetoric of those in power to cover up the sin. God's message will be proclaimed and accepted by the anointed of God, the righteous king, who will seek words and actions that reflect true religious values—such as integrity, humility, peacemaking—and justice for all.

SUGGESTION FOR MEDITATION: In what ways are the words and actions of the most powerful of today's world in harmony with God's justice? In what ways do I seek God's justice in my dealings with others around me?

If we seek God's justice, we need to recognize the implicit critique of power that this portion of the psalm articulates. In the last analysis, for the Christian, our only hope for justice is that through God in Christ there is a new creation.

I remember sitting in my backyard watching moths being drawn to a lightbulb. The moth simply cannot help but be drawn to the bulb's brilliance. Whenever God's glory is revealed in the world, people, from the greatest to the least—the most powerful to the most powerless—are drawn to its brightness. Throughout history the people of God have struggled to reveal God's glory to the world. We struggle yet today. Sometimes we seem to be much better at concealing it—keeping it to ourselves. We sometimes squabble about it, sometimes ignore it completely. We must allow the pull of God's Spirit on our lives to challenge and lead us as we seek ways to reveal God to the world.

In the nation in which I am blessed to live, I have opportunity to take pride in the biggest chariots and the most powerful horses. Yet I know that God may work as effectively through other people with smaller chariots and less powerful horses. Scripture teaches me this again and again.

We must work constantly to take pride only in God and God's justice, God's chariots and horses. Realizing that the things the world values will collapse and fall, the justice of God will rise and stand upright in the world through faithful ordinary people empowered by God's Spirit. By this work of God through us a new creation can and will become reality.

PRAYER: God of ordinary people empowered by your Spirit, whose ways are not the ways of the world, empower your people—empower me—to be a witness to you and an instrument of the perfection of your love in the world. Amen.

God Is Our Refuge

June 19–25, 2006 • Martha Boshart[‡]

MONDAY, JUNE 19 • Read 1 Samuel 17:1a, 4-11, 19-23, 32

A giant of a man, Goliath stands 9 feet, 9 inches tall. In addition to his body weight, his armor weighs 272 pounds, 13 ounces. He emerges from the Philistine army camp with an arrogance befitting his intimidating stature and calls across the Valley of Elah to Saul's army on the opposite hill, asking Saul to send out an opponent to fight him to the death.

All the Israelites shudder at Goliath's challenge; they know no one in Saul's Israelite army is a match for this monster. But God knew otherwise. Just as Goliath calls out his taunting challenge, a lowly shepherd boy arrives at the Israelite camp with food for his brothers who serve in Saul's army. The boy, young David, overhears Goliath's challenge, and he knows instinctively that God has prepared him for just this moment.

David approaches Saul with an offer so illogical Saul tries to talk him out of it. David declares that with God on his side, he will accept Goliath's challenge and go out and defeat him.

In November 1995, I stood in the Valley of Elah, fifteen miles southwest of Jerusalem, where this event is thought to have taken place. I imagined myself in the various roles of each of these major players. I wondered if I would have the capacity to throw my weight around and intimidate my whole world like Goliath? Would I take my stand, like David, in front of a fearless intimidator if my Lord were challenged? In a test of allegiance, would I obey God or would I go with the flow of family and friends?

PRAYER: Dear Lord, remove any trappings of Goliath I may have in me. Give me the obedient and trusting heart of David. And in every test of allegiance help me always to take my stand with you. Amen.

[‡]Psychologist, author, active member of First Church of the Nazarene, Watertown, New York.

In recent years many bright, capable people have been dismissed from their jobs and have suddenly had to reenter the job market. In search of work, many have discovered they are overqualified. Their extensive résumés, designed to impress a prospective employer, have disqualified some even from the initial interview.

David finds himself in the opposite dilemma. He shows up for the job of fighting the giant Goliath without a shred of credential. Young and inexperienced, he wears no armor and carries only a staff. In short, he is a pip-squeak of a kid who knows a lot about tending sheep but nothing about the art of warfare.

But David knows he's the person for the job based on unlikely credentials only he and God seem to understand. He pleads his case of strength and courage on the basis of having saved his father's sheep by seizing a lion, attacking a bear, and killing both. But Saul remains unconvinced.

So Saul arms David with a brass helmet, a heavy coat of brass plates called mail, and a sword. David discovers he cannot even walk in all these military accoutrements; he cannot fight in this unfamiliar gear. He takes it all off and replaces it with his walking stick and his shepherd's bag in which he puts five smooth stones. He carries a sling in his hand.

The maxim "Keep it simple" surely originated with David in his demonstration of simple obedience, simple faith, and simple military gear—unopposable credentials. When God calls us to service, God equips us. Something remarkable happens to our spiritual growth when we trust in God's salvation.

PRAYER: Heavenly Father, increase my faith and simplify my obedience. Amen.

In November 1996 this account of Jesus' calming the storm became personal. The day was sunny; the Sea of Galilee had hardly a ripple disturbing its mirrored surface when we boarded our ship. But suddenly and without warning, the sky darkened; the winds whipped ferociously; and soon we too were praying, "Lord, save us!" Had another ship not moved quickly to tether itself to ours for mutual support we all would have been dumped into the raging waves. Then, almost as quickly as it began, the storm ended, leaving all on board drenched and shaken.

Such is life! We may live in complete calm and confidence one moment and in complete chaos and terror the next. As I write this, my Florida friends are rapidly storm-proofing and evacuating their homes, hoping to beat the arrival of yet another deadly hurricane blowing toward their lovely coastal properties. And like the disciples two thousand years ago and me in 1996 on the Sea of Galilee, the only guarantee of protection in such storms is the same Jesus upon whom the disciples called.

But there is a caveat. Sometimes Jesus stills storms inside us and gives us an inner peace and calm, even when we find our life in jeopardy or our world falling apart. The final phone calls to loved ones from United Airlines Flight 93 that crashed outside Pittsburgh, Pennsylvania, on 9/11 testify to that variant of this Sea of Galilee story.

No matter what storms surge through our lives, Jesus is ready to command them, always on call with his forceful words to tether us to him. It may simply require that we ask.

PRAYER: My life, Lord, is like the Sea of Galilee—sometimes calm, sometimes stormy. I ask you now to control all of it and calm me even in the storms. Amen.

It is one thing to fear for our lives in a weather-related event where we are not an intentionally targeted victim. We may just be in a normally safe place at a dangerous time, like the disciples on the Sea of Galilee or those in the Caribbean and coastal U.S. in hurricane season. It is quite another thing to have enemies who deliberately wish to harm us, as with terrorists who terrify and kill thousands of innocent people without knowing their names or caring about them.

In these six verses, the psalmist touches briefly on dangers he encounters from his enemies. He focuses on praying to the Lord for mercy and thanking God for being his stronghold in the midst of such dangers. What he does not mention here is how he manages to move with seeming ease and confidence from fear and agony to deliverance and praise.

I cannot imagine how a person might prepare for the chilling eventuality of sitting blindfolded before terrorists, awaiting an imminent and unknown fate. It transcends human reasoning to imagine that in those potentially final moments of life, a person could move quickly and confidently from paralyzing fear to prayer and praise.

I can only imagine that the psalmist makes the shift the same way we must do it: by rehearsing our praises every time we experience even mild and momentary panic. It is comforting to know that we will not be judged on success in overcoming fear but on faithfulness in declaring praise, even in the most frightening circumstances.

Second Timothy 1:7 reminds us that God does not give us a spirit of fear. The psalmist reminds us that God is our stronghold in times of trouble and fear. This God does not forget the cry of the afflicted but is gracious to bring strength and peace.

PRAYER: Whoever may be my enemies and whatever they may do to harm me, thank you, Lord, for being my stronghold. Amen.

In 1981 Rabbi Harold Kushner wrote a book titled *When Bad Things Happen to Good People*. After reading that book I began pondering the somewhat more delicate issue of good things happening to bad people. A book with such a title may never surface because applying the term *bad* to people rather than things sounds much too judgmental.

But the psalmist has no such reluctance about using judgmental and potentially inflammatory terms. Depending upon your translation you will find that the psalmist uses the words *heathen* and *wicked* to name the people God will judge and punish. It is a rare sermon these days that comes close to these incendiary characterizations.

We must not forget that evil still exists in the world, as do people who perform evil acts. Yet those who "forget God" will pay a terrible price for their evil deeds. Some will pay the price they exacted from their victims. Some will feel the consequences of their actions days later. For others, it could be years.

But this psalm testifies to one very important truth: despite all appearances to the contrary, it is God who rules the world. Despite the wickedness in ourselves, in others, or in the world, justice will prevail. The Lord is king—forever and ever. This is our hope and our conviction and the faith that goes with us as we join God's work in the world.

This is the faith we celebrate and honor, the faith that sustains us. This faith bears witness in the face of all that is tough, all that is threatening, all that is bad in our world. This is the faith—God's promise—that has the last word.

PRAYER: Renew my faith, O God, that you are in charge of the world. Amen.

As I write these devotionals about God as stronghold and refuge, I find myself resting securely in the calm eye of a storm that rages madly around my life. I am thankful beyond words that God is my refuge. But I am also aware that only through God's grace is such refuge available.

In these verses, Paul reminds us that once we accept God's refuge, we assume a profound responsibility for ensuring that we have not received this grace in vain. Citing himself as an example, he warns us about putting obstacles in the way of others. We avoid offensive words and actions that might result in a rejection of God's offer of salvation and refuge. God makes that offer to everyone with no exceptions. Yet a single, careless, cruel barb may spawn tragedy.

Then Paul opens the umbrella on everything we do as "ministers" of God. (And don't feel exempt from this comprehensive list just because you are not an ordained minister; as Christians we all are called to ministry based on these criteria.)

Here's the list: we may be sick, poor, imprisoned, or suffering the effects of stress in every conceivable area of our lives. But notice that Paul begins the list with the words: *great endurance.* God provides for these hard times. With God's help, we can remain kind, loving, pure, and truthful. And in the end, we claim victory whether we have been respected or despised, praised or criticized, told the truth or deceived, venerated or ignored, energized or drained, joyful or sad, rich or poor. This is a no-lose formula. A simple yes, and we gain everything.

PRAYER: Thank you, Lord, for inviting me to take refuge in you. With all my heart, I accept. Amen.

In only two other instances in the Bible does Paul address his readers by name. Addressing someone by name usually means one of two things: a gesture of endearment or a prelude to an admonition. Here, Paul intends both.

Paul loves the Corinthians and wants to make sure they know that. Unfortunately, the affection is not mutual and Paul minces no words in letting the Corinthians know he finds it troubling that they do not love him in return. In fact, he seems almost petty about it.

But Paul was seldom given to pettiness, so perhaps there is a better explanation for his expression of love, on the one hand, and his taking those he loved to the woodshed for not loving him back, on the other.

Paul speaks to the Corinthians as a parent to children. Effective parenting from a biblical perspective requires exactly what Paul demonstrates: a combination of love and admonition. Love alone soon becomes indulgent. Admonition without love often scars.

James Dobson in his book *Dare to Discipline* suggests in his introduction that when discipline is properly applied, "tender affection [is] made possible by mutual respect between a parent and child." Within this affectionate, respectful relationship children learn to trust their parents and know they can always go to them for refuge when life gets stormy.

What a powerful prototype of the relationship our heavenly Father desires with every one of us. If you already claim that relationship, thank God for it. If not, it can be yours for the asking simply by opening "wide your heart."

PRAYER: Thank you, Lord, that I can call you Father and that I can always come to you for refuge and know that no storm in my life is beyond your power to calm. Amen.

Out of the Depths

June 26–July 2, 2006 • Fred Oaks[‡]

MONDAY, JUNE 26 • Read Psalm 130

Life can change in an instant. On August 9, 1945, eleven-year-old Koichi Nakajima was swimming with friends in the Urakami River that snakes through Nagasaki, Japan. They were immersed in a diving game called "find the bell." The children dive to retrieve a small metal bell. The one who emerges with the bell is declared the winner.

Koichi had borrowed his sister's bell without permission. No one retrieved it on the first dive. Anticipating trouble if he returned without it, Koichi took his deepest breath and submerged with a resolve not to surface without the prize. He came up moments later to a world he no longer recognized. Buildings were flattened, trees were blackened stumps, and his friends were gone—incinerated by the detonation of an atomic bomb. Koichi's life was preserved because he had been in the depths.

The psalmist calls to God "out of the depths." We usually think of the depths as a place to avoid. However, God entrusts some of the greatest gifts to people who descend to the depths and then resurface by the grace of God. They emerge from grief, suffering, illness, and hardship with perspectives that make them more grateful, more loving, and more whole.

Who best appreciates God's forgiveness? Is it not those who have fallen into sin, plummeted to the depths, and then discovered to their amazement that God meets them even there? After plumbing the depths of sin, the psalmist values God's grace all the more. What gifts might we carry with us out of the depths?

PRAYER: Lord, help us to receive and cherish the gifts and perspectives you entrust to us during times of hardship. Amen.

[‡]Senior pastor, Southport Baptist Church, Indianapolis, Indiana; provides information and encouragement to leaders of older congregations through www.churchover40.com.

Nothing pulls us down like the death of a loved one. And when our loved one dies violently, the shock of loss is compounded.

Wise mourners make time to grieve. Though our culture may reprimand them with messages exhorting them to "get over it," they know that grief cannot be rushed. A significant loss must be mourned over a significant period of time. Counselors suggest that mourning the loss of a loved one or close friend requires up to two years.

Friends are hard to lose because they are so rare. True friendship is precious. In the 2004 Olympic Games, swimmer Markus Rogan was bumped down from gold to silver medalist in the 200-meter backstroke. Judges issued a controversial ruling giving Aaron Peirsol the gold medal. Rogan refused to be bitter, however. "Aaron's one of my best friends," he said. "No medal is as beautiful as friendship."

David and Jonathan shared a lovely friendship. The loss of his friend devastates David. He wails in a song of lament, "How I weep for you, my brother Jonathan!" (NLT). David, a warrior himself, understands the risks of battle. But when Jonathan and his father Saul are killed on the same day, it is almost more than David can bear. Nevertheless, David remains with his grief, refusing the temptation to sidestep mourning. His lament recalls the accomplishments of the deceased, their endearing qualities, and their love. "The only way out," say the counselors, "is through." Not over, under, or around—but through.

In the depths we learn to live with our emotions, even when those feelings encompass anger or sadness. Grief teaches us to cherish the gift of life. The ability to appreciate the wonderful, fragility of life is a precious gift to take with us out of the depths.

PRAYER: Lord, teach us in our grief to appreciate the life you give us now and for eternity. Amen.

A child's serious illness plunges the entire extended family into the depths. Loved ones instinctively maintain bedside vigils and explore every possible source of help.

A synagogue ruler, Jairus is wealthy and influential. He's probably accustomed to sending others on errands. But in his desperation Jairus humbles himself and approaches Jesus directly. His daughter is not only ill but dying. Concern for her compels him to fall down at Jesus' feet, pleading.

Suddenly messengers break the awful news to Jairus: his daughter has died. Yet Jesus ignores them and counsels Jairus, "Don't be afraid. Just trust me" (NLT).

Trusting Jesus makes a big difference in our response to loss and grief. Before Jesus' arrival, wailing fills Jairus's home. Jesus transforms it into a place of rejoicing. Only a few people witness the girl's return to life.

Like the skeptical public expelled from Jairus's home, many people still think of death as cause for bitter tears. But a few know better. What Jesus did in life for Jairus's daughter he did for us all in death. "The sin of this one man, Adam, caused death to rule over us, but all who receive God's wonderful, gracious gift of righteousness will live in triumph over sin and death through this one man, Jesus Christ." (Rom. 5:17, NLT) Certainly we do weep in grief, but not as those who are without hope!

The pain of loss forces us to confront our fears. What happens when we die? Can we trust Jesus' promise that we will share his victory over sin and death? Confidence in the utter trustworthiness of our Savior is a precious gift to take with us out of the depths.

PRAYER: Lord, when my way seems dark and fearsome and others lose hope, help me to trust your promise that nothing can separate me from your love. Amen.

Disease is another life experience that can drag us down to the depths. Unlike wealthy and influential Jairus, this woman with a hemorrhage is unnamed in the text. Her namelessness reflects her isolation. Because of her malady, she is ritually unclean in the eyes of the law. (See Lev. 15:25.) Her venturing out in public is a risky proposition.

Yet the woman takes the risk because of her desperation. She has been sick for a very long time—as long as Jairus's daughter has been alive. Her search for a cure has left her destitute and feeling worse than ever. Nothing has worked for her. She has nothing to lose.

In the depths of crisis, the woman decides to reach out to Jesus in trust and hope. Her fingers grasp the hem of his garment. In that instant, both Jesus and the woman realize that a significant exchange has taken place. She has found help at last!

We are not easily reduced to prayer. Like the woman with the hemorrhage, we are tempted to try everything else before turning to God. We deplete our resources, spend our energy, and exhaust our imagination before coming to Jesus in brokenness and humility.

The remarkable consideration is that Jesus waits for us. He receives us in love no matter how tardy our turning has been. He shares his power freely. In fact, the greater our weakness, the greater the manifestation of his power: "My power works best in your weakness" (2 Cor. 12:9, NLT).

Illness schools us in dependent prayer. The depths teach us a dependence upon the Almighty that we learn in no other way. Surely embracing that dependence is a gift to take with us out of the depths.

PRAYER: Lord, forgive our stubborn insistence upon seeking our own solutions before at last turning to you. Work through our weakness today in ways that bring you glory. Amen.

Sometimes the burden of guilt pulls us down to the depths. From the beginning, sin has been attractive in our eyes. (See Genesis 3:6.) Charmed by sin's pleasing appearance, we succumb to temptation. Then we discover that sin's allure is a false promise of satisfaction that leads instead to bitter disappointment. Our initial excitement gives way to conviction, then guilt.

In the depths with guilt, we have a decision to make. Will we turn toward God in repentance, or will we wallow in despair and self-flagellation? Peter and Judas differed not in their sinfulness but in their ability and willingness to receive grace.

Erma Bombeck called guilt the gift that keeps on giving. Guilt is a gift, for it prompts us to make confession and helps us develop self-control. But guilt over a lapse into sin needn't linger. The scriptures offer a precious assurance: "If we confess our sins to him, he is faithful and just to forgive us and to cleanse us from every wrong" (1 John 1:9, NLT). Guilt has served its purpose once it has led us to make confession and to receive God's forgiveness and cleansing.

The psalmist experiences guilt resulting from sinful acts. But he places his hope in the Lord, and then he yearns for the Lord like a weary sentry waits and watches for dawn. In our church, baptismal candidates enter the baptistery from the west, the direction of the setting sun, which represents all that is over and past and behind them. They proceed through the waters of baptism and exit to the east, the direction of the rising sun, which represents the start of new life in Christ.

Guilt is a gift that can lead us to confess our need for God and to receive God's grace. That's a valuable lesson to take with us out of the depths.

PRAYER: Lord, help us to embrace the gift of guilt until it has led us back to you. Amen.

Falling into poverty is a vexing tumble into the depths. When we lack the means to meet needs and satisfy desires, we feel frustrated and discouraged. We tend to turn inward, to focus on ourselves and our own plight. All the more remarkable then that the Bible commends some poor Christians for their generosity!

The Macedonians are such Christians, giving generously to Paul's collection for the church in Jerusalem. They are poor, but their gifts are great. When Paul writes to the Corinthians about the offering, he points out the Macedonians' good example. He hopes to inspire the Corinthians to do likewise.

To gauge their maturity in Christian love, the Corinthians may compare themselves to the Macedonians. But an even better standard exists, and in our text Paul lifts it high: the example of Jesus himself.

Elsewhere Paul argues that Christians should make allowances for the scruples of less mature believers because "even Christ didn't please himself" (Rom. 15:3, NLT). Here he makes the case that Christians should give sacrificially because such giving mirrors Christ's own generosity. Jesus divested himself of the riches of heaven to be born into a peasant family, living out his life with less comfort than birds and foxes. With a common allegiance to such a kind and loving Lord, believers must care for and assist one another, even at the cost of comfort.

When we have little to give but give anyway, we honor the example of Jesus and inspire the generosity of other Christians. We may not have chosen poverty, but we can choose our response to it. We can decide to hoard and grasp what little we can, or we can be openhanded and generous in grateful response to the gifts of our Lord. Perhaps we can even develop a greater identification with Jesus himself. That would be a priceless gift to take with us out of the depths.

PRAYER: Lord, you became poor to provide me with riches I can never lose. Teach me to be generous. Amen.

The depths of unfinished projects swallow those who start strong but falter before finishing. How many times have we begun worthwhile endeavors and abandoned them?

A year before this text was written, the Corinthian Christians began to receive an offering for the Jerusalem church. Unfortunately, their initial enthusiasm waned. Paul exhorts them to complete what they have started. When churches help one another, everyone benefits from the exchange of gifts.

For Paul, the offering for the church at Jerusalem beautifully illustrates balance and equality. Gentile Christians, having been grafted onto the olive tree of Israel, owe a debt to the Jews. The roots of the olive tree nurture the Gentiles' faith, and the Gentiles in turn help the Jews with material support.

One missionary friend told me that he was riding a crowded bus in central Africa when suddenly a jarring pothole crippled the vehicle. It lurched to a standstill. The driver lacked the necessary parts for repair, and they were miles from the nearest village. The passengers disembarked and sought shade as refuge from the noonday heat. After several hours, an African woman traveling with her young son carefully removed a crust of bread from a cloth wrapper. She broke the bread and offered half to the missionary. "No, thank you," he replied. "Please keep all of the bread for yourself and your son." The woman insisted that the missionary take half of the bread. She said, "Now we have bread, and we will share it. If later we have no bread, we will share the hunger."

Partners like that inspire us to fulfill our best intentions of providing material support. To follow worthwhile projects through to completion is an invaluable resolve to take with us out of the depths.

PRAYER: Lord, help us to finish the projects we have started. We want to be faithful partners with those who count on us, and we want to receive their gifts in response. Amen.

Ordinary People, Extraordinary Things

July 3–9, 2006 • Lillian Daniel[‡]

MONDAY, JULY 3 • Read Psalm 48:1–8

Look up

Sometimes we forget that it isn't all up to us. With our "to-do" lists and calendars, our responsibilities to children, parents, friends, and coworkers, it's easy to forget that ultimately, we are not in charge. We do not have to do it all.

Psalm 48 points us to something greater than ourselves, to the God who created everything. The psalm asks us to look up from the minute details of our own lives and consider something as amazing as a mountain—a sacred mountain—Mount Zion. Look up from your houses, your lists, your garden paths, and even your superhighways, and think instead about this mountain. Who created it and why? Look up from your laundry, your work struggles, your family conflicts, and your worries. It's not that those things are not important. But they are not of *ultimate* importance.

The psalm mentions other things that do not have the last word. From meetings of mighty kings to the pain of childbirth, the psalmist understands that these events, while seeming important at the time, do not define our lives. From the excitement of earthly power to the reality of physical pain, we're called to look up and trust that God is the firm foundation beneath our feet.

Mountains soar to the heavens so that our eyes might follow. We're not meant to shuffle through life looking down at the details. Sometimes we're called to adjust our vision upward, to the powerful God who gave us life.

SUGGESTION FOR MEDITATION: Look for some sign of God's natural creation and meditate upon it silently. Look up.

[‡]Senior minister, First Congregational Church, UCC, Glen Ellyn, Illinois.

God works with people of all ages

Scripture presents an amazing assortment of people called into God's service at different points in the life cycle. The Bible balances a respect for the wisdom of elders with an openness to the gifts of the young. Abraham and Sarah become parents of a newborn at an advanced age, while Mary bears the Christ child when nearly a child herself. God works through people of all ages. Can we human beings do the same?

David becomes the ruler of Israel at the relatively young age of thirty. Can you imagine a thirty-year-old president of the United States? Some churches cannot imagine having a pastor that young. But David's early ascent to leadership comes as no surprise if you remember the story of his first call.

David was a young shepherd in the fields when he volunteered to fight the giant Goliath. People didn't think he could do it, saying, "You're only a boy." But David used his boyhood skills with a slingshot to protect more than sheep. The day he defeated Goliath with a stone, he became a boy who saved his people. By age thirty, he is a natural choice for king. He doesn't stay a young leader, of course. In four decades of service, he grows in wisdom but also makes some devastating mistakes. Yet God used David's gifts throughout his life span.

We live in a culture than tends to pigeonhole people based on their age. Our ideas of beauty are skewed toward the young. Our ideas of wisdom favor the elders. Some companies and institutions privilege one age group over another. But God wants to work with us wherever we are in life's journey, in ways that may upset the world's prejudices.

PRAYER: Christ, your recorded ministry took place over just a few years, and yet we know that every moment of your life was precious. May we see our days as precious and value those around us, wherever they are in life's journey. Amen.

The context matters

Have you ever felt that you cannot please some people? When have you received two entirely different reactions to the same material from two groups of people? You could do the same presentation twice, but most people learn from experience that context matters.

The context is the environment in which we operate. A presentation given to an adult-education class at church may go well, but that same presentation, when offered to the toddlers in the church nursery, may go over rather poorly. The presentation may have been excellent each time, but the context changed.

Jesus, early in his ministry, has this same experience in a more extreme form. As Jesus' ministry begins to take off, people gather to hear his words. But when he speaks in his hometown, the people respond harshly. For Jesus, the context has changed.

Jesus, being human, must have suffered in that moment. It must have stung him when the people who have watched him grow up choose to insult him. It affected his ministry that day. He healed a few people; but in the end, he couldn't turn that crowd around, and he moved on to the next village.

The point is that Jesus continued. He didn't allow the change in context, the change in reaction, to thwart his calling.

If you have been feeling beaten down by the context in which you operate, have hope. Remember that your pain is a pain that Jesus himself felt.

Suggestion for meditation: Recall an incident in which you could not please someone. Ask God to examine your heart and allow you to learn from that time. What might you have done differently?

Prayer: Dear God, bring healing to this hurt and take me onward to the next village. Amen.

Just get out there

Sometimes when I have a sermon to write and only a little time before the deadline, I find myself spending time on the silliest things. Instead of getting straight to work, I make coffee, clean my desk off, check my messages, organize papers that have nothing to do with my pressing assignment. I would rather do anything than get started on my task.

Human beings are great at procrastinating. We tell our children that we will take them camping—but not until we have just the right equipment. We tell ourselves that we will start exercising after we get the right shoes. We will decide whether to attend the event once we have lost the ten pounds that will allow us to wear a certain outfit. We will send out that résumé just as soon as we have it looking perfect. Days and days go by.

Jesus sends the disciples out to pursue much more important work than those. He sends them out to spread God's word. But when you read these words, you have to wonder: *what were Jesus' reasons for telling them to leave money and food behind?*

Jesus sends them out with a message about what is important and what isn't. So, as he sends them out, he makes a distinction between having the "right equipment" and the nonessential equipment.

Don't worry about having all the right equipment—food or clothing or drink, Jesus says. Focus instead on the essential equipment, the basics of ministry: preach, teach, heal—and the rest will come. It's the same for us. Jesus says don't worry about anything but the essentials. Focus on what's most important in our lives as disciples—following Jesus daily. Jesus encourages us to get out there, to travel light. and to take the days as they come.

SUGGESTION FOR MEDITATION: **When has God placed a calling upon your heart that you were afraid to follow? How does Jesus' call to remember the basics make a difference in your approach to that call?**

Ecstasy envy

Paul writes to the Corinthian church about a man who had some kind of mystical experience. "I know a man who, fourteen years ago, was seized by Christ and swept in ecstasy to the heights of heaven," Paul writes in *The Message* translation. "I also know that this man was hijacked into paradise—again, whether in or out of the body, I don't know; God knows." What a tale! Surely his words shocked people. But Paul goes on to state that the man's experience was so amazing that it cannot be spoken of. So he leaves us to imagine what might have happened. Perhaps you find yourself wondering whether or not this could ever happen to you.

The Christian tradition has always had its mystics—people who experience God on a more intimate and intense level than the average person. Saint Teresa of Avila, the Spanish founder of the discalced Carmelites, envisioned souls shooting up to heaven and had connections with God that left her without appetite and close to death. And yet she went on to form an order of nuns and lead them. At a time when women had little access to power, she was negotiating with the pope. What an extraordinary person she was. Yet when as a college student I studied her and wrote my college thesis on that Spanish mystic, at times *her* story made *my* story seem so boring. I found myself feeling so ordinary next to tales of such a passionate faith. What did this have to do with my sitting in the pew Sunday after Sunday? Why wasn't I getting swept up in rapture instead of slogging away in the research library? I had ecstasy envy.

But this word from Paul reminds me that we all experience God in different ways and that we are not the first generation to puzzle over the differences.

PRAYER: Dear God, allow me to experience your presence just as you choose. Please let me notice when it happens. Amen.

Strength in weakness

Sometimes we look at someone we admire and wish we had those same gifts. *I could do that if I had his talent*, we might say to ourselves.

We hear a story on the radio about a famous surgeon who has succeeded in saving lives where others have failed. *What a difference I could make if I had that skill*, we think. We might even begrudge them their amazing gifts.

Yet how often do we envy people for their weaknesses? Most of us don't say to ourselves or to one another, "Oh, how I wish I had his same weaknesses." But perhaps we should.

In this letter to the church in Corinth, Paul speaks about his own weaknesses rather lovingly while acknowledging that he isn't always so comfortable with himself. He tells the church that he knows his own struggle and has even asked God to remove it three times before he realizes that God is using it for a greater purpose. *The Message* translates God's word to Paul like this: "My grace is enough; it's all you need. My strength comes into its own in your weakness."

Paul doesn't tell us what his problem or weakness is. We do know that it truly bothered him, for he says, "A thorn was given me in the flesh, a messenger of Satan, to torment me." Clearly, even Paul, the greatest minister of the early church, had moments of anger, frustration, and irritation. But he finally came to realize that he might wrest meaning and knowledge from his struggle with this thorn in the flesh. He embraced his weakness as yet another aspect of himself that God could use for good.

SUGGESTION FOR MEDITATION: **Before beating up on ourselves, let's take a moment in prayer to ask how God might be using our weakness. Rather than pushing immediately for the answer, what if we lingered more in our questions? What strength might we find in our weakness?**

Noticing God in the midst of the ordinary scenery

The psalmist tells the people to walk around Zion, count the towers and generally take in the scenery, so that "you may tell the next generation that this is God, our God forever and ever." It's a wonderful reminder to us that God doesn't just sit in church waiting for us to visit. God is all around us, in our cities, in our buildings, and out on the mountains. And our responsibility as people of faith is to point that out to others.

Cities are often forgotten as holy places. At the beginning of this week of meditations, we considered the presence of God in a glorious holy mountain. That comes easily to us. We can sense God would be at work in the majesty of nature. But how about in the buildings that surround us, in our own "towers" and "citadels?" When we walk around, can we look for God in our own ordinary paths? We began the week by "looking up," but we end this week by looking around at what surrounds us, and finding God there as well.

God does not reside just in beautiful structures, not just in the buildings that tourists visit and visitors admire. Might God be at work at the motor vehicle administration building as well? Couldn't God be at work in the long lines of the Social Security building? God is at work there because God is at work in us. In that long wait to renew a driver's license, could God be presenting us with the opportunity to meet another person and offer some Christian kindness and encouragement?

The message from the psalm strongly affirms that because of God's love and power, we can with faith discern God's presence everywhere.

PRAYER: Lord Christ, you lived among us in the ordinary places of life and there you did extraordinary things. Help me to find your calling for me in the midst of life, so that I can with my life tell the next generation that you are indeed my God and my guide. Amen.

Lifting Our Hearts to the Face of God

July 10–16, 2006 • *Glory E. Dharmaraj*[‡]

MONDAY, JULY 10 • Read 2 Samuel 6:1-5

The Bible is an inspired text for a pilgrim people who seek rootedness in God. People who feel rootless, spiritually or otherwise, seek in it a home. Today's reading tells about David's recovery of the ark of God and its journey to Jerusalem.

Some years ago, I taught a mission study on "Refugees and Global Migration" to a group of mission study leaders in the American Midwest. At that time my husband got a long-awaited (six and a half years) transfer to New York to join me. The thought that I would have a home again was a matter of excitement. When I left the school of mission to drive with my husband from the Midwest to New York, someone offered well wishes, saying, "May you have roots!"

The ark of the covenant symbolizes God's presence with a traveling people, a sign of rootedness to a rootless people. An assurance that God understands the experience of rootlessness, the ark serves to remind the people that God is a traveling God who dwells in a tent for the sake of God's rootless people. The ark itself is called by the name of the Lord of hosts who is enthroned "on" or "between" the cherubim. God is the dwelling place (Ps. 90:1) for the resident aliens as well as native residents. God searches for sanctuary among the people, and David establishes a dwelling place for the ark of God. Home is as much a pilgrim people's search for God as the seeking of God for the people. It is the face of God turning toward those who turn to God.

PRAYER: God, our eternal home, we cherish your love for us today and all days. Amen.

[‡]Women's Division staff, General Board of Global Ministries, The United Methodist Church, Church Center for the United Nations, New York, New York.

TUESDAY JULY 11 • **Read 2 Samuel 6:12b-19**

Today's text describes the procession of the ark of the covenant through the streets of Jerusalem. The epicenter of the procession is the ark, the physical symbol of God's divine presence. David has planned a spiritual and strategic moment. He creates a liturgical context for all Israel under the lavish skies on the streets leading to Jerusalem and into the tabernacle where the ark will rest. As the anointed king leaps, dances, and sings before the ark, all the house of Israel joins him in the sheer joy of worship. The slave maids and the royal heads join in one community of dancers and turn the street Godward by creating liturgical space.

The arrival of the ark in Jerusalem is a gathering point of all the tribes of Israel. David's sacred act of bringing the ark is also a strategic way of making Jerusalem a spiritual as well as a political center. From the streets, David views the journey of the ark with an eye toward the future. The story of the ark and the story of Israel are inseparable for him. However, from the windows, David's wife, Michal, the daughter of Saul, only sees her husband dancing like a street urchin. A pawn in her father Saul's household, Michal's limiting royal vision fails to glimpse the spiritual power of the procession, the ark, and the future of Israel.

Guatemalan poet Otto Rene Castillo has written,

> Being ahead of your time
> means much suffering from it.
> But it's beautiful to love the world
> with eyes
> that have not yet been born.

Sensing spiritual power and energy through the eyes of those yet to be born marks a difference in the perspectives we adopt and the actions we take.

PRAYER: Awesome God, help us discern the Holy shaping us for your future. Amen.

Imagine a sanctuary where you worship. Today the summer worship centers around the theme, "The Cosmic God's Local Entry into Our Sanctuary." As part of the preparation, the minister and the choir stand at the entrance. So does the entire congregation on this day. The minister invites all the gathered company to join in an opening confession of faith saying, "People of God, the earth belongs to God. The creation belongs to God. The whole humanity belongs to God. Amen." Then the congregation processes into the sanctuary singing the entrance liturgy found in today's reading, Psalm 24:1-2.

These verses remind the faith community of the sacred relationship between God and humanity—one between the owner of the universe and the caretakers of the earth. In this respect, someone referred to humans as "earthlings."

The God of the cosmos chooses to be present to a local community of believers. The God of the cosmos chooses to localize God's self for the people. This is risk-taking love. The vision of the holy entering the archway of the ordinary provides an event for celebration. It lifts the believers to a new and expansive sense of belonging: we are children of the God of the universe, and therefore, what Ivone Gebara calls "cosmic citizens." That entry leaves all of us in the faith community forever changed. God reigns! The earth is the Lord's!

We are invited, in a direct and unmistakable way, to be part of God's reign. Recognizing God's power, we know with certainty that the world belongs to God, that we belong to God. This is cause for great rejoicing, cause to dedicate our lives and efforts to God.

PRAYER: God of the universe, we celebrate your infinite love and hallowed presence among us. Keep us mindful of being your responsible children and stewards of creation. Amen.

On the last Sunday of August, my husband and I attended an open church service in front of the Central Station of Oslo, Norway. The sky provided the roof. There were no enclosures. The electronic billboard across the station flashed ads for cars and sports goods. People walked from and into Central Station. Against this backdrop, four women, two clergy and two lay, set up a table and poured coffee for the wayfarers before the service. Then they set up a cross on the concrete floor by laying blocks of stones and placing candles on them. The youth who accompanied them began the singing at the set time. The four leaders formed a procession, walked to the "altar," and led the worship service.

I looked around. Some of the congregation sat on chairs, some on the steps of the train station, some smoked cigarettes and some talked. The minister preached and then conducted the Eucharist. At the service's end, my husband and I thanked the volunteers who conducted this service for wayfarers and tourists.

One of the volunteers Eva, a middle-aged woman, said the service was meant for drug addicts, prostitutes, the poor, and the homeless of the city. She said when the singing started, the place became a church for her. The church "happens" when a company of believers seek the face of God. The church happens when the faith community seeks to restore the image of God in its unlikely neighbors. The ordinary becomes sacred and the mundane becomes holy when believers practice dignity and integrity in their neighborly dealings and seek to demonstrate love and establish justice on the street corners. Their affirmation comes from God. So does their identity.

The psalmist makes a radical declaration: People who try to live out God's love in the world boldly seek not just God but the very face of God. It is they who will come to understand what it means to live in love in the world.

PRAYER: God of the least of these, open our eyes to seek your face in the faces of those at the margins and to follow you as you process into their midst. Make us your temples. Amen.

Today's reading sets forward God's goal statement for the faith community. God's purpose for the believers is that they take their place in God's new family as children of God. "How-to" steps accompany the goal statement. Being children of God or adopted into the family of God is both the point of departure and the destination. God knows, for most of us, it is a comparatively easy task to accept that we are God's children. The hardest part, however, is to accept one another as brothers and sisters, siblings in the large family of God. God directs us to our oldest sibling, our elder brother, Jesus the Christ, who leads us into this new life assuring us that it is possible, since it is he who has broken down the walls of separation on the cross.

Under Christ's leadership we are to live as children of God. The way we treat those we love—and those we don't like—measures the effect of God's grace upon us. Adopted as children of God, we find ourselves reoriented. We see things, people, and circumstances in a new and different light.

Often God's goal remains an unrealizable ideal because of the prejudices and injustices of one group against another. Mahatma Gandhi, the foremost leader in the freedom struggle of India, called the most discriminated against people of India *Harijans*, "God's children." Caste and racial prejudices in India have assigned them the lowest place in society. This group of people chose another name for themselves, *Dalits*, the "broken" people. Neither Gandhi's endearing term *Harijan* nor the church's claim to be one in Christ have attracted the broken people of the land because of long years of discrimination.

God's goal for believers remains an enlarged new humanity where old barriers of race, culture, class, and other distinctions are broken down. This new human family is God-designed; sealed by Christ's death; delivered daily by the guarantee of the Holy Spirit.

PRAYER: Christ, our eldest brother, make us one in your broken body on the cross. Amen.

Bishop Serapin of the fourth century prayed, "We beg you, God, make us fully alive." Today's passage enjoins us to be fully alive to Christ's redemptive work of the human soul, the world, and the entire creation itself. Being fully alive to God's cosmic design is to feel, fathom, experience, and celebrate the person of the Risen One in the depth of one's self and the presence of the same God in the vastness of the cosmos.

Being fully alive to God means that we participate in God's design and will for the world, carrying that grace with us in the world. It allows us to do this. Grace allows us to recognize Christ's magnificent love in our lives. Indeed, the grace that has been given to us is not just given but lavished upon us. The word *lavished* used here refers to something beyond any fixed measure. A grace so lavish changes us. Gifted by God's kindness, we find our speech and our actions reflect and evidence grace.

When our eyes are opened this way, we can see clearly that God's grace is infinite, unmeasurable, embracing the whole world. This clear-sightedness gives us hope even when we face the toughest part of our lives and the toughest part of our world.

This is the true measure of God's love for us: having been given the gift of Christ, we can hope. We can live. We can love others. We can help heal the world.

PRAYER: Praise be to you, God, for the great gifts you have given us. Fill us with hope so that we may live in love today. Amen.

The story of John the Baptist's death is one of a list of court intrigues: mutual spouse-stealing, a youthful dancer used as a pawn, a rash oath given in the heat of a seductive moment, a mother/daughter team outmaneuvering a drunken ruler, the ruler's defense of a supposed family honor code, and the onlookers witnessing the final command performance of the servants. That is, carrying the gory head of the Baptist on a platter as a gift to the dancing girl.

John's call to ministry came before his birth. The shaping of his spirituality took place in the wilderness of Judea. His travail of vocation is best described as a " voice in the wilderness." What is remarkable is that John the Baptist refused to keep religion in the isolation of wilderness, insulated from the world. He dared to bring his witness to the court circles in Jerusalem.

In his travail of vocation John bore witness to the reign of God—on the banks of the river Jordan and in the center of power in Herod's court. His calling to bear witness to Jesus summoned forth enormous energy and commitment under extraordinary circumstances. He paid the ultimate price for his witness: martyrdom. The Old English word *martir* and the Greek word *martyr* mean "witness." John the Baptist is dead, but the prophetic tradition is not. Most of us live as witnesses to the reign of God with courage and love. In North America we confront the hydra-headed monster of our times and culture, bringing faith to bear in "courts" of power, affluence, and complicity. Julia Esquivel, a poet and advocate from Guatemala once said, "I am no longer afraid of death. . . .I am afraid rather of that life which does not come out of death."

PRAYER: Lord, direct our lives Godward every day in the crucified spirit of Jesus. Amen.

A Dwelling Place

July 17–23, 2006 • *Jessie M. Jones*[‡]

MONDAY, JULY 17 • **Read 2 Samuel 7:1-7**

David has an idea. David is "settled in his house . . . . a house of cedar" but "the ark of God stay[ed] in a tent." David wants to build a house for God. It seemed a generous and respectful wish, and Nathan approves. But God does not want a house. God sends a message to David: "Whenever I have moved about among all the people of Israel, did I ever speak a word . . . saying, 'Why have you not built me a house of cedar?'"

We, like David, sometimes imagine God as an extension of ourselves, a God made in our image. We have what seem to be good and generous impulses, ideas of service that we think are service to God. If these ideas do not flow from God's direction, however, but from our own pale image of the service God would have us do, they are self-service, not service to God.

How can we know whether the service we would give is within the will of God? We can begin by answering God's question: "Did I ever speak a word, saying [I wanted such a service]?" Have we emptied ourselves in prayer and meditation so that we can hear God's direction and have an image of the persons to be served? We might also ask: Is the service likely to feature us or can we do it quietly? Does the service require a yielding of our will, a surrender to God's will? Are we dwelling in God and allowing God to dwell in us? Are we praying with all our hearts, "Hallowed be thy name. Thy kingdom come, thy will be done, on earth as it is in heaven"?

PRAYER: Creator of the universe, dwell in us so that we dwell in your spirit. Lead us always to say "not my will but thine be done." Then help us to know your will. Amen.

[‡]United Methodist laywoman, church school teacher, Bible study leader; living in Clarksville, Tennessee.

Having declined a house built by David, God sends a message to David: "I will appoint a place for my people Israel and will plant them, so that they may live in their own place, . . . The LORD declares to you that the LORD will make you a house. . . . [And] raise up your offspring."

More than anything else, we want a place. It is part of our human condition to long for secure ground on which to stand, a spot to be rooted, a foundation. We want to be planted and live in community.

Without a "place" we feel alienated and lonely, compelled to address our rootlessness by trying to build our own place. But in our own wish to be builders, we, like David, forget the greatness of God. God creates and plants. God is the builder, the originator of covenants.

God provides a place for us, promising a place to dwell and to be. God does not promise a life of ease in the face of our iniquities. The Holy One does not prevent our periods of exile. But as God said to Jeremiah in the face of the coming Exile and devastating loss of place for God's people, "Surely I know the plans I have for you, . . . plans for your welfare and not for harm, to give you a future with hope" (29:11).

To find a dwelling place in God, we must give up self and allow God to be the builder of a house for us, permit God to plan for our future. In following God, we will travel paths unimaginable—as far from what we imagine as David's being king over God's people was from the pasture from which God took him.

PRAYER: God of creation, take us from the place we would imagine and design for ourselves and lead us to our dwelling place in you. Thank you for knowing that we need to be planted, rooted firmly in you. Keep us restless until we are ready to come to you. Amen.

Imagine God saying to you: "I have found you, my servant/ my hand shall always remain with you; / . . . . My faithfulness and steadfast love shall be with you. / . . . Forever I will keep my steadfast love for you, / and my covenant with you will stand firm."

Hold those images in your mind. Imagine being found by God, identified, known, called by name. Imagine being guided by God's hand, not wandering, stumbling, losing the way—but finding a sure path. Imagine being surrounded by God's faithfulness and steadfast love forever, shielded from fear if not from all danger for all time. Imagine dwelling in God's covenant, believing that the Holy One will be your God, and you will be God's child.

To be found by God, known by the divine, should be all that we ever want. Our understanding of the greatness of these promises might allow us then to rest forever in God. But we often do not want to imagine the breadth and scope of God's promises. Such promises require a complete and total response, not with a small part of our lives but with our whole lives. We resist, wait, delay. We come a little way forward and then pull back. Responding to God's promises means being enveloped in God's love. We feel the energy and power of God, while holding fast against the pull toward God. Responding to these promises requires giving up self.

But giving up self means being freed of self and insistence on self. We don't have to join James and John in asking to sit on the right and left of Jesus in the kingdom. We trust God's plan for our future. We have a place. Freed of self, we can actually become children of God, servants of God.

PRAYER: **God of love, help us not to insist on defining our own place but instead to dwell in your faithful and steadfast love. Thank you for finding us, for allowing us to be your servants. Thank you for the covenant that will stand firm so that we may be rooted in you. Amen.**

God is true and steadfast and has a plan for us. But we must not create a sentimental God, a god that requires nothing of us. This One who speaks of keeping covenants "forever," of never violating the word that goes forth from God's mouth—this very God requires that we walk according to covenants and statutes and commandments or receive punishment with a rod, a scourge for our iniquity.

We do not like the image of the rod and scourge. We would prefer a place to dwell that does not include the rod and scourge. In Jesus, we have the final gift of David's line, the inheritor of David's throne. Jesus intercedes for us so that by grace the rod and scourge are not the final word.

But God continues to make demands of us: that we love our enemies, that we become servants. God insists that we turn the other cheek, forgiving not just seven times but seventy times seven. God demands that we invite all to the table, leaving the comfort of our usual guests and going into the highways and byways to find new guests for our banquet. God requires that we give up classifying by the world's standards and classify according to love.

God may ask that we give up all to follow Christ. We may be required to leave all that is familiar and respond to the call to a new place in the tradition of Abraham who left his country. He left his kindred and his father's house to go to a land that God would show him and the tradition of Ruth who did not return to her mother's house but instead claimed the place, the people, and the God of Naomi. As we respond to the divine call, God will not forsake us; the Holy One will not remove from us God's steadfast love.

PRAYER: God of our lives, we thank you that you continue to make demands of us, that you call us out of ourselves and lead us to you. We thank you for your promise never to withdraw your love from us. Amen.

Modern life produces weariness, demands beyond our bearing. We fear we will never rest. Our world seems to move at a pace not imagined in first-century Palestine. But in the short transitional passages we read today, we learn of demands made on the disciples and Jesus, a pace we may not have imagined for them.

In the first passage, when the disciples return from a mission telling Jesus "all that they had done and taught," Jesus' first response is to understand their weariness. He issues an invitation: "Come away to a deserted place all by yourselves and rest a while." Jesus treats his disciples with compassion. Regardless of their weariness, however, the work remains. The people hurry on foot, ahead of them. And when Jesus goes ashore, great crowds come. Jesus has compassion for the people, as sheep without a shepherd. In the second passage, Jesus is weary; but people keep flocking to him wherever he goes, bringing the sick, hoping only to touch the hem of his garment for healing.

Even in these short passages, we can sense the depth of the weariness that the disciples and Jesus feel. As to the disciples, the writer tells us: "For many were coming and going, and they had no leisure even to eat." People come to Jesus not just to hear his teaching but to crowd around him, to touch him or "even the fringe of his cloak." Jesus receives not even the personal private space we believe we are entitled to.

Some cycles of our lives offer little rest. We also can be grateful for Jesus' invitation to come away to a deserted place all by ourselves for our own rest and healing. Even more, we can be grateful for the very deep weariness we feel. As we serve and are weary beyond our own ability to manage, we may be led to give up control and return to God. The place to which Jesus invites us is a place where God dwells.

PRAYER: Thank you, God, for your compassion toward us, for understanding our weariness and our need for a place by ourselves to rest. Amen.

In this hymn of thanksgiving. the writer praises God for divine redemption of the whole world through Christ. Early Christians struggled with the question of whether Gentiles must become Jews first, being circumcised before becoming Christians. Paul and those influenced by Paul insisted that circumcision of Gentiles was not a prerequisite for their following Christ.

This writer, though in the Pauline tradition, recognizes the power of the covenant represented by the circumcision and the power of the isolation of uncircumcision: those outside the covenant are "aliens from the commonwealth of Israel, and strangers to the covenants of promise, having no hope and without God in the world."

Our understanding may differ from that of the writer of Ephesians related to God's power to reach all peoples in all times. However, metaphorically and actually, we are these Gentiles of whom the writer speaks. We try to hold the image in our minds: being aliens, strangers, without hope, without God in the world. We cannot hold it very long. We grieve; our tears overflow. We cannot bear the sense of loss or take even the first steps without the knowledge that God is with us. Life without God in the world seems untenable.

Go into the world today, conscious of God's presence there. Look for signs of God in the world, for a place to be and to serve. Be a sign of God to those who feel alienated, strangers to God's hope. Embody divine promise. Allow God to dwell in and through you. Sense God's love flowing through you to those without hope. Christ's death and resurrection redeem us and all of creation.

PRAYER: Thank you, God, for the basic understanding that your action in Christ is for the whole world. Through our service we can bring God's love to those who feel isolated, alienated, and without a place. We give thanks that the whole of creation "will be set free from its bondage to decay and will obtain the freedom of the glory of the children of God" (Rom. 8:21). Amen.

We began this week with the house David wanted to build for God. In today's reading, we see that God does, after all, want a dwelling place.

In Christ, the inheritor of David's kingdom, now redefined as the whole creation, God has brought together the peoples of the whole world, broken the dividing wall between the people of Israel and Gentiles, brought peace to all—those near through the covenants and those far off, aliens, strangers, without the covenant. All peoples are reconciled to God.

In Galatians Paul issued a message for both Jew and Gentile, for persons in all classes long thought divided: "in Christ Jesus you are all children of God through faith. . . . There is no longer Jew or Greek, there is no longer slave or free, there is no longer male and female; for all of you are one in Christ Jesus" (3:26, 28). The commonwealth of Israel no longer claims a superior covenant, nor are the Gentiles separated from the covenant and without hope. Christ declares peace to all, access to the Spirit and to God for all. Boundaries of nation, ethnicity, tribe and household are gone; the household of God, accessible to all, provides the only meaningful boundary. In Christ, "the whole structure is joined together and grows into a holy temple in the Lord; in whom you also are built together spiritually into a dwelling-place for God."

God has a place for us, a plan for our future. The plan includes not just us but all the peoples of the world. With all others in the world, in Christ, we now become the temple that David wanted to build, a dwelling place for God.

PRAYER: **God of all the world, thank you for bringing all peoples of the earth out of alienation and into your household where all may dwell. Thank you for allowing us to be built into your dwelling place. Touch us with your grace so that we may be able to surrender to your will and become your dwelling place. Amen.**

Live for God

July 24–30, 2006 • Blessings Magomero[‡]

MONDAY, JULY 24 • Read 2 Samuel 11:1-5

Close the opening; live for God

When I was a child, peanuts were my favorite food. I grew up in rural Malawi, and our village survived on what we could grow. My parents grew peanuts, what we call groundnuts. During my childhood, my parents would give me a hundred-pound bag of groundnuts at the end of the harvest season. But in 1970, the harvest was bad, and they could not give me the usual allotment. Our village houses had thatch roofs, each one supported on the inside by poles that also served as a storage system. That year, my parents put all of our meager harvest high up near the roof, out of my reach. Putting the peanuts out of reach did not reduce my appetite for them, and I began to look for ways to satisfy my appetite. I noticed one bag had a small hole; I began to poke the hole with a long stick and thus steal the peanuts I wanted.

We often allow an appetite to overtake us and lead us to wrong action, which compromises our integrity as God's children. King David allows lust to overcome and control him. From my understanding, sin is an action of wrongdoing. Biblically, our sins alienate us from God. Often we humans rationalize our wrongdoing, and our reasons seem valid as we commit sin! When I took peanuts as a child, I got some nutrients for survival, but the stealing was wrong. David misused his authority as king in order to satisfy his desires, and the outcome led him deeper into sin. We, like Paul, ask: "Who will rescue me?" (Rom. 7:24).

PRAYER: Forgiving God, give us our daily bread. Keep us from evil and separation from your love. Amen.

[‡]Student, Drew Theological School, Madison, New Jersey; pastor and organizer of thirteen local churches; former Council Director for Malawi Mission Area of The United Methodist Church.

Always on duty

One of my evangelism trips took me to a district in Malawi where I encountered a strange custom. When a death happens in that village, everyone who is present, even visitors, spend the night with the bereaved family.

Every community has rules and customs that bind the people together. These customs form culture and may have the useful function of protecting a community from corruption. Such is the situation with Uriah. While loyal to King David, he also honors the military code by remembering his fellow soldiers in the battle camp. Uriah, however, dies because of his loyalty in observing the ritual regulations of the battle camp. He rejects King David's suggestion to go to his home and lie with his wife, a trick David devised to veil the conceived child in Bathsheba's womb. Uriah carries instructions for his own death in a letter from King David to Joab, commander of the Israelite armed forces.

Like Uriah, people today can choose loyalty and obedience to community custom and morality codes over the direction of an individual supervisor with different values. Such a choice brings unknown risks and problems. What a challenge to us today when we encounter a situation filled with lying and hatred. We cannot take Uriah's death for granted; it teaches faithfulness before the Lord despite problems that might separate us from God. We are invited to be faithful to God despite the difficulties that surround us. Do not be overcome by fear, but trust in God at all times.

PRAYER: Eternal God, give us the courage of conviction when we are faced with hard choices. Help us to live by your rules and yours alone. Amen.

The first testimony

My daughter, Gift, suffered from tuberculosis in 1996, when she was just six years old. Both my wife Jeanie and I lost hope that this beautiful daughter of ours would survive. A pastor friend came to visit us and to pray for the child, "I know that you have left this house of my friend, Lord, for such a disease cannot affect families of the righteous ones. Lord, forgive them."

Sometimes we feel that God has deserted us. Problems seem bigger than we can handle. We pursue our dreams, but things just don't go the way we planned. Obstacles mount up, and we see no way out. We lose our understanding of God's presence in us. Sometimes we are misled by reasoning because God does not do what we expect God to do. We start to question God's existence.

Like the psalmist, my friend's prayer reached the climax of this thinking when he prayed that God had left our house. Jesus Christ suffered on the cross of Calvary for our salvation. Therefore, every human being is a witness and testimony to God's love. We do not need to look far to discover God's existence and presence. We start with you, and I mean *you*. We look at the things around us, including the people. Christian theology calls this the natural revelation. Doesn't everything tell us of the glory of God in our midst? Whenever we have problems, remember the word of the psalmist, "Fools say in their hearts, there is no God." We hold on to the claim that God is God because we see the divine revealed in Jesus and that love endures forever.

PRAYER: Eternal God, keep us from being distracted by our problems. Do not let our thoughts limit your power. May we always seek you. Amen.

We are because they are.

My first trip to the United States was full of new experiences. It was the first time to fly on a large plane where each passenger had an individual TV monitor. I did not know exactly what to do to open and operate the TV. I asked my neighbor who was busy watching a movie. He replied, "Mind your own business and do not interrupt me." I immediately remembered a phrase from the story of Cain and Abel. God asked Cain the where-abouts of his brother and Cain answered, "I do not know; am I my brother's keeper?" (Gen 4:9)

Today, as I read the psalm, I wonder if people know how much we need one another. We must remember the importance of each person before the Lord. Each day we might ask ourselves these questions: How have we treated the people we met today? Where have we seen the poor? How have we worked with those we supervise or those who supervise us? What is our relationship with other people, especially those who differ from us?

The psalm straightforwardly acknowledges how easily we lose sight of who God intends us to be. The psalmist uses the word *evildoers* to describe those who "confound the poor" and who treat others with disrespect and disregard. The Lord is the refuge of those in need, therefore, we are to live kindly and justly in the world.

A short and simple self-examination each day can be the start of remembering that the center of our relationship with God begins with how we treat other people. Our poor treatment of others calls into question our relationship with God. Daily reflection raises our awareness and helps us develop new habits that lead to better relationships. Our perception and experiences of how others treat us shape our self-image.

PRAYER: Precious God, I thank you because you first loved us through Jesus Christ. Help us consider this love as our model of how to treat others. Amen.

Everybody's responsibility

I completed my first theological studies in Zimbabwe in 1994 and returned to my home country of Malawi to await a formal ministry assignment. The United Methodist Church had just started in Malawi and there were few established churches. I was assigned to an area to build a church. From 1994 through 2004 with the help of God, thirteen local churches were developed in the Bethel circuit; these now form two pastoral charges.

One thing I have learned through these years is the power of prayer during difficult times. The committed sisters and brothers whom God raised up for this mission set their hearts and minds on the importance of prayer for leaders. Just as the writer of Ephesians prayed for the leaders of the church in Ephesus, the leaders of the Bethel circuit prayed for me and for new leaders of the Bethel circuit. The charge has grown both qualitatively and quantitatively through the power of prayer.

The writer reminds us that leaders must develop the spiritual discipline of prayer. Sometimes we wonder in awe at the large number of people in the early church who risked their lives to become Christians. Christianity in the twenty-first century is challenged again to weather the winds of change with a discipline of prayer. We must be careful to remember that head knowledge and our own resources are not as powerful as prayer and a close connection with God.

As Christians, we must not be distracted by endless criticism of our leaders, but rather we must pray for leaders in the church and in the world. Just twenty minutes of prayer per day can make a big difference to the world. Start today. Reschedule your busy calendar and include a time of prayer for your church leaders, political leaders, and other leaders. Make a difference in the world through prayer.

PRAYER: Lord Jesus, help us realize the difference it makes when we pray for our leaders in this world. Amen.

The faith challenge

Imagine the day described in this scripture. The disciples of Jesus line up, waiting for a word from their master to start feeding the five thousand. Read verse 11 carefully. What do you imagine the disciples and the people think that Jesus will do with five barley loaves and two fish in his hands? Are they even paying attention to Jesus or simply wringing their hands at the impossibility of feeding so many people?

I believe the miracle comes when the disciples step forward to act on Jesus' suggestion. There is such a small amount of food and so many mouths to feed! Consider the boy who gives all that he has. We do not know how big the fish are, but we assume this is the boy's lunch. What does he think will happen when he chooses to give up his lunch?

Today a serious challenge faces the world. Many people die every day because of starvation. Jesus sees and acts to diminish the problem of hungry people. This scripture challenges *us* to open our eyes to the problem that is right before us. According to the Web site of the Children's Defense Fund, each day in America, 2,171 babies are born into poverty. Can you imagine how many people in their families go hungry?

This challenge to our faith calls for our response. Remember the little boy who gave up his lunch. We can share what we have in many ways. Some congregations sponsor an exchange table for excess summer produce. Many communities have food banks that need donations and volunteer hands to sort and package food. Recall the disciples' actions, and consider the places you can step out in your community.

PRAYER: Eternal God, help us recognize hunger in our communities and to step forward as Jesus' disciples. May your love in Jesus Christ shine through us. Amen.

No fear

Twenty-five years ago, a missionary visited my home village. He made a big impact by helping our people develop a supply of clean water, teaching skills to produce more food, and setting up a system to improve health. After five years, his mission term ended, and the time came for him to return to his country. His leaving was difficult for the whole community; we had all come to love him. We wondered how we would continue.

In today's passage, the disciples have to deal with the absence of Jesus. They have just participated in the great miracle of feeding five thousand people. The miracle convinces the people that Jesus is the expected Messiah who will liberate them from the Roman Empire. They want to make Jesus their king.

Then suddenly Jesus retreats to the mountain to pray, leaving the disciples alone to cross the Sea of Galilee. Just like the people in my home village, the disciples feel uneasy when their leader leaves. They place all their hope and comfort in their master, Jesus. For them, the absence of Jesus and the beginning of the storm seem like the beginning of chaos.

When have you experienced a beloved leader leaving you to work in another place? How did you feel? Sometimes we experience the loss of a significant person as a problem, and the loss seems insurmountable.

We can take comfort from the rest of the scripture story. When the storm seems ready to destroy the disciples' boat, Jesus appears. They are terrified, but he reminds them not to be afraid. Listen, children of God; do not lose hope when your plans don't go your way. Continue calling on Jesus, and watch for the ways he will appear. May your terror turn to a song of joy.

PRAYER: Dear God, we ask you to increase our faith day by day. Let your Holy Spirit fill our hearts so we keep strong our relationship with you. Amen.

A Clean Heart

July 31–August 6, 2006 • *Ciona D. Rouse*[‡]

MONDAY, JULY 31 • **Read Psalm 51:1-12**

In a Bible study group, we discussed David's spirals of sin in 2 Samuel 11. David's actions surprised members of my class, and they couldn't understand God's favor upon him. How could a man of God be so captured by sin? Why did God so greatly favor someone who betrayed God so boldly?

Their questions, however, were not mine. After all, aren't we like David in this way? Maybe our sins do not destroy others' lives in the same way. Maybe we do not try to cover up an affair or murder another person. But we do sin, yet find ourselves favored by God and constantly pardoned for sin. Often I feel like David, enjoying the blessings of life I do not deserve.

At times I would like to be more like David. When the prophet Nathan delivers a message from God to David about his deeds, David responds saying, "I have sinned against the LORD" (2 Sam. 12:12). He then elaborates his confession of sin and deep repentance as the attributed author of the penitent Psalm 51. David no longer flees or covers his deeds. He recognizes that his sins have harmed others and deeply displeased the Lord. Covered in humility, David sincerely pleads for God's mercy.

When confronted with our wrongdoing, we sometimes make excuses for our actions. Someone says we have hurt them, and we may give a quick apology to make things better. Sometimes we cover our deeds so they are never disclosed. Oh, to be like David! What glory it is to recognize our sins against God. What freedom it is not to flee from the confrontation our sins will surely bring but to face God with profound repentance.

SUGGESTION FOR MEDITATION: With my transgressions before me, I pour out my heart to the Lord; I want to be more like David.

[‡]Writer, speaker, and workshop leader for youth and young adult retreats; member, Belmont United Methodist Church, Nashville, Tennessee.

Were they blind, this crowd following Jesus? "What sign are you going to give us then," they ask, "so that we may see it and believe you?"

This same crowd, however, has witnessed Jesus' signs as he healed the sick (6:2). They watched as Jesus took five loaves and two fish and fed all five thousand of them. With the miraculous feeding the people recognize the sign, proclaiming Jesus as "the prophet who is to come into the world" (6:14). They even realize that Jesus cannot have made it across the sea to Capernaum without a miracle because only one boat left and arrived on shore, and Jesus was not on it when it crossed (6:22). They saw sign after sign after sign from Jesus.

Still the people ask Jesus for a sign. I imagine he has tired of showing signs soon forgotten. He is ready for them to stop needing more healing, more power, more bread, more works, and more signs in order to believe. While not tired of giving, Jesus is probably weary of proving. Jesus stands before them—a wonderful feast of life—and the people expect manna from heaven like Moses provided in Exodus 16. Instead of filling their souls with the presence of the bread of life, the people want Jesus to do something else for them. They desire that he provide bread that will not fully sustain them but will surely awe them.

God performs miracles in our lives daily. Do we see them, or do we simply ask for more? Or do we count the miracles as blessings but count the greatest of all blessings as the opportunity to be in Jesus' presence? Do we feast joyfully, prayerfully, and wholeheartedly on the body of Christ given to us daily?

SUGGESTION FOR MEDITATION: **Be still before God, enjoying the presence of the Lord.**

"Lead a life worthy of the calling to which you have been called," the author writes to the church in Ephesus. How do we lead a life so worthy? We respond to the call.

Our calling takes us all over the world. We are called to be one in Christ, one in the Holy Spirit, and one in God. We are called to be one with each other. To be so connected to the Trinity means that we walk in unison with the Trinity.

When Jesus goes through Samaria to get to Galilee, we go with him. Others find ways to dodge Samaria and avoid interacting with the people there, but Jesus walks from Judea through Samaria to get to Galilee. Then he spends time with a woman there. We go with him.

When the Holy Spirit comforts in the midst of disaster, we go with the Spirit. Others may flee hardships and tears, but the Spirit goes to the heart of the pain. The Spirit comforts, consoles, and loves. We go with the Spirit.

When God shows mercy to David, sparing his life and granting him another son, we go with God. Others may find David's heinous murder appalling and turn away in disgust from his sin, but God goes to him with grace. God displays inconceivable forgiveness. We go with God.

Our humility, gentleness, patience, love, and peace are synchronized with the attributes of the Trinity. The one baptism that unites us as people of Christ calls us to a place of unity with one another and unity with the heart of the Trinity. Only then can we lead a life worthy of our call.

SUGGESTION FOR MEDITATION: Reflect on your faith community. In what ways does the community's connectedness to God, Son, and Spirit foster a life worthy of the call? To what places are you going with the Trinity? Where does God lead but you do not follow?

A woman called the radio talk show host for advice about her wedding. She wanted to let go of one bridesmaid. Nobody in the wedding party liked the woman, bride and groom included; the bride had asked her out of pity. Listeners called the show spilling their wisdom. Get over it, some said. Just be honest, others advised. Here is a formula for the best lie, another said. The caller was most pleased with the lie.

We love the infomercial promise of a firm body in just three weeks even if the witnesses are paid actors. The dramas and fairy tales we see on television shows capture us. Even when television offers us truth through reality shows, the enthralling shows include a deceptive apprentice or a bachelorette who lies for weeks to a man, making him believe she loves him. The other reality shows—the raw documentaries—just don't provide enough entertainment for most of us.

We crave honesty from our presidents, our employers, our family members, our friends. The healthiest relationships in our lives speak the truth to us. Yet many of us are most comfortable with the little white lies.

God calls us to build up the body of Christ by speaking the truth in love. The body should not lie to itself. It openly talks about its wounds, its joys, its concerns. When my knee is injured, it lets the rest of my body know it's time to stop running. When my stomach is full, it tells my mouth to stop chewing. When it needs to eat again, it rumbles to let the body know. When the body does deceive, cancers and other illnesses may spread unknowingly.

Beyond simply speaking the truth, God calls us to be the truth in love. The good news of God is the truth, and we are to live in that good news.

SUGGESTION FOR MEDITATION: **Reflect on what is true. What is the difference between honesty and truth in love?**

Take care of yourself! Look out for *numero uno*! I hear this all the time in our world of corporate ladders, self-help, and spas. David may have subscribed to this psychology. He has a plan to take care of himself. He desires the beautiful woman bathing, so he helps himself to her. To cover his misbehavior, David makes sure Bathsheba's husband Uriah is killed in war. David allows Bathsheba time to mourn and then takes her into his care, making her his wife. For David, the plan is coming together. He gets all he wants, any way he wants it. He is taking care of himself, and he feels good about it. He likely even feels a bit noble for bringing Bathsheba into his home and doing what he deems the right thing.

But David's actions and behavior displease the Lord. David got what he wanted, all the while breaking God's heart. His deeds ignore God's laws and betray God's goodness.

The things that seemingly satisfy us most may not satisfy God. They may oppose the depth of who God is calling us to be. Our deepest, truest form of happiness comes in pleasing the Lord. God does not call us to the simplest life. Some of the things that most please God make us cringe. Maybe God takes pleasure in our going into uncomfortable places and there loving the people whom others ignore. Maybe God delights when we let go of comfortable salaries to follow the Lord's plan. Some of God's pleasure comes simply when we neglect our schedules to praise God. These things may frighten or inconvenience us.

At the heart of God are the things that please the Lord the most. When we meditate on God's pleasures, we experience the deepest satisfaction.

PRAYER: **May the deepest satisfaction I seek, Lord, be the satisfaction of pleasing you. Amen.**

I heard a story about a man who never misses a worship service. After each service, he tells the pastor, "You told them! They needed to hear it." One service he's the only person at church. The pastor happens to have prepared a sermon about humility. When the service ends the man tells the pastor, "Too bad they didn't come. They needed to hear it."

Are we sometimes like that man, looking for ways the word of God speaks to *other* people? David is. Nathan's clever tale of the greedy rich man outrages David. *How can someone be so despicable?* David may be thinking. Clueless as to how God is speaking to him, David stands ready to punish this rich man for his evil deeds.

How often are our fingers ready to point at those who need to be rebuked? How often might those fingers point back fairly at ourselves?

Nathan could have simply shared this story with David and hoped that it resonated at some point. But Nathan goes an extra step in order to fulfill God's command. He honestly tells David that his theft and crime is much like the rich man's. He holds David accountable for displeasing the Lord.

As people of God we are to approach the word of God eager to hear what God would reveal to us. We should be alert to God's truth. When our ears and hearts are closed to God's voice, we need people who will speak the truth in love to us. While God is the ultimate judge of our actions and our love, we need accountability as we journey together in faith.

SUGGESTION FOR MEDITATION: **Am I more often like Nathan or David in this story? When I am like Nathan, do I speak with the love of God or make my own judgments? When I am like David, how can I still myself to hear what God is saying to me?**

The psalmist wants to be clean—not physically but spiritually. He wants God to free him from the iniquity that holds him captive. In order to be cleansed, though, the psalmist has to reveal his dirty places. Like all of us, David, the attributed writer, may feel uncomfortable revealing his dirt. I cannot count the many times someone I know who has been outdoors or at a gym will refuse to hug me. My friends have obviously been running or lifting weights and do not want me to embrace their odor. Few of us want to share our dirtiness.

My room stays messy most of the time. It's rather embarrassing how messy it gets: unfiled papers, discarded clothing, and trinkets piling up. I keep the rest of the house much more livable, but my room gets all of the mess. So when people visit my place, I let them see every part of my apartment except my room. I just can't have them in my dirty place.

Sometimes we do this with God. We want God everywhere in our lives, but we are afraid to unveil those dirty places. We fear the stench of our sins, so we do not allow God to embrace us. But God sees all of who we are. The Lord wants an invitation into every aspect of our lives, the clean and the dirty places. Only as David let God see how dirty his heart was could God truly create a clean heart for him.

SUGGESTION FOR MEDITATION: Do you invite God only into your clean spaces? How does it feel when you allow God to see the messiness in your life?

Costly Discipleship

August 7–13, 2006 • *W. Scott McBroom*‡

MONDAY, AUGUST 7 • **Read 2 Samuel 18:5-9, 15, 31-33**

I am the parent of two young adult children who have matured into responsible individuals, and I am enjoying the opportunity to relate to them in new ways. As they grew up, they occasionally tried my patience or stirred my anger; but my love for them never wavered. Likewise, at no time did I question their love or feel that they maliciously opposed me.

David is not so fortunate. His son Absalom not only rebels against David, he takes up arms against him. Absalom gathers supporters and enlists an army. Outnumbered and outmaneuvered by David's forces, Absalom flees into the forest of Ephraim. While passing under an oak tree his long hair becomes entangled in the branches; he remains suspended. Despite David's explicit instructions not to harm Absalom, Joab's armor bearers kill him. When David learns of his son's death, he utters one of scripture's most heartrending cries: "Would I had died instead of you, O Absalom, my son, my son!"

In spite of Absalom's betrayal and rebellion, David grieves the loss of his child and longs for the opportunity to restore a broken relationship. This tragic story brings to mind the parable of the prodigal son and Jesus' lament over Jerusalem. Each depicts a love that transcends the disappointment caused by another, a glimpse of amazing grace and God's persistence in loving us no matter what our transgressions. God fervently desires restoration of relationship broken by our sinfulness.

SUGGESTION FOR MEDITATION: Examine your heart and reflect on broken relationships in your life. How is God calling you to an act of reconciliation to restore a relationship?

---

‡Licensed professional counselor; spiritual director; former campus minister; member, Providence Baptist Church, Charleston, South Carolina.

As a psychotherapist, I frequently serve as a companion to clients who are trapped in the pit of depression. I can best describe this common mental illness as feeling as if you have fallen into a deep, dark hole. You may see a shaft of light far above you but all around is darkness. You may yearn to climb out of your prison, but efforts to ascend the steep walls surrounding you seem futile. Most of all, you feel the agony of failure or worthlessness; you believe you are a disappointment to yourself, to others, even to God.

The writer of Psalm 130 reveals a personal look into his own struggle with despondency. From deep within his soul, he cries out in pain to the Lord. He pleads with God to listen to his appeal for relief from his plight. Realizing that his own actions have contributed to his condition, the psalmist begs God to hear his petition for forgiveness. While aware of how far short of God's intention he has fallen, the psalmist clings to his belief in God's forgiving nature.

At times, each of us faces trials that test our faith and challenge our belief in God's abiding love for us. In such times, we may feel that God has withdrawn or even abandoned us. Were God to demand perfection as a condition for divine love, we would be doomed to despair. Fortunately God's mercy is not conditional upon our merits. God's ears indeed are "attentive to the voice of [our] supplications." Clinging to God's grace and forgiveness, we find ourselves lifted from darkness into the light of redeeming love.

PRAYER: O God, we give you thanks that your love for us is unconditional. However much we may feel abandoned, you are always with us. Help us to cling to you in times of trial, even when we cannot sense your presence. Amen.

My brother Doug served in a variety of settings during his years in the ministry. He once shared a memorable story from his first pastorate located in a small, rural community in eastern Kentucky. A man in his congregation was deeply troubled. Doug patiently persisted in his attempts to offer encouragement and support to this distressed parishioner. In time, there was a break-through, and the man's condition improved. On a subsequent visit, the man took Doug's hand and said, "You have hoped me." Thinking the man had misspoken, Doug asked, "You mean I've helped you?" "No," the man replied, "you have hoped me." Doug later learned that this colloquial expression described a level of caring that far exceeded helping.

Like this troubled man, the psalmist has spent considerable time longing for relief from his despair. Having spent countless hours in spiritual darkness, he awaits the coming of forgiveness with an anticipation that exceeds that of a night sentry longing for dawn when he gains relief from his duties. He waits with expectation, believing that, even in the darkest hours, the light he longs for will come.

What sustains us in our desolation? It is hope, the belief that we will soon be delivered from the darkness. The persistent love of God will penetrate our troubled lives and restore us to whole-ness. Notice, however, that redemption comes not only as a bless-ing for individuals but also to the community, even the nation. To experience the full benefit of hope, we must collectively seek and await the presence of God.

SUGGESTION FOR MEDITATION: When you honestly examine your heart, in what do you place your hope? How will your source of hope sustain you during the dark times in your life? If someone "hoped" you, what broken places would be made whole? How might you be a source of hope to hurting persons in your community?

This letter to the church at Ephesus contains some down-to-earth instructions about how to live as Christians. The writer boldly confronts the errant behavior of the believers, while encouraging them toward choices congruent with faith in Christ.

Two thousand years have passed since the composition of these words; time seems to have eroded their impact upon contemporary followers of Christ. We tend to reduce stern admonitions to pious pabulum. We are far more likely to read these pointed directives as applicable to others rather than ourselves. Seldom do we stop to consider how our behavior affects others.

I listen faithfully to public radio's *A Prairie Home Companion*. In one of his monologues about Lake Wobegon, Garrison Keillor described the effect of a town resident's extramarital affair on Lake Wobegon: it was as if someone had poisoned the town's water supply. The couple thought their behavior affected only them; yet soon, even people who did not know them were tainted.

This passage from Ephesians particularly addresses how we speak. When we engage in critical, negative conversation, we not only harm the one about whom we speak, but we undermine the whole community. Such talk invites the devil (*diabolos*—slanderer) to work among us.

Some of the most malicious talk I have ever heard was spoken during church conflicts. Such behavior grieves God and causes great damage to the witness of the church. The writer reminds us that our words should help build up the body of Christ, not tear it down. All of us bear a responsibility to monitor our mouths and to consider the effect our behavior may have upon others.

SUGGESTION FOR MEDITATION: Which of your personal behaviors are most likely to grieve the Spirit? How might you control these behaviors so they do not cause harm to others? What conflicts in your life need to be dealt with redemptively?

One of my earliest recollections of Sunday school is the recitation of the week's "memory verse." While I cannot recall the name of the sainted lady who taught the preschool children's class, I remember well her patient perseverance in making sure that we left the room able to recall the scripture for the week. Of all the verses we learned that year, the one that still echoes in my mind is the singsong rhythm of "Be ye kind one to another, tenderhearted, forgiving one another" (KJV).

That emphasis upon kindness created a lasting impression on me. The writer probably made an intentional play on words to remind the church at Ephesus that Christ (*Christos*) expects us to be kind (*chrestos*) to one another.

For years, friends of mine organized a ministry on the ski slopes of western North Carolina. The ministry team trained volunteers to encourage frightened beginners and to assist the ski patrol and lift operators with crowd control. Often the volunteers would help those who had fallen to recover lost skis or mittens. The value of this ministry of assistance was not lost on our friends' young daughter Casey. Her parents once observed Casey making numerous stops on her trip down the mountain. When they asked why she had often interrupted her run, Casey replied, "I was stopping to help people. That's what Christians are supposed to do."

Children imitate others. If mentors act kindly toward others, those they mentor will likely duplicate that behavior. As we age, we often lose the desire to emulate our teachers; we adopt an air of sophistication. The writer calls disciples to imitate God and regain the childlike desire to follow Christ's example of demonstrating faith through acts of kindness and compassion.

PRAYER: Lord, help me surrender my internal obstacle of self-importance and become an imitator of Christ. Open my eyes to opportunities to practice acts of kindness today and give me the desire to respond to the needs I see. Amen.

This passage follows on the heels of the miracle of the feeding of the five thousand. On that occasion, Jesus provided bread for the crowd to eat, but it only satisfied their hunger temporarily. While concerned about physical hunger, Jesus desired that the people understand that spiritual hunger was a more serious malady. This passage also brings to mind the earlier dialogue Jesus had with the woman at the well. On that occasion, he had spoken about living water that quenches a deeper thirst.

As a child I helped my mother make homemade biscuits. She carefully measured and mixed the ingredients. Then came the interminable waiting for the dough to rise before rolling it to just the right thickness. Only then was I allowed to press the cookie cutter into the dough and lay the resulting circles onto a cookie sheet for baking. Today I can buy prepackaged frozen biscuits from the supermarket that are ready in minutes, but they pale in comparison to the homemade biscuits of my childhood.

Like the Hebrews in the wilderness seeking food for survival, we often cry out to God for solutions to immediate problems. We look for a quick fix, giving little consideration to the greater need that lies beneath our yearning. In my therapy practice, I sometimes encounter clients experiencing family conflict. They call with great urgency for the first available appointment and attend several sessions. As their situation begins to improve, they often drop out of therapy, only to call several months later with another crisis. Their focus upon relieving the symptoms rather than changing the behavior makes lasting progress unachievable. Lasting change always costs something.

The living bread that Jesus offers us cannot be obtained cheaply. It cost him his life. For us to receive the full benefit of Christ's sacrifice, we must look beyond a superficial piety to the practice of costly discipleship.

PRAYER: Lord, forgive our desire for superficial solutions to inner hungers. Give us instead a desire for the bread of life, which can transform us into a new creation. Amen.

Most of us love heroes, folks who acquire a larger-than-life quality as a result of some act of bravery or self-sacrifice. Typically, heroes are people we do not know personally or have little contact with. In our ignorance, we imagine that they are somehow different from us; their lives are far from routine, and they seldom have to deal with mundane matters. In our admiration, we place our heroes on a pedestal and believe them to be better than we are.

In contrast, we often respond quite differently to people we know well who achieve some special recognition or move into a position of prominence. We may become jealous or even critical of the one receiving special attention. Such is the case when Jesus begins to claim an unrivaled authority and a special relationship with God. Were we to update the language, the Jews' indignant response might sound like this: "We know this guy. He's Mary and Joseph's son. Where does he get off acting so high and mighty?"

To the crowd, Jesus is a hero because he performs a miracle and gives them what they want: food to pacify their hunger. But when Jesus shifts from giving bread to proclaiming himself the bread of life, he challenges those who think they know him. He defies their assumptions and declares himself to be unique. That distinctiveness, however, makes salvation available to us. Jesus not only gives to us, he is also the gift. Those who accept Christ's gift of himself will receive eternal life.

PRAYER: Lord, forgive us when we impose our own conceptions of who you are upon you. Open our hearts to new ways of receiving you so that we may experience the fullness of life that only you can offer us. Amen.

The Silence between the Drumbeats

August 14–20, 2006 • Larry G. Jent[‡]

MONDAY, AUGUST 14 • Read 1 Kings 2:10-12

A star falls to earth

At 4 A.M. in the dead of winter I rolled out of a warm bed, drove to a deserted hay field, and lay down in the back of my truck. My seeming madness soon received its reward: a night of spectacular meteor showers. A shooting star streaked across the sky: first red, then gold, then blue, then red. Then there was nothing but a glowing orange trail where that light had just pierced the sky.

So it was when David—the man after God's own heart—fell to earth. His life was a blaze of glory. First he blazed with naiveté and bravado, a shepherd boy who dared to slay giants. Then came an unblinking moral light as he refused to lift his hand against God's anointed. The light shifted to blood red as he burned with adultery, then deception, then murder—yet God's light continued to shine through him.

Finally this star fell—still and cold—back to the earth. As Israel watched, David's son Solomon prepared to choose his path. What sort of light would he shower on those around him? How long would his arc light the sky?

Someone will watch your light today and behold the colors with which you burn. Even after you are gone, the paths you choose in life will be marked in their minds. Native American elders say our choices affect seven generations: ourselves, three generations to come, and the three generations that have gone before us. Our choices reach across time and space to affect more lives than we will ever know.

SUGGESTION FOR MEDITATION: Your life will glow with something today. What will it be?

[‡]Associate Director of Communications, Virginia United Methodist Conference, Glen Allen, Virginia; former chair of the Native American Ministries Committee.

Solomon's dark side

At first blush it appears that young Solomon was only a humble lad who wanted to be a good king. The lectionary skips over this dark portion of the story, full of bloodshed and intrigue.

Like his father, David, before him, Solomon's reign was a blaze both of glory and shame. His quest for wisdom was much in style for monarchs of his day. People were looking for someone to make wise decisions on their behalf. Solomon wanted to seal big political deals and construct huge public monuments to demonstrate his power. He established Israel as a regional power, but his accomplishments also sowed the seeds of destruction. His marriages, while politically wise, opened the door to foreign gods. Solomon's policies of high taxes and forced labor soon split the kingdom. His wisdom gave Israel her golden age—and led to her downfall.

If the wisdom of Solomon is also the counsel of fools, what hope do we have for our own decisions? How can we possibly bear the responsibility of choices that will touch seven generations? John Wesley said Christian conversation is a path to God's grace. When we talk about our plans and worries with other believers, we gain more than the wisdom of those persons present. God actually speaks in between the words. Native American elders say God speaks in the silence between the drumbeats.

Think about this the next time you find yourself in a small group of believers. The room may not be full of brilliant minds—yet it contains wisdom more profound than Solomon in all his glory. God is in the midst of every Christian conversation, speaking in the silence between the drumbeats. The only question is whether we are willing to listen for the wisdom of God.

PRAYER: Lord, I am not wise enough to choose my own paths today. Let me be wise enough to listen to your voice among other believers. Amen.

Looking for wisdom

God promises young Solomon wisdom to lead a nation, along with all the worldly trappings of success. At first it seems that Solomon needs no help from anyone to make this happen—after all, he is already the wisest person around. However, Solomon is wise enough to realize that he needs the help of others. His greatest moments of wisdom seem to come by listening carefully to all concerned before opening his mouth to speak.

Among traditional Native American societies there were few absolute rulers. Those who tried to force their will upon others were not considered true leaders. Instead, the greatest leaders listened carefully to all sides of a discussion. When they finally spoke, they expressed the thoughts and feelings of all present.

We can see some of this wisdom in young Solomon, but as time went on he listened less and spoke more. His gift of wisdom faded as he spoke only for himself. What sort of wisdom do you exhibit in life? Do you try to lead by convincing others that your views are correct? Or do you listen carefully—particularly to those who find it difficult to speak for themselves?

True leaders still listen carefully to others, knowing that this quality does not signal weakness or indecision but the greatest sort of wisdom. They invest the time and effort to understand before they speak. They embrace friends who can offer many different perspectives. Their greatest reward is not personal power but the opportunity to hear the silent ones whisper, "Yes! Amen!"

Someone will need your leadership today. When you need the wisdom to lead, will you be listening or speaking?

PRAYER: O Lord, it is too easy for me to speak quickly for myself. Grant me the wisdom to take time to listen, that I may gain real understanding. Amen.

Praying the ABCs

This psalm is an acrostic: each phrase begins with a successive letter of the Hebrew alphabet. Why was it written this way? Perhaps it was meant to make it easier to memorize. Perhaps it was written to help students learn their Hebrew *ABCs*. Or perhaps there is a deeper lesson.

As a youth I heard stories during revivals about a man who stumbled up to the altar of a tent meeting one night. He hadn't been in church for years. In fact, he and God had not been on speaking terms for decades. The preacher leaned over to pray with the prodigal and heard him softly sobbing the alphabet. When he asked why, the man replied that he did not know how to pray anymore so he was trusting God to put the words together out of the letters he was repeating.

In college I learned that this story went all the way back to the earliest rabbis. When a disciple lost the ability to pray, the teacher would say, "Recite the *aleph beth*—all words are contained there. God will form the words." I am sure that both stories are true. People of all ages have trusted God to supply the words when pain kept the words from forming.

This is such a happy psalm. It seems that all is well in the psalmist's world and that praise flows naturally. Could it be that this happiness and contentment are a direct result of allowing the Spirit to form the words? Could this be the prayer of a person who knows how to recite the alphabet through tears and trust God for the blessing?

Could this be the day that you become such a person as you learn to let God form the words too deep for you to utter?

PRAYER: *A, B, C. . . .* **Amen.**

The gift of fear

I never met a motorcycle I didn't like. Zippy Japanese bikes, thunderous American mounts, cowled in plastic or dripping with chrome—it does not matter—I like them all. Over the past few years I have logged tens of thousands of accident-free miles on two wheels. Some of my friends have ridden hundreds of thousands of miles without a scratch.

No one can guarantee such a safety record, but all safe riders have one common teacher: fear. This is not the paralyzing fear that takes the joy out of life but a healthy fear that brings wisdom. Fear teaches riders to respect the power of the machine, expect the unexpected, honor the laws of physics, and understand human limitations. With those things in place, fear can do something wonderful: open the door to exhilarating freedom.

That is the meaning of "the fear of the LORD," as used by the psalmist. No hellfire-and-damnation fear but a respect, honor, and reverence that interweave to form wisdom. People use wisdom born of fear every day when they drive on the freeway, swim in the sea, or fly in the skies. Fear can allow human beings the freedom to enjoy—but never master—the elements of nature. Forgetting one's place brings a swift reminder that we are guests upon this earth, not lords over it.

How much more powerful is our spirituality than the laws of physics? We dare to touch the very hand of God every time we pray. Such power demands honor and respect even as it offers freedom and possibility. Approaching God with that special wisdom opens a doorway to exhilarating freedom.

PRAYER: Lord, teach me always to honor and respect the power at work in my prayers. Open my heart to the joy of fear and wisdom as I take my place in your world. Amen.

To know God

Paul—the attributed writer of Ephesians and a good Jewish boy trained as a rabbi—is trying to explain the Christian faith to Greeks, Romans, and other foreigners. They hunger for knowledge and wisdom. Their sages wrote often on this topic, so they expect Paul to teach them all about God.

This Western quest for knowledge left its stamp upon our modern faith as well. Ask any number of Christians why they attend church on Sunday morning. Many will answer, "To learn more about God." But look closely at Paul's response: we do not gain wisdom through knowledge *about* God but through life *with* God. Faith is not something we learn through study. It is something we learn by doing.

Think of someone learning to drive. A beginner should know the rules of the road before taking the wheel, and it helps to know a few things about the way an automobile works. But if someone never takes the wheel, that person will know nothing about driving. Experience is still the best teacher.

That is what Paul tells us in this passage. To really know something about being a Christian, put your faith to work. Fill your words with God's encouragement. Let songs of praise come bubbling out. Become a blessing to those around you. Let the rubber meet the road. Let Christ shine in your life. That is the way to really know God.

PRAYER: Lord, let me be wise enough to put faith in motion through my life today. Amen.

SUNDAY, AUGUST 20 • Read John 6:51-58

The gift of life

In the Gospel of John, people seem rather dense. Time after time, Jesus tries to speak about heavenly things but folks assume he is talking about ordinary water, perishable bread, or physical birth. This passage is no different. Jesus speaks about giving himself as heavenly food and baffles his audience. As we read these verses we find it hard to imagine that anyone could be so dense—how could these people miss his point? Why did they not understand God's offer of abundant life?

In our daily lives, do we miss Christ's point just as often? Jesus calls us to receive the gift of God's presence at all times and in all things. In the mystery of Holy Communion, we realize that God's very life is poured out that we might have life; that is true beyond the elements of Communion and the walls of the sanctuary. All of life is eucharistic; that is, full of sacred thanksgiving.

When we realize that everything—from the food we eat and the water we drink to the clothes we wear and the walls we call home—is God's precious gift poured out for us, then every moment fills with sacred awe. We live in constant gratitude. Because we are loved so lavishly, we can give ourselves freely.

In this material world, we feel pressured to covet more and more things, even though they never bring satisfaction. The race for success never allows time for gratitude. But those wise enough to listen hear another voice. God calls us to receive love in all things, to experience awe and gratitude, and to give our love to others. What could be wiser than that?

PRAYER: God, you have poured out your life that I might live. Fill my heart with gratitude for that love, so that I might become wise enough to pour out love in your name. Amen.

Acknowledging God's Presence

August 21–27, 2006 • *D. S. Dharmapalan[‡]*

MONDAY, AUGUST 21 • Read 1 Kings 8:1, 6, 10-11

One evening a little fellow looked up at his grandfather and asked, "Grandpa, what is the wind?" His grandfather replied, "I cannot tell you what the wind is, but I can tell you when I should hoist the sail of my boat!" Such is the presence of God in our lives. We cannot explain it, but we can feel the difference when God is present.

We do not know what happened on the day that King Solomon dedicated the temple in Jerusalem, but we read about the event in today's passage: the people feel God's presence fill the Temple. In God's sphere, our feelings outrun our logic and our spirits overshadow every definition. Logic and definition have no place when experiencing the presence of God.

Dear friend, today you may be seated as you read your devotions or perhaps you stand as you hurriedly take a moment of quiet in the day. Whatever posture you assume, no one would doubt the presence of God being right where you are, kindling your soul and bringing peace and joy into your life this day.

Just as the cloud of God's presence filled the Temple on the day of its dedication, may you feel God's presence with you along with the great "cloud of witnesses" (Heb. 12:1) who have already run this race and who now encourage you on your way.

PRAYER: Dear Lord, may your presence fill me with joy and peace that my life will show forth your countenance. Amen.

[‡]Pastor (retired), New England Conference of The United Methodist Church, General Board of Global Ministries mission interpreter, writer, Bible study leader, artist; pastoral assistant, Osterville United Methodist Church, Cape Cod, Massachusetts.

TUESDAY, AUGUST 22 • Read 1 Kings 8:22–30, 41–43

Early in their history, the Israelites learned that God is too great for spatial limitations and that faith cannot rest solely on spectacular interventions similar to the parting of the Red Sea. However, both King David and King Solomon sense that spiritual worship combines the heart and the visual. That is to say, symbols and definitive spaces play a significant part in worship. This perception may have prompted Solomon to build the temple in Jerusalem. Perhaps he believed that assembling all God's people in one special place strengthened the awareness of God's presence. The author of the letter to the Hebrews seems to endorse this concept when he says, "Let us hold fast to the confession of our hope without wavering. . . . And let us consider how to provoke one another to love and to good deeds, not neglecting to meet together" (Heb. 10:23-25).

Our moods fluctuate; our thoughts wander; at times we become cynical about everything. For this reason a community of faith assembling in one place facilitates the keeping of sanity and a focus on faith. Although in the book of Revelation, John the Divine saw "no temple" in the New Jerusalem (Rev. 21:22), and Jesus said: "God is spirit, and those who worship him must worship in spirit and truth" (John 4:24), yet the Temple, as does the church, stands as a trysting place with the Infinite.

In his dedicatory prayer, Solomon makes several requests, including a petition that the Temple be a place where foreigners may offer prayer and, in a larger sense, witness to all the people of the earth. The Temple will be a house of prayer for all people.

PRAYER: Dear Lord, make me a conduit of your love that even those whom I meet casually in life's path may find me to be a source of strength and consolation. Through Jesus Christ our Lord. Amen.

In this poignant psalm, a man expresses his deep yearning to worship at the Temple of Jerusalem during the festival. His words bear witness to his deep desire: "I would rather be a doorkeeper in the house of my God than live in the tents of wickedness."

One may compare the psalmist's desire to a little girl who wished very much to be in a school play in which her siblings were taking part. Because of her age, she was not included. But on the day of the play, at the conclusion of the performance as her brother and sister were going offstage and the curtain was coming down, the little girl ran onstage, looked out at the audience, and said, "Do you know something? They are my brother and sister!"

Similarly the psalmist wants to join the happy throng of pilgrims going to Jerusalem, there to view the beauty of the city and the Temple. God's dwelling place receives and welcomes all. Those who make their way to the city of Zion *ascend* to Jerusalem, experiencing both a physical and a spiritual "high." And it is here that the psalmist feels most at home, his true home.

May we, like the psalmist, have the same desire and yearning to live in God's presence and to serve God faithfully all the days of our lives.

PRAYER: Dear Lord, grant me that deep desire so I may seek your presence fervently, whether at worship or at work or at play. Through Christ Jesus our Lord. Amen.

THURSDAY, AUGUST 24 • Read Ephesians 6:10-20

This passage seems to imply that recognizing the majesty of God's presence enables us to withstand the wiles of the devil, because God provides "weaponry" to the faithful. The metaphor of the "whole armor of God" would be clearly understood by early Christians.

In a way, the writer is saying, "You are waging spiritual warfare against the evils of these days. You cannot run away, but you can be equipped to face them." That is so true about our present day; we cannot run away, but we, like those of old, can withstand evil with the "armor of God." As Jesus prayed for his disciples: "[Father], I am not asking you to take [the disciples] out of the world, but I am asking you to protect them from the evil one" (John 17: 15).

"To take up the whole armor of God" means that we believe that the cosmic powers and the spiritual forces of evil cannot withstand the power of the Christian's witness to God's word.

Ultimately, whenever we respond to angry words with more words of anger, we virtually bring out the "darts" of the evil one; but words of love and mercy can bring out the goodness in us. This passage from Ephesians encourages all Christians to live a life of faith—to live with joy and confidence, strength and hope, kindness and mercy. This applies not only to our words but to our actions as well. Only then have we put on the whole armor of God.

PRAYER: Dear God, help me to bear your "armor" all the while, that I may live a life that embraces your will. O Lord, create in me a clean heart and renew a right spirit in me. Amen.

John's Gospel focuses on the flesh and blood of Jesus. This writer moves beyond the arena of symbolism of the flesh and blood to emphasize Jesus' corporeal existence, his giving of his entire self. Our relationship with Jesus is a life-giving one that connects us, through Jesus, to the Giver of Life.

When God took on human form in the flesh and blood of Jesus, God was also taking on the task of facing human situations and battling human temptations, while working out the salvation of the human race. As you read this passage, you can almost hear Jesus saying: "When you are discouraged and in despair, when you are tired of life and beaten to your knees, when you are disgusted with your life, remember that I took your very life and struggles on me!"

If we come to this realization as we partake of Holy Communion, then life and flesh are clad with glory and touched by God's majestic presence. We then understand that God is with us, through all the good things and the bad things that happen. We know with certainty that we are loved and protected by God. We know that God will strengthen us to answer the call to witness to our faith.

When we partake of the Lord's Supper, we abide with Jesus. This passage reminds us that at the heart of the sacrament lies the urgent need for relationship with Christ. The next time you kneel at the altar to receive Communion, remember that Christ is present, renewing you and filling you with new life.

PRAYER: Giver of Life, may your presence in the breaking of the bread and the drinking of the wine saturate my life with your everlasting love, that others may see Christ in me and come to love him too. Amen.

Jesus' sayings often seemed difficult, difficult to understand and difficult to follow. Perhaps that's why certain eternal truths elude us, and people turn from Christ. Robert Browning knew about this difficulty. His opening line in "Easter-Day" reads, "How very hard it is to be a Christian!"

Whenever we fail to follow Christ in our lives, as the disciples did at times, we will also fail to understand him. The Spirit gives life, John writes. To focus solely on the flesh is to focus solely on what the flesh is able to do. To focus on the flesh limits your imagination and God's endless possibilities.

When Jesus asks his disciples, "Does this teaching offend you?" we get a glimpse of what it's like when God's intention and human choice come to odds with each other. We do have a choice—to follow God's intention or not. The Lord's Supper strengthens us and helps us understand Christ better. The Lord's Supper, shared in fellowship with other believers, gives us the courage to follow Christ.

Jesus takes on a simple act of breaking the bread and sharing of the cup to instill in his disciples a place of return. Jesus did not wish to leave his disciples without a point of reference they could turn to and remember him. The Lord's table is exactly that: a sacred point of reference.

PRAYER: Dear God, open my heart that I may grow closer to you, that I may understand your will for me. Through Jesus Christ our Lord. Amen.

Although Peter has spiritual highs and lows, he is one of Jesus' closest companions. Like some of us, Peter can be passionate and impulsive, daring and risk-taking. But he makes no bones about his allegiance to Jesus, as evidenced in his response to one of Jesus' difficult questions: "Do you also wish to leave me?" Peter answers, "To whom can we go? You have the words of eternal life. We have come to believe and know that you are the Holy One of God." What an overwhelming statement of faith.

What's interesting about the question Jesus puts to the disciples—Peter included—is this: While the disciples have faith, they also experience doubt. And Jesus addresses their doubt by reminding them in plain and direct language that being faithful means making the choice to be faithful every day.

The story is told about a man who set out to walk a tightrope across Niagara Falls while pushing a wheelbarrow. He asked the gathered crowd whether they thought he could do it. One young man assured him, "Sir, I believe you can do it." "Are you sure?" asked the tightrope walker. "I am confident," the young fellow replied. "Then," said the tightrope walker, "get in the wheelbarrow!"

To grow in faith and to answer Jesus' question, we must trust and get in the wheelbarrow. We open ourselves to experience Jesus, to experience the faith, to experience the grace God gives us through Jesus. Peter believes in Jesus not only because he has heard Jesus' teachings or has seen Jesus' mighty acts of love and mercy but also because of his personal experience of the Holy One of God.

Only through personal experience can we cultivate a spirit that not only recognizes but acknowledges the presence of Christ in our lives. By putting our faith and trust in Jesus we can come to know his power in our lives.

PRAYER: Grant me, O God, a share of your nature that I may venture into the unknown, knowing that you have gone before me to prepare the way. Through Jesus Christ our Lord. Amen.

Falling in Love with God

August 28–September 3, 2006 • Gary Holloway[‡]

MONDAY, AUGUST 28 • Read Song of Solomon 2:8-13

"It's about sex." That's the shocking discovery some of us have made about the Song of Solomon. However, for centuries Jewish rabbis and Christian teachers have also understood these words as poetic descriptions of our relationship with God. That relationship is much like a romance. God does not choose to rule us with an iron fist or set demanding standards for approval. God does not condemn but invites and woos. The Divine Lover asks us for a date, an opportunity to know each other better. The Holy One offers enticements and asks only to love and cherish us. For our own good, might we offer our love in return?

If the idea of falling in love with God sounds strange to you, remember the Bible often describes the relationship between God and God's people this way. The Old Testament speaks of God pursuing the beloved Israel with gentle words of intimacy. Jesus uses the language of romance when he calls himself our husband and us his bride. Paul and John also use this romantic, relational marriage imagery.

Christian spirituality involves falling in love with the God we see in Christ. The mysterious process of God's loving work in us is not a trick, a shortcut, or a technique. It is a way of life. Spirituality is living our faith and believing from the heart, the very center of our being, that we are loved by God. To live that way means we hear the voice of God our beloved, saying, "Arise, my love, my fair one, and come away." If we truly hear God's loving voice, we will make time each day to be alone with God, alone with the one we love.

PRAYER: God of love, may I listen for your voice and follow wherever it leads me this day. Amen.

[‡]Professor and Associate Director, Center for Spiritual Renewal, Lipscomb University, Nashville, Tennessee.

If God is our beloved who gently calls us to come away with him, then Jesus is the anointed king of our hearts. As the superscription suggests, Psalm 45 is a wedding song or love song for use at the marriage of a king, a king who rules under God's control. The noted handsomeness of the king calls to people's minds the penultimate ruler of Israel, King David (see 1 Sam 16:7). God bestows blessings and grace upon the king, who through his rule executes God's command. Christians have long applied this psalm to Jesus, thereby referring to Jesus Christ as "the most handsome of men."

Such intimate romantic language may offend us. How can mere mortals fall in love with Jesus? Yet the deepest human emotion we feel is that of true romance, where we love someone so deeply that we willingly commit to him or her for life. So too in our relationship with Jesus. His handsomeness is not physical but spiritual: "grace is poured upon your lips; therefore God has blessed you forever" (Ps. 45:2). Jesus attracts us as embodied grace, God made flesh, the very face of love.

Thus, Christians are called to unashamed affection for Christ. This is what Christian mystics through the ages have understood. As with romantic love, that affection should grow into a committed relationship in which we willingly forsake all others for Jesus.

The regular practices that sustain long-term relationships are unromantic. You cook the meals every day, clean the house every week, pay the bills every month, and do the taxes every year as tangible ways to express love for each other. These regular jobs, while not thrilling, are necessary for the good of those we love.

So also with those regular practices or spiritual disciplines—prayer, Bible study, and service to others. They may not always be exciting, but through these regular practices we express our love for the most handsome of men, graced and blessed by God.

PRAYER: Lord Jesus, your grace outshines them all. Accept my praise to you this day. Amen.

Anointing seems such a primitive custom. Few today would sign up to have olive oil poured upon their heads. Yet in ancient Israel, anointing symbolized the direct blessing of God. Prophets, priests, and kings were anointed not just with oil but also with the power of God. Christians have understood the evocative words, "God, your God, has anointed you," as appropriate to Christ, the ultimate anointed one (Heb. 1:8).

Anointing is central to our understanding of Jesus. Both *Christ* in Greek and *Messiah* in Hebrew mean "the anointed one." As prophet, priest, and king, Jesus reveals God, atones for sin, and reigns over creation. His throne truly endures forever and ever.

Anointing is therefore more than an ancient custom. God has anointed us too, anointed us with the Holy Spirit (Rom. 5:5; Titus 3:6). The Holy One has poured God's love, God's very self, into our hearts through the Spirit, so that we might be in intimate relationship. Like the Davidic king praised in the psalm and like Jesus the anointed one, God lavishes the oil of gladness upon us. In light of such a marvelous gift, what can we do but praise the One who anoints?

But our anointing, like that of the king and of Jesus, is not merely for our benefit. The king's scepter is one of equity. Ruling in God's Spirit, the king loves righteousness.

Jesus begins his ministry by reading these words from the prophet Isaiah: "The Spirit of the Lord is on me, because he has anointed me to bring good news to the poor. He has sent me to proclaim release to the captives and recovery of sight to the blind, to let the oppressed go free, to proclaim the year of the Lord's favor" (Luke 4:18-19). As the anointed and beloved of God, we, with Christ, proclaim good news to the poor and exercise the authority favored by a scepter of equity.

PRAYER: Father, this day pour out your Spirit upon me through Christ, so that with your power I may serve others with equity. Amen.

"Be doers of the word, and not merely hearers." Such advice can be misunderstood. The Pharisees of Jesus' time were neither the first nor the last who based their relationship with God on their own ability to do what God required. By contrast, James does not moralize and urge us to be better through our own power. It is God who empowers us to control our speech and anger. God births us through the word of truth. A loving God draws us into relationship. That is gospel, or good news.

The good news not only saves but guides our behavior as saved persons. Or as James would say, the perfect law brings freedom from sin but also mirrors the soul, reflecting areas for improvement. The persons who do the word (that is, obey the gospel) gaze into the law and do not forget what they see but change their lives accordingly. Such doers are blessed by God, as Jesus himself said, "Blessed rather are those who hear the word of God and obey it" (Luke 11:28).

This discussion of hearing and doing serves as a corrective to the cheap grace practiced by many in the church today. Salvation by grace does not mean that moral standards are lower for Christians. Indeed, Jesus calls his disciples to a higher righteousness (Matt. 5:20). In James's day, as well as ours, some have deceived themselves into thinking they are saved by virtue of hearing the gracious words of salvation. James reminds us that grace requires an active response. That response includes control of our speech, care for those in need, and rejection of the world's standards.

PRAYER: Holy God, give me clear eyes to see myself, a pure heart to love you, and an active faith that cares for others. Amen.

We live in the time of the domesticated church. When one thinks of a dangerous subversive group, the church doesn't immediately pop into the mind.

Jesus, a dangerous subversive, threatened the establishment and questioned authority. He built his movement on the rabble, the downtrodden, the worst of sinners. No wonder the religious authorities, the scribes and Pharisees, dogged his every step looking for a reason to arrest him.

And what reasons Jesus gave them! He healed on the sabbath. He ate with prostitutes. He didn't keep the fast. He claimed he could forgive sins. He even threatened to destroy the Temple.

Here the Pharisees get on to Jesus because his disciples do not wash properly before meals, their concern being not hygienic but religious. The phrase "thoroughly wash" seems to imply a prescribed way of washing before meals. The Pharisees question Jesus about his disciples' oversight in this matter: "Why do your disciples not live according to the tradition of the elders?" Jesus replies with words that indict the people for following human teaching rather than giving true devotion to God. Jesus then turns to the crowd and says in effect, "You've got it all wrong. It's not what goes into a person that "dirties" him or her; it's what comes out. Don't worry so much about unclean hands as unclean hearts."

That battle between inner devotion and outer piety is still with us. God invites us into an intimate relationship—on God's terms, not ours. The Pharisees then and now confuse outward obedience with heartfelt relationship.

This doesn't mean we can ignore God's word of truth as long as we think our hearts are right. It means we trust God to cleanse our hearts, make us right, and inspire our actions. God wants more than outward observance; God wants us.

PRAYER: God of love, thank you so much for wanting me. May your love turn my heart toward you. Amen.

Barney Fife said it first. In explaining the workings of the Mayberry jail ("The Rock"), he told some dangerous criminals, "We have two basic rules. The first rule is 'Obey all rules.'"

That pretty much sums up the attitude of the Pharisees. After all, what would life be like without rules? Without order, nothing gets accomplished. Besides, they follow *God's* rules.

Jesus doesn't keep the rules.

Or so say the Pharisees. Jesus doesn't even make sure that his disciples wash the right way. Refusing to wash clearly violates God's law as interpreted by the Pharisees. While a seemingly insignificant violation to some, it could lead to wholesale disregard of the Law; Israel would forsake God and face the terror of divine wrath. What Jesus allows is the first step down the slippery slope toward destruction.

But the ideas of Jesus can never catch on. It's just too ridiculous to think that God's law (or our interpretations of the law, as Jesus would say) could oppress people. Anyone can see that it's impossible for God-fearing people to be corrupted by religious power, to put down opposing views by force, and to be overzealous in enforcing godly rules. Extremism in the pursuit of holiness is no vice. To think that those trying to enforce God's laws can crush people is ludicrous.

Simply ludicrous.

So say we Pharisees.

As a recovering Pharisee, I must admit that I at times am blind to my own traditions, confusing them with the voice of God. But like those Pharisees we need constantly to hear the voice of Jesus who tells us not to judge others by our own self-proclaimed standards but to love others (even Pharisees) as God loves them. To love them as God loves us, bull-headed and misdirected as we are.

PRAYER: Lord Jesus, forgive us as Pharisees. May we forgive those who sin against us. Amen.

When we struggle with temptations, particularly one that often overpowers us, we can easily try to shift the blame to others, to our social environment, to the devil, or even to God. We despair of ever overcoming our weaknesses. We might even wonder, *Why did God make me this way?*

But James makes it clear that the idea that God leads one to sin is deception. The divine nature prohibits God from doing evil toward humanity. God is consistent in giving only good and perfect gifts. James uses the metaphor of "lights" for the consistent goodness of God. The Holy One is the "Father of lights" because God created the heavenly lights—sun, moon, and stars—in the beginning, the first of God's good and perfect gifts. However, the light from these heavenly bodies changes from an earthly point of view. The moon has its phases. Sometimes the planets and stars cannot be seen. Even the sun finds itself eclipsed. By contrast, the Giver of Light is not changeable like the gift. God's goodness always shines on God's people. "God is light and in him there is no darkness at all" (1 John 1:5).

This reference to heavenly bodies may also be James's version of the later Shakespearean quote: "The fault . . . is not in our stars, but in ourselves." Neither fate nor astrology guides human lives—but God, whose nature is unchangeably good. If we are tempted, the fault resides with us, not God.

God's consistent goodness shines for all to see. The greatest gift of all is the new birth we experience through the Son. Although we are subject to temptation and sin, by God's help we become a "kind of first fruits of his creatures."

PRAYER: God of light, pour your light within me, so I may shine with your goodness to others. Amen.

A Share in the Household

September 4–10, 2006 • *Elaine Eberhart[‡]*

MONDAY, SEPTEMBER 4 • Read Proverbs 22:1-2, 8-9, 22-23

He stood outside of the donut shop of my building at the university, wanting a dollar or a cup of coffee. His name was William, and we talked each morning before I left to deal with e-mail, calendars, and meetings. He would be absent for days at a time and upon his return would tell me that he had been sick. I wondered if his sickness involved drugs or alcohol.

Most mornings I bought him a cup of coffee when I bought my own. Sometimes I was busy and gave him a dollar. And sometimes I was too late to do more than wave. Whatever I did, I always had a sense of guilt. Was I doing enough?

Dennis, a colleague, and I shared the same office coffeepot. Though our paths didn't cross often, we sometimes stopped to say hello when crawling over each other in the tiny break room. I saw him talking to William one day, taking my place as the coffee buyer. I asked him about the situation when we got to our office. Yes, he knew William. He knew he had a drinking problem; they talked about the lost days when he would go on a binge. Dennis tried to get William a job at the donut shop. He talked to the manager and took William to meet her. William wouldn't apply, but Dennis was working on him, he said.

What accounted for the difference in the way we talked about William—Dennis with his determination that William get a job, I with my fear of not doing enough for him? We were both concerned about William, but I saw William as someone I felt obligated to help in just the right way. Dennis saw William as he saw himself, someone who needed others to make it through life's challenges, large and small.

PRAYER: Thank you, God, for those who teach us to help and those who teach us to accept help. Amen.

[‡]Member, Pilgrim Congregational UCC Church, Birmingham, Alabama.

The writer of Proverbs warns against robbing the poor merely because they are poor. Those who don't heed that advice will have a hard time because God pleads the cause of the poor and afflicted; and that same God will despoil the life of those who despoil the life of God's chosen.

We rob the poor by ignoring them when they ask for a dollar and by pretending that we don't see them when they offer to clean our window for change. We rob the poor, sometimes without thinking, when we forget the donation for the rescue mission campaign or the cans for the food bank drive. We rob the poor in these small individual ways, but together our harm is much greater.

We rob the poor when we allow check-cashing businesses to thrive in poor neighborhoods, charging exorbitant fees to cash paychecks. We rob from the poor when we cannot find ways to connect the working poor with traditional financial services so they aren't victimized by an industry that makes their economic progress impossible.

We rob the poor when we build subsidized housing over sites of former chemical businesses. Oily liquids that can't be identified leach up in the yards where children play. The raised levels of cancer and other diseases come as no surprise. Only when a television camera shows sludge draining from a playground does anyone question the apartments' location. Even then, few residents are relocated.

Giving cans of food is important, but we are called to address those who despoil the lives of our brothers and sisters. Advocacy in areas of public policy can seem overwhelming, but perhaps it is the avenue of the most help. What if our only choice was to live with our children in the apartment over the chemical dump?

SUGGESTION FOR MEDITATION: **How are the poor robbed in your community? How can you and your church address the problems?**

I struggle to understand the psalmist's worldview. He has known political occupation. Aside from the days around September 11, 2001, I have never thought about the possibility of another country invading mine. He writes as one entitled to land through a covenant between God and his ancestor, Abraham. He knows that if intruders conquer the land, they will not dwell there long because God has promised the land to the just. I can't view my country as particularly chosen by God while others are not.

I don't have to return to the psalmist's time to broaden my perspective. Innocent people in recent years have lost their homes and lives to tyrants concerned only with amassing more power and money. The fighting in Kosovo left children without parents and with bombed-out shells of family homes. In Uganda, parents live in constant fear of their children's abduction. Landowners are routinely thrown off their lands and if allowed to remain, huts and crops are burned.

The psalm writer affirms that those who trust in God will not be moved, just as Mount Zion cannot be moved. God will lead away the evildoers while doing good to those who are upright in heart. More important, God will surround those who trust in God as mountains surround Jerusalem.

What does it mean to live with uncertainty about my survival and know that God surrounds me as mountains surround Jerusalem? I won't presume to speak for someone in Kosovo or Uganda whose experiences I can't imagine. But when I think about the possibility of facing overwhelming loss, assurance of the Creator's care makes life bearable.

PRAYER: Your care surrounds me as mountains, O God, and I am comforted by your presence. Amen.

This text discomforts me. I can't quite reconcile the Jesus who was sent to the nations and who bids the children come to him with the Jesus who calls this woman and her people dogs. Calling someone a dog was probably a racist remark in Jesus' day, used to malign the Syrophoenicians and their ancestors, the Canaanites. Why would Jesus use this term to reject a woman who bows at his feet earnestly seeking help for her daughter? Scholars offer no firm answer. Some contend that the word *dog* here refers to a family pet or lap dog, which softens the blow of Jesus' words a bit. Others disagree: to label a woman a dog was to revile her.

Whatever the severity of Jesus' words, the conclusion of the story is the main focus. The Syrophoenician woman willingly bows before a man who is her cultural enemy because she believes he may help her daughter. Then Jesus dismisses her, telling her that the children must be fed first. But she responds from her place at his feet with an audacious claim, "Sir, even the dogs under the table eat the children's crumbs."

The Syrophoenician woman does not ask for the privileges of a family member. She will take her place under the table with the dogs, but she asserts her right to a share of the household food. She is at once humble before one who holds her only hope and bold to ask for what she needs for her child. Surely Jesus has time enough for her daughter to offer one crumb of his power!

Jesus, moved by her response, grants the woman's request; she receives much more than crumbs. He sends her home to find her daughter well.

PRAYER: O God, with humility and boldness I ask for the fullness of life that is found only in you. Amen.

Through the crowd some people bring to Jesus a man who can neither hear nor speak. Jesus takes him to a private place, puts his fingers in the man's ears, and touches his tongue. Looking toward heaven Jesus says, "Be opened." As quickly as he says it, the man can hear and speak plainly. Jesus sends him on his way and instructs those with him to tell no one.

With a word and a touch, Jesus restores the man to life and to his community. The man can now participate in worship since he no longer violates the purity laws. Daily tasks will be his again. He will not depend on someone else's schedule to pursue activities that require listening or speaking. He can enjoy the fullness of life through hearing and speech. He can listen to the sounds of nature, music, and crying. He can whisper, argue, and sing.

We can imagine that the man and his entourage maintain their silence—until they get past the city limits. Then they buy a loudspeaker for their wagon so more people can hear what has happened. They hold an impromptu meeting in a market along the road. When they reach a larger town they rent out a stadium and announce to growing crowds that Jesus does everything well. Jesus opened a man's ears, and the man speaks again.

Jesus has urged the man and his friends to tell no one, but they can't remain silent. The change they have witnessed is too dramatic. And isn't the removal of any impediment that keeps us from fullness of life dramatic? When we witness it, aren't we astounded beyond all measure?

We who have known the transformation of our lives can't be quiet. We who have witnessed healings large and small that have enabled us to be more fully human can't maintain silence. Thanks be to God.

SUGGESTION FOR MEDITATION: Consider the ways you have been healed to live more fully.

Many of us learned about social boundaries in our high school cafeterias. We sat at tables depending upon what sport we played, or if we played at all. We sat at other tables if we were deemed popular or unpopular. Sometimes we sat at a table because of our race or the language we spoke at home. If we were studious, we chose one area; if we had more or less money, we sat in another. After our short lunch period, we went back to class where we didn't have the safety of our little group. Our best chance to cross a social boundary had just passed. Around those tables we could have examined our labels face to face if we had talked to someone new. Teenage social boundaries are difficult to cross.

Adult social boundaries are not much easier to negotiate. Now we wonder how to reach out to the woman downstairs who doesn't speak English. Driving onto the ramp of the interstate, we see a man with a sign asking for food and work. We can't imagine how to cross our social boundaries to include him in our lives. A man and his partner visit the church today. Will we be the first to cross a social boundary to welcome them?

James urges his hearers to honor the poor in accordance with God's plan. We invite poor and other oppressed people to our tables and ask to sit at theirs. As in high school, we find it tempting to stay in the comfort zones of our neighborhoods, our biases, and our past experiences. If we can cross our social boundaries and care for those who have been dishonored by our world and even by our churches, we will fulfill God's command to love our neighbors as ourselves.

PRAYER: Allow me to cross my social boundaries, O God, so all may be invited to your table. Amen.

Christian belief and action are linked inextricably. Informed by the Spirit, belief in Christ's love motivates love of neighbor. Experiences in the love of neighbor reinforce belief in Christ's love. When this cycle of belief and action occur in community, it deepens both communal faith and outward ministry.

Many teenagers reared in The United Methodist Church spend a week each summer on mission trips. Whether at a mountain location, in an inner city, or on a barrier island, the jobs are usually the same. Teenagers and adults repair homes and churches. They lead Bible schools for children. The work usually is both strenuous and fun.

Sometimes, a teenager experiences her first cross-cultural exchange on the trip. After meeting people who seem strange to her, she wonders why she decided to come. She promised Jesus that she would do anything to serve him at the closing service of the fall retreat, and she signed up for the trip while her belief was strong. Her belief isn't holding up well after two days in a strange land. She feels afraid of the people she came to serve.

Enter her community of adults and teenagers, many of whom have made this trip before. Their belief has called them to love the neighbor. Listening to an elderly man through a window as they replace the boards on his porch reinforces their belief. They know that he has gifts to share with them that are as important as the work they will complete on his house.

Tomorrow someone will notice that young woman, and they will ask her to join the group going back to work on the porch. The man's gift will remind her of her belief, and her group will help her put her belief into action.

PRAYER: Transform my faith, O God, into one that actively seeks to love you and my neighbor. Amen.

Listening to Wisdom

September 11–17, 2006 • Craig Gallaway[‡]

MONDAY, SEPTEMBER 11 • Read Proverbs 1:20-33

"Wisdom calls aloud in the street" (NIV). "Whoever listens to me will live in safety" (NIV). To receive wisdom we are called to listen. This week's lections lead us to think about the importance of listening, really listening, whether we are reading scripture, looking at creation, teaching others, proclaiming the gospel, or just trying to follow Jesus in our lives. The appeal of Wisdom in Proverbs and its echo in the other readings pulls us from hyperactivity and busyness to a place of attentive and expectant receptivity. But, oh, how difficult this can be in a culture addicted to action, production, and efficiency.

How often do I slow down enough really to listen to anyone: to my children, to God, to my spouse, to a friend? How often when I come to a place where I might listen am I more focused on what I have to say, what I have to do, what I have to accomplish? Here in Wisdom's plea is the great message of contemplative spirituality for our time, caught up as we often are in the noisy and busy cacophony of contemporary social, cultural, and ecclesial life: Listen.

What are we finally listening for? The wisdom of the Creator who knows us better than we know ourselves? The wisdom of the Spirit who can keep us from the arrogance of proud speech? The wisdom of the Son who must change our ideals of life in order to save us? When we listen, surely the Wisdom of God will teach us many things over time; but first we must simply listen.

PRAYER: God of all wisdom, help us listen in new ways so that we may receive your gifts, your presence, you. Amen.

[‡]Artist, theologian, teacher, and leader of courses and workshops on the practices of Christian spirituality and creative arts; living in Birmingham, Alabama.

TUESDAY, SEPTEMBER 12 • **Read Proverbs 1:20-33**

There is a difference between wisdom and knowledge. In our culture we place a great deal of emphasis on education. We say that "knowledge is power." And anyone who has tried to get a good-paying job without a degree can attest to the power of this dictum in our marketplace. Yet we also know that knowledge and degrees do not make us good. Many smart and educated people have been featured in our newspapers over the last year as a result of using knowledge for selfish and even criminal purposes. Knowledge is simply information gathered; knowing how to use knowledge for the sake of health, community, and happiness is wisdom.

In Proverbs, Wisdom cries out in the middle of the city, pleading for someone to pay attention. "Stop following the accepted ways of a wasteful and harmful culture," Wisdom seems to say, "Seek the way of health, peace, and genuine community." We recognize, however, that few if any are listening. Everyone is too busy keeping up with the current way of life, which though harmful in many ways, everyone depends on.

What a poignant picture of our culture today in North America: we have vast resources of knowledge and goods, yet we are dying of obesity and destroying our environment. Richard Foster says that what we need today is more deep people, not more knowledgeable or intelligent people. Mother Teresa once said of America that she had never seen a place more materially wealthy yet more spiritually impoverished. Surely Wisdom is crying out in our streets, "Listen to me and I will show you the way of life." Are we listening?

PRAYER: Maker of heaven and earth, we confess that we are usually absorbed with our own passions and agendas. Do what you must to shock us awake so that we might seek and find again the place of wisdom in our lives and in our world. Amen.

"The heavens declare the glory of God" (NIV). Clearly, the intricacies and magnitude of creation have profoundly affected the psalmist. This poet has paid attention to the wonders of the sky; his response is inevitably one of metaphor and imagination. The sun comes forth "like a bridegroom." And the poet knows no words can sum up these wonders. So he is led outside of himself in praise to the Creator who can make such a world and set it in order according to the Creator's own wisdom and law. This is the first great movement of the psalm: the movement of the soul through meditation on creation to praise for God and God's law.

But where are we today? Given our schedules and deadlines, how often can we stop in this way and tune in to the works of creation? How often do we take time to pay attention to the natural world around us so that we are led outside of ourselves in praise to the Creator? Do we sense with even small wonder the holy gift of the place wherein we walk? Are we capable of such a meditation today in the heart of the city? Annie Dillard is a contemporary poet of the same order. In her book *Pilgrim at Tinker's Creek*, she seems to say, "Stop; tune in to the wonder and mystery of creation; see where this leads you." How might this practice help reorder our priorities as individuals, as communities, and as a nation?

SUGGESTION FOR MEDITATION: Take a pencil and paper. Go apart in a local park or trail. Find a place to sit and draw any of the objects that you find lying about—a leaf, a stone, a branch. Take time to recognize how little you really see of these small and usually ignored creatures. Listen for the Creator's word as you attend to what the Lord has made.

If the first part of Psalm 19 is a hymn of praise to the Creator for the amazing order and law of creation, the second part is a prayer of confession, repentance, and trusting dependence. "Who can discern their errors?" This rhetorical question has an implied answer: "No one, least of all me." The vast wonder and order of creation has led the psalmist to an awareness of how little he really understands, how little he really knows—even of his own life. And so he prays, "Forgive my hidden faults" (NIV). (That is, hidden to me, O God, not to you. For as John Wesley also knew, even in his definitions of Christian perfection, we are all guilty of unconscious sins all the time.) And then comes the final petition, based again on the poet's knowledge of unfailing incompetence if left to himself, "May the words of my mouth and the meditation of my heart be pleasing in your sight, O Lord, my Rock and my Redeemer" (NIV).

Do we live today with this deep sense of compunction, this sense of our infallible capacity for self-deception? Or are we confident that we have the world figured out and, given enough technology, we will control it? Too often our way of life as individuals and congregations is dictated by a marketplace that cares only for short-term profits, not the long-term health of our families and communities. Can we rediscover the psalmist's pathway, through the meditation on creation to this profound sense of God's law and our fallibility? Or do we fear being grouped with the tree huggers?

SUGGESTION FOR MEDITATION: **Contact a local environmental conservation agency and ask about the most pressing problem in your area at this time of which most people are unaware. Ask the Creator to guide you about what to do with what you discover.**

James says we must learn to "tame our tongue" if we want the wisdom needed to teach others. A student once explained to me that he wanted to show the love of Christ to his older brother; but he found it difficult because his brother had so many "improper" and "indefensible" opinions. I wondered if one of the reasons the older brother continued to avoid church was the high-minded and condescending attitude of his Christian sibling. By contrast, John Wesley made a point of emphasizing that no one is saved by his or her opinions. On the way of salvation we need words, thoughts, and teachers; but we also need deeds of humility, wisdom, and peace. (And perhaps we need these even more in our highly educated and technical culture.) James goes on to recommend these virtues in chapter 3.

Luther called James an "epistle of straw" because, to him, it did not seem to contain the language of imputation and atonement that he found in Paul. But this abuse of James fails to understand either James or Paul. The faith that the apostles recommend always suspects big talk backed up by small lives. James's command to tame the tongue is surely anticipated in Paul's words, "If I have . . . all knowledge, . . . but have not love . . ." (1 Cor. 13:2, NIV). As teachers, our silence, patience, and submission (even to a cantankerous adversary) are sometimes a stronger proof of God's unmerited grace than any argument we could win.

PRAYER: O Lord of James and Peter, Sons of Thunder, you who put up with so much boasting and hot air, thank you for your patience with me. Forgive me when I bluster and pontificate. Teach me again and again your way of grace, peace, humility, and wisdom. Amen.

One of the most curious things in the Gospels is Jesus' decision at times to conceal his identity. In several places, Jesus tells someone not to tell others who he is. Here, after Peter's confession of Jesus as Messiah, he tells Peter not to tell anyone. Scholars refer to this as the "messianic secret." But why does Jesus keep things quiet? Why doesn't he just shout the good news about himself from every rooftop and encourage his disciples to do the same? The contrast with some of our programs of evangelism could not be sharper.

A pastor friend once scoffed at a parishioner's idea that a person might in some cases practice evangelism better by the way one lives than by words. "No one's life is good enough," the pastor declared, "to represent the gospel." But Jesus' practice differs. His words and his life go together. Likewise, he teaches in parables because of his concern with the preparation of a person's heart and life to receive the seed of the gospel. "He who has ears, let him hear," he says (Matt. 13:9, NIV).

Eugene Peterson says that it is often more important to ask how many people we have listened to in Christ today than how many people we have told about Christ today. Our eagerness to speak can mask our lack of real concern for another person, and the other person may sense this lack within our so-called "gospel." What really is the good news if it is not the news of healing and new life that Christ brings into our lives? Surely our ability to speak of Christ is grounded in our capacity to listen in and through him.

PRAYER: Lord, as I seek to be your witness, give me wisdom and insight into my own life and the lives of others, that I may know when to speak, when to listen, and in all things how to love as you love. Amen.

The second part of Mark's passage offers another reason for Jesus' practice of the messianic secret: words about being the Messiah and bringing salvation are so easily misconstrued. Peter proclaims Jesus the Messiah. Yet, when Jesus begins to explain his mission through suffering and death, Peter takes him aside. I imagine Peter's objection like this: "Lord, don't talk this way. Are you trying to scare away all of your potential followers?"

This week's scriptures have allowed us to meditate on several reasons why listening is a prerequisite of wisdom. Here we see the summation of it all. Jesus must save us from our own ideas of what wisdom is. In the traditions of contemplative prayer, this is known as the purgative stage. We must be cleansed again and again of our fallen self-regard if we are really to hear and see the great good that God has in store for those who love God.

Like Peter, we balk at spiritual disciplines that require restraint, self-sacrifice, and even suffering. This is not the way of consumer culture, which promises that we can always have more and should demand what we want as soon as possible. But if we are to follow Jesus—in the way we look upon the created world, or in the way we try to teach or evangelize—we must learn the way of self-sacrifice. Jesus said to Peter, "Get behind me, Satan." To us he still says, "If you follow me you must deny yourself."

The brash and defensive Peter eventually became an apostle of peace, wisdom, and self-sacrifice, as the epistles of his name testify. The same way opens to us as we listen to our Lord.

PRAYER: Lord of heaven and earth, help us listen to you, so the truth of your good news, your wisdom, may find its way into the deep motives and desires of our hearts. Amen.

Who Is Wise?

September 18–24, 2006 • Thomas C. Ettinger[‡]

MONDAY, SEPTEMBER 18 • Read Mark 9:33-37

Reversal of fortune. A radical change in the order of things. Surely the disciples are upset about having been found out. After their failure to exorcise a demon and the revelation of their inability to pray, the disciples' conversation on the way to Capernaum definitely seems inappropriate: they argue about who is the greatest among them.

The disciples know it's wrong to argue about such a matter; when Jesus asks them their topic, no one will say. To their silence, Jesus responds with two sayings. The first, "Whoever wants to be first must be last of all and servant of all," might not sound too drastic; they have probably heard this before and can at least pay lip service.

But the second saying sounds rather off-putting and a bit frightening. Jesus takes a child in his arms and says, "Whoever welcomes one such child in my name welcomes me." A child? A child in Jesus' time was a nonperson. For an esteemed male teacher to introduce a child to male disciples is outrageous. It offends their sensibilities. They move from surprise to shock.

If we understand this teaching and its implications for our lives, we may be shocked too. To follow Jesus, we must accept not only little children but also an outsider, someone we don't know, someone we consider far beyond the bounds of our usual community.

Our treatment of these outsiders indicates the discipleship we claim and now must live. First to last. Outsiders welcomed inside. That's the Christ we follow.

SUGGESTION FOR MEDITATION: Imagine the faces of the outsiders God might be calling you to welcome.

[‡]Coauthor of *What about God Now That You're Off to College*; living in Lakemont, Georgia.

"Draw near to God and God will draw near to you." "Cleanse your hands, . . . purify your hearts." These sound like high and lofty goals. Right-minded goals. Important goals. But maybe too high, too lofty, too right-minded. Maybe just a bit daunting—until you consider James's audience, his hearers. He writes to Christians who struggle day by day to live the faith. They are ordinary people. Their lives aren't high, lofty, and right-minded. Their lives resemble our own. They tried to be faithful. They tried to grow closer to God. They tried.

And so do we. We try to be faithful. We try to grow closer to God. We try.

So what James tells them becomes important to us. Draw near to God? Yes, that is what we want. Cleanse our hands? Yes. Purify our hearts? We try; if only we could.

James's words relate the significance of drawing near, cleansing hands, purifying hearts. All these actions help us become more like Christ. And becoming more like Christ is a lifelong endeavor, a lifelong journey in which we turn wholeheartedly toward God. James states clearly that the process is gradual. It doesn't happen overnight, and we don't have to accomplish it overnight. Nothing in this world grows overnight. Nothing. Not trees, not children, not love in a marriage, not friendship, not athletic skill or ability as a nurse or doctor or teacher or truck driver. None of it comes overnight. But it does come, with practice, repetition, and discipline and by just showing up every day.

It's like that with our discipleship too. We must turn to God—every day, over and over again; from hour to hour, day to day, week to week. Only then will we settle into the simplicity of heart and singleness of purpose that God yearns for us to have.

SUGGESTION FOR MEDITATION: Use James's image of clean hands and a pure heart as you pray today. Ask God to help make you single-minded in your life as a Christian.

It certainly isn't what the disciples have been expecting. Their work with Jesus' ministry seems promising. Much has been accomplished—healings, teachings, crowds eager to hear what Jesus has to say.

So when Jesus tells them that he will be betrayed and killed, it brings them up short. And when he talks about his resurrection, they are no less surprised. They do not understand what he is saying . . . and his words conjure up such fear in them that they don't dare ask questions.

The disciples don't understand; they're afraid. They're coming to understand that their relationship with Jesus might turn out to be different—very different—than they have imagined.

The relationship between Jesus and his followers isn't smooth, seamless, and untroubled—not always. And if his followers who walked, ate, and talked with him daily experienced rocky, jarring, and troubled days with Jesus, then we might too.

On our worst days, we may feel abandoned, alone, and forgotten. Yet we go on, because we have the disciples and their misunderstandings of Jesus before us. On better days, we may go through our life and work without much thought of Jesus or with thoughts we wouldn't want Jesus to overhear. Yet Jesus continues to reach out to us with a power and passion that ultimately brings us back again.

Because these first disciples had to work hard to figure out Jesus' place in their lives, we can acknowledge our feelings of lostness, separation, or estrangement from Jesus. We know we can continue following Jesus even when we don't understand.

SUGGESTION FOR MEDITATION: **Recall a time when you had to work hard to understand your relationship with Jesus or Jesus' relationship with you.**

"Who is wise?" James asks. "Who is wise?" Albert Schweitzer was wise. A remarkable man—brilliant organist, philosopher, and theologian—he saw work that needed to be done in Africa and he set his heart there as a medical missionary.

Mother Teresa was wise. She looked deep inside people and saw God. She understood service as a good path to God. Anne Frank, the young teenager who fled the Nazi occupation of her country, exhibited wisdom. She looked deep into herself and others to discover that she could say with confidence in the face of the world's evil, "In spite of everything I still believe that people are really good at heart."

Martin Luther King Jr. was wise. Minister and civil-rights activist, King traveled the long, hard road with so many others in pursuit of justice. His wisdom came in his reliance on God. The night before his assassination he made this statement, "I just want to do God's will."

Children display wisdom. Children early on know instinctively what's important and what isn't. Jesus treasured the time he spent with children, and he reveled in their wisdom.

My first-grade school teacher was wise. With great love and tenderness, she taught each of us the joy of learning. She loved each of us into doing our best. Beyond that, her only expectation of us was that we show kindness to one another, to our sisters and brothers, to the children in our neighborhoods. We all can name people in our lives who are wise: people who bring out the best in us, people whose lives make our lives gentler or more noble or more inspired.

Who is wise? Those who show by their good lives "that your works are done with gentleness born of wisdom." People whose wisdom leads them to a deeper discipleship and whose discipleship changes the world in ways that are kind, generous, and good are all around us.

Suggestion for meditation: Give thanks for the wise ones in your life. Pray for wisdom to make a difference in the world.

It's traditional. It happens in all cultures, in all countries, across all centuries. Wisdom, captured in short sayings. Wisdom, passed on from one generation to the next.

"Blessed are the meek, for they shall inherit the earth." "The early bird catches the worm." "God helps those who help themselves." (No, this last one is not in the Bible. It's a uniquely American proverb.)

These verses from Proverbs put together a variety of sayings under the title "Hymn to a Valiant Woman." Its rich and energetic images describe a woman who "makes her arms strong" and "girds herself with strength." This valiant woman "opens her hand to the poor" and is "not afraid for her household" because she has provided vigorously for them.

This hymn praises women, but it also gives a clear signal to men about their treatment of women. In the time Proverbs was written, women—no matter how strong they were—were vulnerable to the whims of men. Society offered little protection for a woman. This hymn, in addition to recognizing women's worth, reminded men of their duty to care for and respect women.

No doubt many valiant women have been part of your life. Other women in your life have needed protection, care, and justice. What images of strength come to mind when you think of these women? What images of vulnerability? What words would be in your "hymn?"

Wisdom, in itself, is beautiful. But wisdom is not content to stay within itself. Instead, wisdom lays a path, shows the way, points the direction to the ultimate way of wisdom: the path that leads toward God. An important aspect of that path is protection and justice for women. God's wisdom is valiant. God's wisdom protects the vulnerable. God's wisdom is powerful.

Suggestion for meditation: **Choose a word or phrase from this "Hymn to a Valiant Woman." Carry it with you as you go about your activities and as you pray.**

Noble, capable, trustworthy, industrious. That's how these verses from the book of Proverbs describe her. She opens her hand to the poor and cares for the needy. Her children's lives pay tribute to her and make her happy. Her husband praises her. She works so hard and faithfully that her works are spoken of even in the city gates—the center of the city's life.

For this woman in Proverbs, it is clear what moves her, what motivates her, what sustains her. It is her relationship with God. Because God is in the middle of everything she does, she can perform difficult and even heroic tasks. She is strengthened for whatever the day ahead holds for her.

People throughout history have lived difficult and remarkable lives. Some names we know: Dorothy Day of the Catholic Worker Movement, Helen Keller, Oscar Romero of El Salvador.

Others who have lived difficult and remarkable lives are less well-known: the woman in the neighborhood whose husband is on disability and who has three young children; yet her kind demeanor lightens the load of all she meets. The five-year-old who lives part-time with his mother and part-time with his father, a child who befriends kindergarten classmates who are ignored or teased. The layperson who recently lost his wife and still checks in weekly to see how his own pastor, whose wife is away at school, is doing and what he might need.

In Proverbs the wisdom and fear of the Lord comes to fullness in daily activity. We live heroically every day because we live for God.

SUGGESTION FOR MEDITATION: **How does my daily life reflect and serve God? How can I, with God's help, meet what lies ahead of me today?**

"Save me, O God, . . . Hear my prayer, O God." Strong words. Deep cries from the heart, from the deepest part of the pray-er. This psalm starts out in despair. "The insolent have risen against me, the ruthless seek my life."

Any of us, at some time in our lives, can pray this psalm with certainty. The world is out to get me—at least today. Meanness, unkindness, and badness dominate my life. If the psalm says anything about prayer, it says this: go to God with all your heart, with what's most troubling in your life, with those who would do you harm always in mind.

Go to God in that way and make this affirmation: God is my helper. In the midst of everything. Surely my helper. Surely.

In the midst of laying out our troubles, our ability to affirm God as our helper gives witness to God's power and strength. To say, in the midst of difficult times, that God is our helper implies a complete dependence on God. It means that we as Christians experience even now the life God desires for us, even alongside the world where our brokenness is real.

And that brokenness is very real. Sometimes it is there on the large scale: tsunami, terrorist bombs, genocide. Sometimes it strikes closer to home: the death of a child, loss of a job, a devastating accident. It comes sometimes from the outside: a co-worker's lie about us, the racial slur on the street, the home that pretends all is well even though an alcoholic lives there.

Lay out your troubles and complaints. Let God know you're afraid, alone, or vexed. Let God know, and ask God to give you strength to let someone else know.

Lay it all out, and say these words: "God is my helper. Surely. God is my helper." Say them, even when you can't believe them. Say them, and let God be there, somehow, for you.

SUGGESTION FOR MEDITATION: In quiet prayer, give over to God a particularly troubling or hard part of your life. When this person or situation comes to mind, say quietly, "God is my helper."

Right Word, Right Time

September 25–October 1, 2006 • Marilyn E. Thornton[‡]

MONDAY, SEPTEMBER 25 • Read Esther 7:1-6

The preservation of life and the ability to survive in the midst of oppression and death-dealing circumstances requires radical, sacrificial behavior. Esther decides to gather up her spiritual strength through fasting and prayer and to petition the king for the sake of her people. She risks her position in the kingdom, and indeed her life, by daring to go before the king without being summoned. Through her action Esther experiences spiritual deliverance. Rather than being bound in secrecy about her identity, she is freed to be herself. As she claims her identity as a child of the Jews, she delivers them from death.

Esther's action prefigures God's radical action of sacrificing a glorious position in heaven and becoming Immanuel. Similarly, Jesus' sacrificial work on the cross created new possibilities for our existence. The Holy Spirit provides a continuing presence, enabling us truly to be that which God created us to be, children of the Most High God, created in God's image.

In turn, when we sacrifice ourselves on behalf of someone else, when we empty ourselves before the King, that radical action reflects God's ongoing work of salvation in the world. Sacrificial behavior gets to the root of how we ought to relate to one another. By giving up the insistence that our life, needs, will, and desires are more important than those of others, we participate in their ability to be, to discover life and their own identity in God, even in the midst of a world that seeks to destroy.

PRAYER: My God, help me live in sacrificial love, remembering that through your grace we all have life everlasting. In Jesus' name. Amen.

[‡]Developmental editor, African American resources, The United Methodist Publishing House; Director of Christian Education, South End United Methodist Church, Nashville, Tennessee.

Mordecai's words thwarted a plot against the king, so the king honored Mordecai and hanged Haman. All of Haman's plans to murder Mordecai and oppress the Jewish people came to naught. By the words of one man, justice prevailed and deliverance from oppression was effected.

It goes against the grain of polite society to speak when everyone else remains silent. "Why stir up the waters?" one might ask. Let sleeping dogs lie. Just keep your mouth shut! Yet over and over we see the results of the right word spoken at the right time. Sometimes the right word is spoken at the wrong time.

When Martin Luther King Jr. wrote his "Letter from a Birmingham Jail," many people thought it came at the wrong time. Some in the Birmingham community had already objected to his words and actions, indicating their belief that black people should wait, that moderation and negotiation should reign. Some felt that accommodation was key. King and his ilk seemed too radical. These people believed that it was the wrong time. But it was the right word. Words of justice often appear wrongly timed. But sooner or later they are remembered, like Mordecai's words.

Mordecai and King remind us to speak out against injustice. When we stir up the waters on behalf of the poor, the sick, the children, the undereducated; when we speak out against injustice of any kind, against violence and greed, those words are not spoken in vain. They may rest awhile in the minutes of the meeting, but words are living things. Like the word of God, they offer hope to the oppressed with the knowledge that someone sees, someone knows, someone cares. They are not alone.

PRAYER: Open my mouth, dear God. Give me the courage to speak your words in season and out of season. In Jesus' name. Amen.

The Jewish people have much for which to be joyful. They have been delivered from the possibility of mass slaughter, multiple funerals, and unending sorrow. It is time for celebration. The people respond to Mordecai's decrees by establishing Purim in order to remember God's deliverance.

The root of much griping, depression, and sorrow lies in our failure to remember, claim, and celebrate God's graciousness. Sorrow surrounds us; persons stand ready to demoralize, to slay in body and/or spirit. We always have some event or person to mourn, a reason for sorrow. Most any news report acquaints us with items that move us to sadness. We often choose to concentrate more on things that bring tears of sorrow than of joy. However, Jesus tells us, "Blessed are those who mourn, for they will be comforted" (Matt. 5:4).

Indeed, God can turn the tide every single time. The sun rises, and the trees bloom in spring. Babies are born. Old skin cells are shed, and new skin grows every single day. What a revolution! What a radical change! How God turns darkness into light! We must remember to celebrate. Celebrate life, celebrate love; celebrate God's loving-kindness and ability to turn our sorrow into gladness. Let us count blessings instead of grievances. Let us smile rather than frown.

Make today a holiday, a day holy to God. Set it aside. Sanctify it for praise and thanksgiving in everything that you do. Bless God for being a God of joy who wants us to play, give gifts, and fellowship with one another. God is able to deliver us from aching hearts, depression, and the blues. "The joy of the LORD is [our] strength"! (Neh. 8:10).

PRAYER: O God of joy, help me to remember how you delivered the whole world from sin and death. Let me be glad in the joy of your salvation. In Jesus' name. Amen.

In attempts to mold the world toward a particular point of view, we usually invoke the name of God: If it had not been for the Lord on our side! We thank God for the inspiration of plans laid to silence enemies and snuff out opposing views. Our self-righteousness becomes a hatred that we feel is justified because we believe God approves of our way of thinking and doing.

How does it feel to escape from a trap that has been laid by an enemy? Certainly those who survived the calamity of The World Trade Center in 2001 know. In this disaster, those who considered themselves enemies of anything American, made plans and laid a trap that resulted in three thousand dead. As tragic as it was, disaster by hatred is nothing new.

Through the ages enemies have been burying their opponents alive, gassing, lynching, bombing, and chasing them down to annihilate them. In recent years enemies are so hateful they commit suicide in order to murder the hated.

Our deliverance, rescue, help in times of trouble come from God. So we proclaim with the psalmist, "Our help is in the name of the LORD, who made heaven and earth." When we are delivered, when we understand and claim God as our deliverer, we make a strong and liberating confession: We cannot go it alone. We must rely on God, and God is love.

What if we sought to be on the Lord's side and chose love? Only by God's hand can we escape hatred, whether as the hated or the hater. Only the love of God can remove the poison of hate and deliver us all to love.

PRAYER: O God, may we seek to become lovers of life. May we be delivered from hatred that causes death. May we desire to cultivate a love that is perfect because it includes all of humanity no matter the color, religion, ethnicity, culture, size, hair texture, eye shape, gender orientation, locality, and/or any other characteristic we are so bent upon using as an excuse to hate. May we learn to be radical in our love. Our help is in the name of the Lord who made heaven and earth. Amen.

Most people have suffered in their bodies from physical illness or disease. Usually, the first thing we do is reach for a bottle of pills. We try the heating pad, therapy, pain shots, herbal regimens, surgery, anything and everything to gain relief from physical discomfort. Too often the last resort is reaching out to the house of prayer and turning our illnesses over to the One who knit us together in the womb.

This James passage does not admonish us just to pray, going into a secret closet to find solace in God; it encourages us to call on the faithful, to open our spirits to the healing power of corporate prayer, and to trust our fellow sojourners, all of whom have known suffering of some kind. Our communal God operates in community to bring wholeness and harmony. An African proverb states, "A single bracelet does not jingle." By the Word of God, the world was fashioned by the Creator when the Spirit of God moved over the face of the deep. If our triune God operates communally, who are we to snub the community of faith at a time of direst need?

Trusting God to act through the community of faith requires radical obedience, humility, and love. In our time of vulnerability we empty ourselves of pride, anger, and distrust. This is not to say that we do not avail ourselves of the great blessings of modern medicine. At the same time, when we submit ourselves to the prayers of the people and the songs of the saints, our spirits, minds, and bodies can find a deep peace that makes us whole. Regardless of any external circumstance, we are delivered from the soul-killing effects of bitterness, self-pity, tension, anxiety, and depression that illness and suffering can bring.

PRAYER: O Lord, may my prayers join the community of faith as we lift up those who suffer in body and spirit. In Jesus' name. Amen.

The media often portrays evil (opposition to God) as a man in a red suit with a pointed tail and horns, carrying a pitchfork. And don't forget the goatee! How easily we could fight evil if its identity were so obvious. The disciples do not recognize what is evil and what is good. Caught up in their special status as followers of Jesus, they complain that people are using Jesus' name to cast out demons. The disciples' complaint is quite ironic: they are trying to prevent someone from doing what they, just a while before, had failed to do.

The irony is not lost on Jesus. The disciples have become possessive and perhaps feel threatened by this outsider who heals in Jesus' name. They want to restrict the activity of salvation to their group alone.

Their small-mindedness prevents the disciples from realizing that Jesus' ministry and power are not the property of their "in crowd." Jesus draws the circle to include as many people as possible: "Whoever is not against us is for us."

This could be a word of grace for the disciples; but they have missed the point entirely, so Jesus reinforces it. He declares that there will be those outside the disciples' small group upon whom they can depend for a cup of water, given in Jesus' name. They can depend on those among whom they minister.

This word is a hard one for the disciples to hear; it is sometimes a hard word for us to hear. We too become possessive, wanting to restrict the work of God to those in our group alone. But the name of Jesus gets in the way of all that. The name of Jesus is so powerful that any encounter—not just with Jesus but also with his name—can bring about a radical change in the human heart.

Jesus calls us, like the disciples, to broaden, deepen, and widen our understanding of his work and our vision of how salvation might come about.

PRAYER: Open my heart and my mind to be see all the ways you are at work today, O God. Amen.

In this passage Jesus utters an emphatic declaration concerning the temptation to sin in what we do (hand), in the lifestyle in which we walk (foot), and in how we use our intellect (eye). The eye is the light of the body (Matt. 6: 22-23). Kingdom living sometimes requires radical action in order to keep our gifts in line with the will of Christ.

The kingdom of God is the goal! Our busy, self-righteous, know-it-all attitude often prevents others from seeing Jesus. Jesus tells us to cut it out! He wants us to eliminate our tendencies to use our gifts in ways that create division and competition. Rather, we must become seasoned disciples, finding opportunities to uplift and bring out the gifts of others, thereby being delivered from the sin of arrogance and self-aggrandizement. By accentuating the gifts of our companions we engage in a more peaceful and loving journey.

Western culture requires promotion of self, often to the extent of generating humiliation and insecurity in our coworkers, friends, and family. We are encouraged to toot our own horns. But Jesus requires that we be as salt—the essence that helps preserve the table of Christ's love, inviting others to taste and see that the Lord is good. In other words, we are not the main dish! So get over it and let God be glorified.

As Christ's disciples, our role is not to prove how capable, bright, and righteous we are. Our gifts will not deliver or redeem anyone. Our hands, feet, and eyes are given for the purpose of revealing the grace and redeeming power of Jesus Christ.

PRAYER: "I looked at my hands and they looked new. I looked at my feet and they did, too!"* Dear God, use my hands and my feet and every gift you've given me for your glory. Amen.

---

*The above quote is part of African American religious lore.

Shaken but Unshakable

October 2–8, 2006 • Marshall Shelley[‡]

MONDAY, OCTOBER 2 • Read Job 1:1; 2:1-7

God assigns people some incredibly tough, even severe, situations. In Genesis, at God's direction, Ishmael and his mother are evicted from their tension-filled home into the desert. Young Isaac is bound as a human sacrifice. In Exodus, all firstborn sons of the Egyptians are slain by the death angel. And in this passage, we see Job lose his possessions, children (probably grown children), and health because of Satan's test, sanctioned by God.

As a parent who has grieved the loss of two children, I wrestle with God's seeming severity. In the story of David and Bathsheba, the adultery and the arranged murder of Uriah no longer interest me. Now I fixate on God's treatment of their two sons—one, a nameless son, died as God's judgment on David's sin; the second, Jedidiah (meaning "loved by God"), grows up to become Solomon and enjoys God's most lavish blessing.

In John 9, in front of a man blind since birth, Jesus is asked if this suffering is due to the man's own sins or to those of his parents. Jesus explains it is neither but rather "that the work of God might be displayed in his life." A childhood of blindness in order to bring glory to God. That answer—especially from Jesus, known for his love of children—is no cheap comfort.

Ultimately the Divine sends God's own son to die upon a cross. Living for God's glory is not for sissies. God's purposes, require a high price. Redeeming the world of sin's contamination must be ever so much more costly than we imagine.

PRAYER: Our God, help us see how you are redeeming the world of evil even as we offer compassion and consolation to those who suffer. Amen.

[‡]Editor of *Leadership*, a practical journal for church leaders; a vice president of *Christianity Today* International; member, Parkview Community Church, Glen Ellyn, Illinois.

People's suffering compels their faith to become more intentional. Throughout the book of Job, and especially in this passage, we see Job choosing to trust God, even when he has no earthly reason to do so. This choice changes the nature of his faith.

Do you remember the classical distinction between virtue and innocence? Virtue, unlike innocence, has successfully passed a point of temptation. Perhaps a similar distinction can be found in faith—innocent faith can trust God because it hasn't seen the abyss; virtuous faith has known the terror and chooses to trust God in the midst of it. As Abraham Heschel observed, "Job's faith was unshakable because it was the result of being shaken."

Even as a child, I enjoyed reading novels. I quickly recognized that the opening chapters were the most confusing. They introduced new characters. Disparate, seemingly random events took place. Subplots didn't seem to make any sense in relation to the main plot.

But I learned to keep reading. Why? Because I knew that the author, if he or she wrote well, would weave all the disparate parts and pieces together by the end of the book. Eventually, each element becomes meaningful.

At times, such faith has to be a conscious choice. That's what Job does. Even when he can't explain the loss of his wealth, his offspring, and his health, he chooses to trust that by the last chapter, the Author will make it clear.

As God said through the prophet Jeremiah, "For I know the thoughts that I think toward you, says the LORD, thoughts of peace and not of evil, to give you a future and a hope" (Jer. 29:11, NKJV).

Clinging to that promise, even when the weight of sorrow makes our knees buckle, is what makes faith intentional.

PRAYER: Lord, give me grace to cling to you even when things go against me. Amen.

How do you respond when attacked or accused? It's easy to become defensive, to counterattack, to return charge for charge.

But Thomas à Kempis observed centuries ago, "It is good that we at times endure opposition and that we are evilly and untruly judged when our actions and intentions are good. Often such experiences promote humility and protect us from vainglory. For then we seek God's witness in the heart."

Though the psalmist lived almost two thousand years before Thomas à Kempis, he seems to practice that same understanding. While pleading for God's vindication, he spends the rest of the psalm examining his motives, actions, and associations.

The writer searches his heart and mind to determine whether his love for God is vital and alive; he concludes that he has been and continues to be "blameless" (NIV). Does this mean the psalmist is without sin? No, as he acknowledges elsewhere; when comparing himself with God's perfect standard, he must confess his sin (Ps. 51:3-4).

But here, when viewing himself on a human level, the psalmist sees nothing that warrants this treatment. As best he can tell, his trust in God is strong. His attitudes and thoughts are without guile. He is neither conspiring with others to do evil nor does he tacitly approve those who do by associating with them. After his self-examination, he professes that he has acted with integrity before both God and humankind.

The psalmist asks God to redeem him and be merciful. This is not a request for a quick escape from his situation but a plea to see good come out of the present struggle. The psalm closes with a word picture of standing on level ground, praising the Lord—an image of solid confidence, not only that God is on his side but that he continues to seek God's will.

PRAYER: Lord, search me and see if there is any wicked way in me. Amen.

For centuries, God had spoken to people through prophets who used a variety of means—pronouncements, poetry, symbolic action—with almost always the same result. Despite occasional instances of people hearing and heeding God's word as spoken by the prophets, in most cases the prophets and the word they communicated were rejected, often violently.

But eventually God spoke more directly through his son, Jesus. This Jesus didn't just present God's words; he was himself "the radiance of God's glory and the exact representation of his being." Jesus too met violent opposition. But after his death and resurrection he provided purification for the sins of the world; he returned to his position of highest honor in heaven.

This passage introduces Jesus in a significant way: as the heir of all things and creator of the universe. What can we learn about Jesus by looking at his creation? Of the many possibilities, consider just one—the built-in repetition.

The sun rises every morning without fail. If you were born in 1956, you have seen over eighteen thousand sunrises and sunsets. Days, sabbaths, seasons, and years—over and over. And on a more personal level, think of life-sustaining heartbeats, one hundred thousand per day. A lifetime of repetition. What does this tell us about the Creator—that God is boring? Hardly.

G. K. Chesterton observes in *Orthodoxy*: "A child throws a ball up in the air over and over again because of genuine pleasure, not because of boredom. . . . A child always says, 'Do it again'; and the grown-up person does it again until he is nearly dead. For grown-up people are not strong enough to exult in monotony."

Perhaps there's so much repetition in the universe because Christ has the eternal creativity of a child. He delights in each heartbeat, in each sunrise. He loves you anew each day. Indeed, as Chesterton concludes, "We have sinned and grown old, and our Father is younger than we."

PRAYER: Each day, Lord, help me to live for your glory. Amen.

What does it mean to be human? In today's world, many people consider human beings as just another part of the animal kingdom. But the Bible indicates that God had something special in mind for human beings.

In lyrical Psalm 8, an anthem to the Creator God, the writer marvels, "When I look at your heavens, the work of your fingers, the moon and the stars . . . what are human beings that you are mindful of them? . . . You have made them a little lower than the divine beings, and crowned them with glory and honor. . . . You have put all things under their feet."

While today's secular society assumes that humans are only a slightly higher form of animal, the psalm indicates that we are created by God as just a bit below *elohim*, the "heavenly ones." So to be human is a privileged, exalted position.

But today's passage interprets this psalm with a different emphasis. "At present, we do not see everything subject to him" (NIV); but we see Jesus who came to earth and was made "a little lower than the divine beings" and suffered death to restore lost and fallen human beings to a position of glory.

Yes, before original sin, there was original glory, a place of honor in God's created order. Because of human rebellion, we have not fully experienced God's intention for us. As G. K. Chesterton observed, whatever else is or is not true, one thing is certain: human beings are not what we were meant to be.

Christ, by assuming human likeness and through his life, death, and resurrection, enables us to experience what God created us for.

PRAYER: We praise you, O God, for creating us and, through Jesus, for recreating us for eternal glory with you. Amen.

Charlie Gordon is a janitor with a mentally handicapping condition who lives in New York City. A cheerful man, he enjoys his work and takes night classes to learn to read and write. Charlie's life, however, dramatically changes when two doctors tell him that they can give him the one thing he desperately desires: the chance to become smart.

After a quick and painless operation, Charlie's doctors begin to see signs of his improving intelligence. He writes better; he spells better; and he even begins to read college-level textbooks and enjoy them. Soon after that, the doctors tell Charlie that he has more than tripled his original IQ; he is an official genius!

Unfortunately, Charlie's newfound intelligence doesn't bring him the happiness he thought it would. He begins to understand that his friends have been making fun of him all his life, and soon he is forced to quit his job because his coworkers fear his dramatic change. Even worse, Charlie is horrified when he discovers that the effects of his operation are not permanent and that he will slowly sink back into his original mental condition with no memory of his brief intellectual awareness. As you have probably guessed, Charlie Gordon is not a real person. He is a character in Daniel Keyes's short story "Flowers for Algernon."

Are those the only two options: misery that comes from awareness and intelligence versus happiness that's a result of being oblivious to your true situation?

No. The same Jesus who praised childlikeness also told his followers, "I am sending you out like sheep among wolves. Therefore be as shrewd as snakes and as innocent as doves" (Matt. 10:16, NIV).

The life of faith does not require intellectual suicide. In fact, Jesus wants disciples with sanctified shrewdness. But above all, he longs for followers whose love for him is pure.

PRAYER: Lord, even as I strive for wisdom and street-smarts, keep my heart pure. Amen.

In this passage, two very different groups approach Jesus. First some Pharisees come with a hardball question intended to embarrass or discredit him: "Is it lawful for a man to divorce his wife?" The Pharisees probably think they have him cornered. Whether he answers yes or no, they can charge Jesus with discounting either the law or the sacredness of marriage.

Jesus responds by reframing the issue and saying in essence that while divorce, because of the hardness of human hearts, may be permitted according to the law of Moses, it is never God's intention. Jesus elevates the question beyond what is lawful to what is right.

After that encounter, a second group comes to Jesus, parents bringing children, desiring that he touch them. This group may remind us of people today who crowd in asking for autographs or looking for a chance to shake hands with a famous person.

Jesus' disciples assume Jesus doesn't want to be bothered with these unimportant people. But Jesus quickly corrects them: "Let the little children come to me, and do not hinder them, for the kingdom of God belongs to such as these. I tell you the truth, anyone who will not receive the kingdom of God like a little child will never enter it."

The contrast between the two groups couldn't be more dramatic. One comes with trick questions wanting to trap him; the other simply wanting to enjoy his presence. One group has impressive credentials but a cunning intention; the other has no credentials but a spirit of wonder and delight.

Compared to the shrewd, sophisticated Pharisees, the children exemplify the kind of spirit that Jesus wants. Not conniving. Not driven by masked motives and guile. But a simple desire to be near him and be blessed by him. Hardball? Or heartfelt?

PRAYER: Jesus, I have lots of questions, many that emerge from my own selfish agenda. But I want to be near you just because of who you are. Amen.

Lay Aside Hindrances

October 9–15, 2006 • Jerry Lowry[‡]

MONDAY, OCTOBER 9 • Read Job 23:1-9, 16-17

Have you ever waited for God to reveal God's self in a time of darkness or despair? We find Job in anguish of soul and spirit as he waits on the unknown God. His perception of God differs greatly from that of his three friends who think they know exactly how God orders and measures the universe. In this time of waiting for God, Job pours out his soul, saying, "Oh, that I knew where I might find him."

There is perhaps no stronger complaint against God's absence in the face of abuse and evil than the one here in Job. For Job and for other people of faith, to believe in God is to believe in justice. When evil and injustice surround Job, and God does not respond, life stops making sense

All of us have found ourselves searching for God's presence, peace, and power. Jesus had a similar experience during his Passion. He cried out, "My God, my God, why have you forsaken me?" (Matt 27:46). Both Job and Jesus felt at times bereft, abandoned, hopeless. Like them, our faith in God and in a God of justice is tested mightily How then can we live, trying to believe in God when everything around us witnesses not to God's presence but to God's absence? For Jesus, for Job, and for us there are no ready answers. But one thing is certain—we can hold on fiercely to our faith, demanding in our prayers that God answer us. We join the procession of saints who have believed that God exists and is worth finding and serving.

PRAYER: Ever-present God, help us this day to know your presence, even when you seem absent. May we lay aside anything that would keep us from knowing you. Amen.

[‡]Sanford district superintendent, North Carolina Conference, The United Methodist Church; Native American Lumbee Tribe; living in Sanford, North Carolina.

My wife and I are blessed to have my ninety-year-old mother-in-law living with us for the present. She recently had to sell her home of sixty-one years to the North Carolina Department of Transportation. The state needed the additional land for a new interstate highway. All the necessary transitions have over-whelmed her. But in the midst of her grief and mental anguish she has reminded herself and us of her faith. She says, "Dark times will come, but God will see you through. I wonder why God has allowed this to happen. At times I feel God has forsaken me, but it is only a feeling and not a fact. I have trusted God since my childhood, and I will trust God now."

My mother-in-law's words reminded me of the psalmist's cry: "My God, my God! Why have you forsaken me? Why are you so far from helping me, from the words of my groaning?" Despite his circumstances, the psalmist also expresses his faith and trust in God: "In you our ancestors trusted; they trusted, and you delivered them. To you they cried, and were saved; in you they trusted, and were not put to shame."

I wish I could always trust God when the hindrances of life come. Maybe God placed my mother-in-law within our home to let me see faith in action. Faith affirms that God is and that the Holy One comes to the aid of those who seek God. Faith chooses, acts, and endures.

SUGGESTION FOR MEDITATION: **Think about the most recent event in your life journey that called for faith alone. What do you face in the present that calls for faith in God alone?**

Some years ago I read about Jim Elliot, a missionary in Ecuador. Prior to his death he shared this invaluable bit of wisdom: "He is no fool who gives up what he cannot keep to gain that which he cannot lose."

The highest calling in life is the call of Jesus Christ to come and follow him. Jesus reveals this again in our Gospel lesson. Draw your own conclusions about this story, but it says to me that being a disciple is costly. Jesus is on the way to Jerusalem to die in obedience to God's call upon his life. Before his departure he must tell his disciples what they must do if they want to be his true disciples. Seemingly neither the disciples nor the crowd understand the cost of discipleship and the matter of self-denial.

In an emotional fever, a man comes to Jesus and asks, "Good Teacher, what must I do to inherit eternal life?" Jesus responds, "You know the commandments. . . ." The young man replies, "I have kept all these since my youth." Jesus answers, "You lack one thing; go, sell what you own and give the money to the poor, and you will have treasure in heaven; then come, follow me."

The young man leaves, shocked and grieved, for he has many possessions. Apparently the young man has caused no harm. I like to think that Jesus may have said, "What good have you done with what God has given you? Have you given to the poor? Have you reached out to the orphaned, the oppressed, the captive, and the prisoners?" It costs to be a disciple!

SUGGESTION FOR MEDITATION: **What does it cost you to be a disciple of Christ? What one thing do you lack or what obstacle hinders you from being a faithful disciple?**

What one thing kept the young man from being a true disciple? Could it have been lack of faith in God? Did his possessions possess him? After this encounter with the young man, Jesus looks around and says to his disciples, "How hard it will be for those who have wealth to enter the kingdom of God."

Is not Jesus saying to his disciples, his followers, and to each potential disciple, "I want you to get rid of anything that would keep you from following me"? Or perhaps we might interpret his words in this way: "I want you to put your faith in me and not in things. Trust me! You are too 'stuffed with your own stuff.' You are too possessed by your own possessions, which are here today and gone tomorrow. Give them up, and come follow me. Then you will have the greatest possession. Without me in the center of your life, there will be a 'gaping hole'—a void—an emptiness within.'

Jesus' statement perplexes the disciples. Why? They believe wealth surely affirms God's favor. But Jesus challenges this traditional religious thought. He presses even more, "Children, how hard it is to enter the kingdom of God. It is easier for a camel to go through the eye of a needle than for someone who is rich to enter the kingdom of God." It costs to be a disciple! May God have mercy upon us for loving things and using people, when we should love people and use things.

Why do we let things rob God and us of the joy of being a disciple? A true disciple loves God. This love manifests itself in acts of unconditional love to and for the neighbor. May God help us lay aside hindrances that would keep us from being faithful disciples.

SUGGESTION FOR MEDITATION: **When have you last visited the poor, a prisoner, or a shut-in? Why not spend a week on a mission work team?**

The disciples express astonishment at Jesus' teaching. Rightly so! Jesus calls for radical discipleship. Radical discipleship involves total self-denial. This kind of discipleship is not something we undertake alone. God must be central in order for it to take on flesh. Someone said, "Ninety-five percent of what the church does could be done without the presence and power of the Holy Spirit." Too often, as followers of Jesus, we try to do and be disciples alone, forgetting our source of wisdom and power. Thus we find ourselves relying on our own human limitations.

Notice the disciples seem troubled when Jesus says, "How hard it will be for those who have wealth to enter the kingdom of God." Riches signaled God's favor. But Jesus challenges this traditional concept or belief. When the disciples ask, "Who then can be saved?" Jesus says, "God can save anyone. Nothing is impossible for God" (AP). God calls us; God will equip us, guide us, and nurture us to live out the call to be disciples.

The apparent impossibility of renouncing all things to follow Jesus is possible. Discipleship, which can at times seem impossible, is completely possible—with God. Who can be saved? Anyone can. God can save anyone.

Paul reminds us that we can do all things through Jesus Christ who strengthens us. May our actions reveal God's power at work in us.

SUGGESTION FOR MEDITATION: **"Dear Lord, lead me day by day; make me steadfast, wise, and strong; happy most of all to know that my dear Lord loves me so."** (From "Dear Lord, Lead Me Day by Day," *The United Methodist Hymnal* [Nashville, Tennessee: The United Methodist Publishing House, 1989], #411.)

Peter begins to consider the cost, "Look we have left everything and followed you." Jesus replies, "Let me tell you a truth, there is no one who has left house or brother or sister, or mother or father, or children or land for my sake and for the sake of the Good News, who will not receive a hundredfold now in this age—and in the age to come, eternal life. But many who are first will be last, and the last will be first" (AP).

What is Jesus trying to point out? I think he is saying, "It costs to be a disciple! Count the cost! Be willing to pay the price! There are no discounts! You will be rewarded!"

I heard the following story several years ago. Exxon Corporation searched for a representative to lead their company in the Far East. Eventually they found the ideal person. The person was a missionary. Exxon offered him $100,000 in compensation. He refused this offer. They increased the offer by $25,000; he refused again. The executive of Exxon asked him why he declined the offer. He replied, "Your offer is gracious. But your job is too small. I am a missionary and that is God's call upon my life." This missionary makes a strong statement. For him, nothing is more important or greater than following Jesus. He puts his faith in God, trusting unreservedly with his whole being.

I am learning daily the cost of discipleship. My faith in God helps me experience the rewards of servanthood ministry.

SUGGESTION FOR MEDITATION: **What rewards have you experienced in following Christ? What hinders you from following him?**

The writer of Hebrews has a clear purpose: to encourage or bolster the faith of those who, for one reason or another are considering a return to the Jewish faith. Many Christians were ready to relinquish their faith in Christ because of intense persecution.

Others began to doubt the immediacy of Christ's return and therefore lost faith. The writer encourages steadfastness since Jesus is the greatest revelation of God to humanity.

Life presents many complex and complicated issues that burden humans and our understanding of the Christian faith. We, like the Hebrew Christian community, may question whether or not faith in Christ matters. "Is the suffering worth the reward? Why do I keep following Jesus when nothing seems to change? Hard times, despair, stress, poor health, loss of job, economic plight overwhelm me."

Yet the writer of Hebrews reminds us that the person in whom we believe and place our trust is worthy of our worship because he faced the same temptations and trials we do. "Since, then, we have a great high priest who has passed through the heavens, Jesus, the Son of God, let us hold fast to our confession. For we do not have a high priest who is unable to sympathize with our weaknesses, but we have one who in every respect has been tested as we are, yet without sin. Let us therefore approach the throne of grace with boldness, so that we may receive mercy and find grace to help in time of need."

Jesus Christ has experienced this earthly life in every way we have. He understands and has been where we are. Thus he offers his mercy and grace in unconditional love. So let us lay aside all the hindrances of life and put our faith in Jesus Christ who is worthy of being followed, whatever the cost.

PRAYER: Holy God, your presence lifts us like the melody of a song and comforts us like a parent's warm embrace. Beneath your wings we find shelter from our despair, darkness, and doubt. You strengthen us to live faithfully when we become weary. Thank you for always being near. Amen.

Reverent Submission

October 16–22, 2006 • Pamela J. Crosby[‡]

MONDAY, OCTOBER 16 • Read Psalm 104:1-9

I have exceptional friends who live in Zimbabwe. They are special to me because they seem to delight in my presence. When I visit, they show me a great time. They take me places, show me the beauty and animals of the land, and treat me like part of the family.

Listening to my friends has taught me how to praise children. Their two sons hear, "Excellent, Elliot," or "That's brilliant, Douglas." Superlatives and praise are big in that house and served up often, no matter how trivial the accomplishment. Positive affirmations teach their children that excellence and brilliance are possible.

This passage is an anthem of praise, honoring God's glorious work. How excellent, it seems to say, "that you stretched out the heavens like a tent." How brilliant, to have clouds as chariots, the winds as messengers, fire and flame as ministers! And what an exceptional way to praise God—by memorizing this psalm and speaking it aloud to God. It's a wonderful psalm to offer as a compliment to God when enjoying earth's beauty. How would God feel if superlatives about the Creator's wonderful work were the norm of our conversations?

So much beauty surrounds us that clearly God wants us to enjoy it and be moved by it. The glory of this earth motivates, encourages, stimulates, and challenges us in many directions. Celebrate it by giving God a standing ovation!

PRAYER: God, the beauty of your works extends beyond our feeble language to describe. Your work is incredible! Please accept our humble praise and give us a chance to grow and learn creative ways to honor you more. Amen.

[‡]Writer, producer; member of Otter Creek Church of Christ, Nashville, Tennessee.

In her book *Prodigal Summer*, Barbara Kingsolver uses life in a farming community in southern Appalachia to demonstrate the connection among bugs, moths, birds, goats, coyotes, and humans. When one tries to exterminate another, it upsets God's plan for a working, growing, nurturing earth.

Kingsolver's characters find that they are bound to one another and to the plants and animals in the space they share. As they unearth information, they find their discoveries are implanted inside profound biology lessons, the unfair realities of small farming, and the emphatic truth that humans are only a small part of life on earth.

Kingsolver's book reveals the wisdom of God's creation: every herb-bearing seed and every tree-yielding seed has a purpose that benefits humans and animals; ripping up a field to grow tobacco will often starve out thousands of animals. Kingsolver describes how the things we don't see, like caterpillars and honeysuckle, help us; and the things we try to control, like spiders and varmints, often rear back and bite us.

I didn't know there were two main kinds of bugs: plant eaters and bug eaters. And when humans employ pesticides, they disrupt the balance between the pest bugs and the predator bugs. The predators decrease due to loss of food supply.

Kingsolver's book testifies to God's wisdom and to the majesty of God's handiwork that today's verses describe. God's works are manifold—diverse and stratified—for purposes beyond our comprehension. If we respect and honor the process, we will all benefit from God's incredible work.

SUGGESTION FOR MEDITATION: **We are small and insignificant, but our society tells us we are mighty and important. As we learn more about the intricacies of God's creation, may we respond honorably and respectfully.**

"What's in it for me?" is the tenor of the request from James and John, as well as that of the disciples who later understand what James and John have asked of Jesus. Selflessness and humility are huge orders on the scale of character development.

Examine, however, the way of our world: special achievements deserve great rewards. Accomplishments in the fields of academia, military, theology, medicine, sociology, the arts all deserve special recognition.

You really can't blame James and John for wanting to sit next to Jesus. Being near someone so incredible makes you feel incredible too. Jesus tells them that such privilege is not his to give. His reply offers insight into an important aspect: Jesus does not determine the places people have in the kingdom, because Jesus' work belongs not to him but to God. God has sent Jesus to the world, to serve. But service is not exactly what the disciples think about while they listen to Jesus' powerful preaching and witness his powerful healing. Quite the opposite—they think about power.

Denying the human need for honor and status is not easy—the disciples' repeated fights over their place and status show how difficult it can be. So Jesus explains yet again: the least shall be first; if you want to save your life you'll have to lose it; whoever wants to be great must be a servant; and we're here to serve, not to be served! No view like that had existed for the disciples. How like them we are.

SUGGESTION FOR MEDITATION: **Offer yourself to God today, and ask that you be a servant like Jesus in all the places you find yourself.**

Anger is a useful emotion. Sometimes it gives acrid perception to blunderers and offers exquisite clarity to the inarticulate. Many believe when empowered by anger (at themselves or at an outside force), they can do what, under calmer conditions, seems impossible.

Out of a violent storm, Job 38 and the following two chapters pose nearly one hundred questions from a riled-up God. The rapid tempo and emphatic energy of the questions is razor sharp. Job has ticked off God, and God reads him the riot act.

When I'm dealing with someone who has wronged me, my timing is off and my nerves and language skills don't connect, denying me the opportunity to zap my questions in impeccably timed candor like God's questions to Job. Mine come later when I'm alone delivering an exceptional monologue to the absent wrongdoer.

When I've been on the guilty, dumbfounded side of this scenario, the person's questions to me reveal that I knew absolutely nothing. In their tirade, I learn I had assumed too much or accused inappropriately. I realize I was totally clueless.

This is God's attitude toward Job. From this passage, we gain insight, not only into God's intellect but into God's power. Exquisite details and background unfold about earth's creation: "Who determined its measurements—surely you know! Or who stretched the line upon it? On what were its bases sunk, or who laid its cornerstone when the morning stars sang together?"

God tells Job in so many words, "You don't know the first thing about who I am or my power. So deal with it!"

PRAYER: God, your power is beyond description, beyond our perception. Wisdom and strength multiplied by infinity and taken to the depths of forever would barely give us a glimpse of who you really are. To you be glory forever. Amen.

Through my work, I have been blessed with many trips to Zimbabwe, South Africa, and Sierra Leone. After the job's finished and the meetings are over, I've connected with friends and gone on safari drives in the early morning or late in the afternoon. Once the jeep stops, our whispers cease; we experience complete silence. We sit there gazing at a beautiful African sunset, watching a group of elephants or a herd of gazelles just being themselves in this wonderful world.

Each time, against that backdrop, I have come away with a clear understanding of my place in this world: my world, my dramas, and my issues are so small compared to the concerns of this great world.

I had the same feeling when I visited the Grand Canyon. The people around me felt the same way. As we viewed the vast expanse, a quiet descended; people whispered with an air of reverence and awe.

Sometimes putting yourself in an environment bigger than your immediate surroundings allow you to see your place in the world. You recognize your place among animals, sea life, rivers, anthills, mountains, valleys, a host of cultures and communities, and more.

Once you reflect on and acknowledge that aspect of life, you realize that the One who made you controls all of the world's magnificence, including you and your problems. The One who loves us can "number the clouds" and "tilt the waterskins of the heavens." The One who created human beings also teaches the lioness to stalk her prey and feed her cubs. That One loves and cares for you and me.

SUGGESTION FOR MEDITATION: God is in control. In what ways do we often suggest that we can save the world?

Confessing a sin to someone can be a very intense experience. When I confessed a wrong, I was amazed again at the power of the truth. Aside from the weight of the guilt being lifted, I came away relieved; the self-badgering thoughts left my mind, and I started to feel good again. But better than any of that, the person I confessed to was kind and forgiving, offering more sympathy and concern than I deserved. That person dealt gently with me and my offense.

What a quality God has created that people who are in a place to hear sins and wrongs are to treat sinners and wrongdoers with compassion. What a wonderful commandment to high priests, spiritual leaders, church leaders: to deal gently, have compassion, be kind to people who have done wrong.

Hebrews says the source of this quality is Jesus—his life and work, his struggles and trials. The priests were expected to "deal gently" with the people. These words, used only in the New Testament, translate as "to moderate or control emotion." And the source of this restraint? Hebrews says this restraint is born of the priest's awareness of his own weakness.

So it is with Jesus. His restraint toward us as sinners comes from his awareness of his own humanity. Because he was the Son of God *and* fully human, he can deal gently with us.

Out of his weakness, the priest becomes a strong and forgiving presence. Out of his humanity, Jesus becomes a strong and forgiving presence as well.

This is a great gift to us from God. Surely this gift means we too are called to deal gently with others.

SUGGESTION FOR PRAYER: **Ask God to help you live with restraint, so that you can be a kind and forgiving presence in the world.**

Probably as a wake-up call to a preacher's kid who often felt too comfortable about her spiritual welfare, God has presented people to me whose spiritual depth and discipline humbles me and challenges me to greater obedience.

At the funeral service of a friend, I learned that for eighteen years she and her husband met with a prayer group every Monday through Friday at 5 A.M. to pray for their congregation and its work in the community. Although I'd known her for years, she had never told me this. Other members of the prayer group stayed three or four years, some longer; but Ed and Janice were steadfast, unmovable until her illness. What a gift!

Each time I've been on mission trips to serve people in developing countries, God has led me to spiritual giants whose faithfulness and perception blow me away. Despite my education and spiritual and financial resources, I long to sit at their feet and learn from them.

Jesus anticipated his death. He dreaded it—even begged God on more than one occasion to spare him this challenge. "He offered up prayers and supplications, with loud cries and tears, to the one who was able to save him from death." Bypassing his own choice, Jesus honored and respected God by being obedient and became the "source of eternal salvation." Because of his choice, we are saved.

With the examples of obedient Christians that God offers me, I am more determined to honor Jesus' choice, respect his suffering, and imitate his obedience.

SUGGESTION FOR MEDITATION: Although we naturally choose to do so, resist the temptation to compare your spiritual walk to that of others. Instead, look for ways to imitate and learn from them. Ask God to help you be obedient when your will seeks to challenge God's will.

Living in God's Embrace

October 23–29, 2006 • *Betsy Schwarzentraub[‡]*

MONDAY, OCTOBER 23 • **Read Job 42:1-6**

Strange comfort

In the eye of a hurricane, an eerie calm descends. Just so, everything familiar in Job's life has shattered and been hurled away in chaos. Now, in the eye at last, Job faces the One who creates not only hurricanes but the wind and air, the earth and all creatures: the Creator of all that lives throughout time.

"I have uttered what I did not understand," Job barely breathes, "things too wonderful for me, which I did not know." In one searing glimpse, Job sees God directly and comes to the heart of living in God's embrace. The climax of Job's story is verse 6, which Stephen Mitchell translates most closely from the Hebrew: "Therefore I will be quiet, comforted that I am dust."

This is a strange comfort, indeed. In Job's heart-wrenching encounter with the Divine, he hears a whisper of the Redeemer whose holiness is beyond mortal comprehension and whose personal compassion for each of us comes with every life breath. We wonder that God is mindful of us in the midst of creation!

The answer to Job's questions about God's justice comes in no answer at all but rather in the overwhelming fact of God's reality. This is the One who fashions all that lives (See Job 38-39), from each person to the earth, galaxies and stars, knowing each stirring of our thoughts and every nuance of our fears.

We can trust this awesome, intimate Holy One because God's final, full intention goes beyond justice to love.

PRAYER: God, I bow in wonder before your awesome love. May I look beyond my many questions to trust the sheer reality of you. This I pray through Jesus Christ. Amen.

[‡]Author, Director of Stewardship Development, California-Nevada United Methodist Foundation; living in Davis, California.

Second blessing

Job's first and greatest blessing is the gift of a personal relationship with God. Despite the horrors of his life, Job becomes aware of this blessing and trusts in the Holy One, refusing to accept the easy, mechanistic answers of his friends.

One might assume that Job's second blessing comes in his doubled restitution. Having lived seventy years in affliction, Job now lives another 140 years in fulfillment. He receives back double the number of flocks and herds he had lost. His brothers and sisters and fair-weather friends return to him, eat with him, and show the sympathy they had formerly withheld, each bringing him a gold ring and a substantial amount of money besides. In addition, Job has seven more sons and three beautiful daughters (both seven and three are symbols of fullness), with enough wealth that even the daughters will receive an inheritance.

But this is not the second blessing. If it were, it would surely be hollow, coming after Job's suffering as proof that God's love is not measured by wealth and external well-being. So here is the second blessing: the fact that God pushes Job one more time, after all he has endured! God pronounces judgment on Job's friends for their false statements about God. And then God challenges Job to pray on their behalf.

What a blessing! Job is pressed to pray for his enemies, to pray for those who have hurt him and belittled him. In freely choosing to pray for those who have fundamentally misunderstood and judged him, Job receives a second blessing: the gift of being able to finally and fully forgive.

PRAYER: Dear God, help me to forgive those who have hurt me. This I pray in Jesus' name. Amen.

Prayed up

Yes, we know that the church is the body of Christ. But we also know that people can be sinful and petty, whether inside or outside the church. The same is true for clergy, no matter what the denomination or ordination process. When pastors kneel before God in public worship, we come with the need for personal confession, as well as with prayers on behalf of God's people. Our lives are everyday clay jars that we use to pour out the gospel. (See 2 Cor. 4:7.)

But this is not so with Jesus! With Jesus Christ as our pastor, his prayers save for all time whoever approaches God through him. So we no longer have to come back week after week with fear in our hearts that this human channel for prayer will be deemed unworthy.

Here is why: Jesus prays for us not only as one who is ready to receive God's forgiveness but also as the One who stands ready to forgive. He prays as a human being: vulnerable, trusting, dependent upon God. At the same time, he prays for us as our Loving Parent who yearns for the best for all of God's children. Paul puts it another way: that the Spirit prays on our behalf "with sighs too deep for words" (Rom. 8:26).

These days, people use the phrase "prayed up" to describe their saturation in prayer for a receptivity to whatever God might do next. Human beings need to be "prayed up" every time we come to worship. But when the Living God is "prayed up" on our behalf, nothing can limit the power the Spirit can unleash in our lives.

SUGGESTION FOR MEDITATION: What situations seem impossible to deal with in any way you can fathom? Imagine God's praying for you related to each of these situations.

The death of sacrifice

Sacrifice is a familiar idea to people today. Many parents sacrifice financially in order to provide for their children's present and future needs. Friends do without necessities or additional comforts in order to empower a better life for their neighbors. People give sacrificially for the ministries of the church or for God's family in need of ministry around the world. People sacrifice their well-being for the sake of others during times of war or of protest on behalf of justice issues. These sacrifices can strengthen character and build and shape a faithful community.

But sacrifice becomes a problem when we think we *must* make sacrifices to God—as if God demands suffering as a sign of faith. Underneath such an approach lurks the idea that we might be earning our way into God's heart by our selfless deeds. The fact is, Jesus changed that notion. As Hebrews says, Jesus has no need to offer sacrifices because he himself became the final sacrifice, offering his life for us all on the cross.

Jesus' crucifixion does not turn sacrifice into the standard for the Christian life. Rather, Jesus' gift of his life has made all other ultimate sacrifices to God unnecessary, superfluous, even deterrents to the faith.

This is good news! Jesus has saved us, once for all. Never again will we need to try to earn our way to God or prove our faithfulness! God's love comes to us, not because of our merit but because of God's grace.

PRAYER: Thank you, God, for your incredible love in Jesus and for the fact that we never need to earn our way to you again. This we pray in Jesus' name. Amen.

Claiming mercy

The people crowding in around Jesus think, *That blind man Bartimaeus is just too pushy.* He won't sit meekly while Jesus passes by but persists in shouting, "Jesus, Son of David, have mercy on me!"

"Son of David." What an explosive political term that is during Jesus' lifetime! It refers to the Messiah, God's anointed one, who most people think will overthrow the occupying government someday and establish God's visible rule at last.

But Bartimaeus knows that this is the age of the Messiah, the time of fulfillment when the blind will see, the poor will have their debts canceled, and beggars will become part of the community once more. He dares to claim the mercy he believes Jesus can bestow. He refuses to stay dependent, isolated, and blind.

So what is the mercy (*eleison*) for which Bartimaeus cries out? It is the fundamental relationship that God has toward God's people through the covenant with them. It is God's grace toward particular persons and situations and the very attitude that God requires among human beings.

Further, the word for mercy has a connection with justice. In Greek courts, those who were accused appealed to the mercy of the judge to give a fair verdict. (See Luke 12:1-5.)

So by shouting out for mercy, Bartimaeus recognizes in Jesus' presence the sign that the time of Jubilee fulfillment has come. (See Lev. 25; Luke 4:16-21.) He acknowledges in Jesus the grace of God, interwoven with God's justice. He is clear about his goal of being able to see and about Jesus' ability to make it happen.

PRAYER: Dear God, guide me to trust that you can do all things! In the name of Jesus. Amen.

Deepest yearning

What do you want me to do for you?" Jesus asks the blind man.

The answer to his query is neither automatic nor obvious. Many people today with deep-seated illness, emotional wounds or "dis-ease" would opt for lesser healings. "Give me a lot of money, so I no longer have to beg," they might say. Or, "Make me comfortable here; give me a community but don't dig out my dependencies." Or, "Just change me a little for the better, but don't turn my life upside down."

But Bartimaeus dares to name the deepest yearning of his heart. In an instant, his public bravado voice hushes to a tense whisper. "My teacher," he answers, "let me see again!"

It's as if the moment between the question asked and the answer given stretches into infinity. What do *you* say when you suddenly realize that God is present with you, listening personally to you? What do you want more than anything else?

Bartimaeus's faith has already shown itself in his answer. "My teacher," says this outcast, audaciously exposing the love he has in the closest possible relationship he might claim with Jesus.

"My teacher," he breathes and then speaks his impossible hope.

Looking straight into such daring vulnerability, Jesus says, "Go; your faith has made you well."

SUGGESTION FOR PRAYER: Think of your deepest yearning, then quietly share it with God.

Take refuge

"None of those who take refuge in God will be condemned," declares the person praying Psalm 34. This is joyous news to people who live on the margins, those denied access by the primary structures of human community. These denied ones are "the righteous," people who find their source of help not in society but in God. Here, one of these righteous ones speaks out of personal experience: I cried out to God for help. God answered me, delivered me, and saved me! God saw and heard me, and encamped around me to defend me. I will bless and praise God continually!

Those who seek access and refuge in God know themselves primarily as receivers. It is God who gives us our well-being, and God alone who responds to us in our desperation. Surely this is wonderful news to the brokenhearted and those who have been crushed in spirit!

But there's more. The righteous, whom God sees and hears, are not only recipients. They are also initiators, responsible for reshaping community life according to God's wisdom. Begin with the fear (awe) of God, says the psalmist. Keep from speaking evil and deceit. Do no harm, and choose to do good. Seek peace, living in a way that helps create it. Such personal changes alter human community. As thankful recipients of God's refuge, we invite others to find refuge in God; we overflow with radiance and praise.

PRAYER: Gracious, holy God, I thank you for your gift of life, redemption, and love and for the opportunity to live in your embrace! Guide me to reshape my life and our human community, that others may find refuge in you through us. This I pray in Jesus' name. Amen.

You Bet Your Life

October 30–November 5, 2006 • *John O. Gooch*[‡]

MONDAY, OCTOBER 30 • **PSALM 146:1-4**

Groucho Marx hosted a radio show called *You Bet Your Life*. A combination quiz and talk show, the title has always intrigued me. On what are you willing to bet your life? Whom or what do you trust enough to give your life to?

In one way or another, our texts this week focus on trust in God. Trust is a radical venture. In many ways "you bet your life" whenever you make a commitment to God in Christ.

In one sense "you bet your life" every time you sing a hymn of praise or you pray. You bet your life that the surest way to travel through this world involves trust in God. You bet your life that God is who you've always heard that God is. This does not mean that we fall for the statements about God that we hear from human voices. Those voices may tell us that God calls us to an easy way or to a feeling of superiority over others. The God of the Bible most often calls us to discomfort. Human voices, human institutions let us down. They promise the earth and the sky and fail to deliver. They die and their promises die with them. Governments or other human institutions can guarantee nothing ultimate. Only God is ultimate.

Cardinal Wolsey expressed that truth when he lost all his power to King Henry the Eighth: "O Cromwell, Cromwell, Had I but served my God with half the zeal I served my King, he would not in mine age have left me naked to mine enemies." (William Shakespeare, *King Henry the Eighth*, Act 3, Scene 2)

Trusting human institutions is the opposite of trusting God. So Groucho's show is a call to us. On what do we bet our lives? Whom or what do we trust to bring us life?

SUGGESTION FOR MEDITATION: On what do you bet your life? Do you really believe God deserves your trust?

[‡]Author; adjunct faculty, St. Paul School of Theology, Kansas City, Missouri.

What makes us happy in this life? The psalmist suggests that happiness depends upon whom one trusts. "Happy [blessed] are those . . . whose hope is in the LORD their God." Happiness, ultimately, has nothing to do with wealth or position or lack of pain or illness. Happiness primarily concerns relationships, especially with God.

God cares about human beings and acts for the oppressed and marginalized of the world. In fact, God is best known in the Bible for God's actions. As verse 7 says, this God "executes justice." Verses 7-10 read like the purpose statement for the kingdom of God. Real happiness lies not in what we can accumulate in the way of power or wealth but in feeding the hungry, bringing justice to the oppressed, caring for widows and orphans (the most vulnerable people in the ancient Hebrew world). Happiness, we might say, is coming together as a community, a nation, to support and care for those who cannot care for themselves. We recognize that some people do not have enough to feed their families or to provide shelter and medical care. So we all pull together, giving up some privilege and wealth so all God's children can have the promise of a better life.

This is who God is and what God does according to the psalmist. Surely if this is what God does, and we put our trust in God, we will do the same. The real source of happiness comes in living like God by giving to others. Our truest happiness resides in making it possible for those who have little to be happy too.

SUGGESTION FOR MEDITATION AND PRAYER: **Reflect on what happiness means to you. What does it take to make you happy? In what ways could you find happiness in helping others? Pray for guidance and help in discerning happiness for your life.**

All Saints Day

Moab is a place of death for Naomi. Her family goes there to escape death in the famine, but all the men die. Naomi and her Moabite daughters-in-law are left alone in a world and society that does not value widows. How do they trust God's love in this situation?

Ruth and Orpah are Moabites, foreigners, outside the covenant people. Most scholars agree that the book of Ruth was written in the days of Ezra and Nehemiah as a kind of protest to what those religious leaders were doing. Ezra and Nehemiah, in their attempts to "re-form" Israel's faith, envisioned a pure community that permitted no foreign blood. They called upon men who had married wives outside the Jewish community to send those wives and their children away. Only the pure could be a part of the community.

The author of the book of Ruth challenges the notion of who is acceptable. Look, he says, if we had always had that rule, we would have no King David. After all, his great-grandmother, was a foreigner. Are you going to bet your life that God really wants us to be an exclusive community, locking out everyone unlike ourselves? Or are you willing to bet your life that God desires inclusivity that welcomes all persons into the community of faith?

We face the same question in our day. Do we bet our lives on a God of inclusion or a God of exclusion? Does a person seeking to be in the community of faith have to believe exactly as we believe? Does he or she have to act exactly as we do? In what ways does our manner of speech and practices shut the doors or open them?

Suggestion for meditation: Reflect on what it means to be God's people. Do we bet our lives on inclusion or exclusion?

In spite of what we think, Ruth's song is not about weddings. Rather, it's about betting her life on a relationship with Naomi and trusting the future will be good. Orpah does what Naomi asks of her. She deserves remembrance and celebration, as she returns to her people and her former life, though she returns a different person.

Ruth, on the other hand, is indignant when Naomi asks her to return home. Naomi sees no future for Ruth, no other sons whom she can marry. But Ruth has already bet her life—she has committed herself to YHWH and to Naomi. She doesn't want to give up her new loyalty and turn her back on God. Neither law nor custom required Ruth to remain with Naomi. Orpah follows law and custom when she returns to her life in Moab. Ruth offers an act of covenant love. She goes against custom, against reason, against personal benefit. She knows she will be a stranger and greeted with suspicion when she shows up in Bethlehem with Naomi.

When have you been aware of God calling you to bet your life against custom, reason, and personal benefit? When have you bet your life in your faith community to stand for change? It is easier to say nothing and be comfortable. When have you bet your life by advocating for those who have no voice in public life? It would be a lot easier to take the path of least resistance and not have anyone upset with you. How do you indicate your willingness to trust the presence of God with you?

SUGGESTION FOR MEDITATION: **What is God calling you to do in your congregation? in the public arena? What concrete steps could you take to answer that call? How do you trust God to be with you in your response?**

Since I've retired, I've been helping more with the housework. Every week my wife and I clean house and experience a feeling of real satisfaction for having that job done one more time. But then we remember we have to do it again next week. Wouldn't it be wonderful to have the cleaning done once, for all time, and know the house would always look good?

On a more profound level, the author of Hebrews deals with that question related to salvation. He comes to a new understanding, partly in response to the feeling of loss after the destruction of the Temple in 70 C.E. Perhaps this question is foremost in his mind: "How can we gain forgiveness and relationship with God without the sacrifices of the Temple?"

The author finds the answer in the reality of Christ. Christ entered the Holy Place (the presence of God), offering his own sacrifice. He offered his own blood, shed on the cross—not the blood of calves and goats. As a result, he gained for us all *eternal* redemption, not something that has to be done again and again.

One of the great mysteries of the faith is how Christ's crucifixion almost two thousand years ago can mean salvation for me. For centuries, the greatest minds of the church have struggled with that question and have failed to come up with a satisfactory answer. The best we can say is that we trust that it's true. We don't know how it works, but we're willing to bet our lives that it does. When we commit ourselves to Christ, we trust that his work is true and that his action on our behalf cleanses us from sin and guilt.

SUGGESTION FOR MEDITATION: **Read these verses in Hebrews several times, as quickly as you can. Focus your thoughts— which words or phrases demand your attention? Stop and reflect on those words or phrases. To what do they want you to attend? To what action do they call you? How might they lead you to a deeper commitment to Christ?**

Years ago, before many of you were even born, there was a song with a simple message: "you could be better than you are." It became a hit song partly because we would all like to be better than we are. That's why self-help is one of the largest sections in bookstores and people spend thousands of dollars in seminars and workshops trying to find the secret of life.

The author of Hebrews says that Christ made a perfect sacrifice, once for all, for the forgiveness of sins. In technical language, we call that justification. But the author goes farther to say that Christ's work also will "purify our conscience from dead works to worship the living God." That is, we can be better than we are. In technical religious language, we can be sanctified. To oversimplify, justification means that God accepts us as we are. Sanctification means that God doesn't leave us as we are. God calls us to worship (and I take this as a shorthand way of talking about a whole new way of life) the living God. We can do this because of God's love for us.

One thing a Christian does is to trust (to bet his or her life) that God can keep God's promises. We trust that Christ made a perfect sacrifice for our sins, even though we have no idea how that works. And we trust that we can become better than we are—we can become more like Christ, even in this life. We literally bet our lives because when we trust God to change us, God does. And we will never be the same again.

SUGGESTION FOR MEDITATION AND PRAYER: **Think about the ways in which you'd like to be better than you are. Would you be willing to bet your life that God can help you be better because of Christ? Can you tell God that you're willing to do that—and mean it?**

This delightful story comes in the closing days of Jesus' ministry. The question about the great commandment is easily answered. Jesus and the scribe both know the answer. We know the answer too. We've heard it most of our lives. Our problem comes not in knowing the answer but in living it out. We're not sure that in our world loving God and neighbor isn't too simplistic. Life seems to be more complicated than that.

On the one hand, this seems pretty straightforward. Worship God, and only God. We do that. We don't have an altar to a different god on every street corner. But we often bet our lives on something other than God. We have ultimates in our lives that have nothing to do with trusting God: our nation, our family, our race, political causes, theological systems, and doctrinal standards. Are we willing to bet our lives that the God of scripture calls us to follow? And are we actually willing to do that?

While the scribe is not a disciple of Jesus, he and Jesus share something at a deep level. They both know that the words of scripture are true—we *are* called to love God with everything in us and our neighbors as ourselves. Jesus and the scribe have moved beyond an US vs. THEM way of looking at life. They have bet their lives that the truth of those scriptures can be lived out in this world. Because they have bet their lives on that truth and each can recognize that the other has done so, they go beyond the debates about theological positions. They truly love God and neighbor and willingly trust God to see them through.

SUGGESTION FOR MEDITATION: **What is most important to you? On what do you really bet your life?**

God's Mysterious Grace

November 6–12, 2006 • V. Bruce Rigdon[‡]

MONDAY, NOVEMBER 6 • Read Ruth 3:1-5

These verses locate us in the midst of the fascinating story of Ruth and Naomi. A famine had settled on the land of Israel, and so Naomi, her husband and their two sons had gone from their home in Bethlehem to live in the land of Moab. Among these foreigners Naomi's sons took wives, and then in the space of ten years all three men died. When the famine subsides, Naomi decides to return to Bethlehem. She urges her daughters-in-law to return to their families. One daughter-in-law (Orpah) reluctantly agrees and bids a tearful farewell to Naomi. The other, Ruth, refuses and in powerful and eloquent words pledges her life to Naomi. Naomi cannot prevail against such love and commitment, and so the two women return to Naomi's hometown.

Today's passage reveals Naomi's deep concern for Ruth's safety and security. We see Naomi scheming, as it were, to marry off her daughter-in-law to a well-to-do male relative, Boaz, who has shown compassion on these two women by allowing Ruth to become a gleaner in his fields.

This story is brimful of loving-kindness, mercy, and loyalty (*hesed* in Hebrew). Israelite society was based on the experience that God had extended *hesed* to them as a beloved people and expected them in turn to extend *hesed* to others.

We all live every day from God's *hesed* toward us. We can neither earn nor do we merit God's loyalty, kindness, and mercy. God gives them freely, generously. and unconditionally. The beginning of wisdom is gratitude in the face of God's *hesed*.

PRAYER: Generous and loving God, open our eyes and our hearts to know your grace in our lives and to become truly thankful. Amen.

[‡]President and Professor of Church History, Ecumenical Theological Seminary, Detroit, Michigan.

As the story of Ruth and Naomi concludes, Naomi's plans for her daughter-in-law succeed. Boaz completes the necessary negotiations with kinsman and elders and becomes Ruth's husband. In time Ruth gives birth to a son. Naomi's friends rejoice in the child. They bless the Lord and assure Naomi that this child will be the restorer of her life and the nourisher of her old age. Naomi takes the child in her arms, and the women of the neighborhood give him a name: Obed, which means "the servant." The text concludes with a genealogy that reminds readers that this child Obed is the grandfather of David, the king of Israel.

The theme of Ruth and Naomi's story is that family and community (relationships) are built on *hesed*, loving-kindness. The story mentions kindness a number of times. Naomi hopes the Lord will deal kindly with her daughters-in-law as they have dealt kindly with her; Boaz says that he has heard of Ruth's kindness and Ruth replies that he has spoken kindly to her; Naomi affirms that Boaz has been kind in not forsaking the living or the dead. The word *hesed* appears more than 250 times in scripture. While it sometimes implies that the one who gives *hesed* is in a superior position, it also connotes a sense of mutuality in giving and receiving *hesed* because it establishes a relationship between the parties involved.

In this story, kindness knows no bounds! It flows between Moabites and Israelites. Ruth willingly embraced the faith of Israel, but later Israel would prove unwilling either to embrace her as an individual Moabite or her people as a whole group. Perhaps for that reason the book of Ruth closes with the strong reminder that the grandmother of the great King David was a foreigner.

SUGGESTION FOR MEDITATION: **Meditate on what it means that we are called to practice *hesed*, loving-kindness, toward all of God's children.**

Thirty-five years ago I stood on a steep Galilean hillside near Nazareth with friend Father Elias Chacour. The hillside was rocky and barren with only a few sheep and goats in evidence. "On this hillside I am going to build schools and a college for the children of my people," said Fr. Chacour. The idea seemed fantastic and far-fetched at the time. Fr. Chacour was a young priest of the Melkite Church recently sent to a poor little village called Ibillin, a place with few people and even fewer resources. To make matters even worse, Fr. Chacour belonged to the Arab-Palestinian Christian minority and had little access to power in the state of Israel.

Fr. Chacour's words seemed little more than wishful thinking, an idle dream. But today he is recognized internationally as an outstanding peacemaker, the recipient of awards and honorary degrees from Europe, North America, and Asia. But most impressive of all is that school buildings now crowd that barren hillside, welcoming some five thousand students from kindergarten to university. I am most amazed by the fact that these students and teachers are Moslems, Christians, Druze, and, yes, even Jews. They study and play and work together daily as a community, something unheard of in a deeply divided Middle East. On that barren hillside Fr. Chacour has built a community that shines like a beacon, offering hope for a future not yet visible in Israel—and in other places experiencing conflict and violence.

Fr. Chacour would be the first to say that unless the Lord builds the house (the community) those who build it labor in vain. Thirty-five years later it is clear to me that God wanted to build a peaceable community on that rocky hillside, and God gave that vision and purpose to Fr. Chacour and his friends. God has blessed their struggles to build the schools and to establish the community. And the dream goes on.

PRAYER: Lord, inspire us to build houses and communities that are a blessing to others. Amen.

Today's passage comes at the end of Jesus' public ministry. It follows his triumphal entry into Jerusalem and culminates in the events leading to his arrest, crucifixion, and resurrection. The context is one in which the religious leaders of the day challenge Jesus' authority and seek to discredit and entrap him.

Jesus responds by confronting them. The issue is that their pretentious behavior—walking about in long showy robes, taking the best seats at synagogues and the places of honor at banquets—masks their simultaneous exploitation and abuse of the poor, especially widows who had no one to protect them in a society like that of first-century Palestine.

Jesus' words and actions recall the fiery prophetic message of the Hebrew prophets who denounced the rich and powerful for their failure to practice justice and mercy in behalf of the poor. It raises serious questions for each of us in the church at a time when religion is being used to justify policies that ignore the growing numbers of people in our own society who suffer hunger, homelessness, unemployment, and grinding poverty.

Jesus' words remind us of the church's charge to preach good news to the poor. The question is this: What is the good news, and how are Christians to practice it as well as proclaim it?

SUGGESTION FOR MEDITATION: **Meditate on what is "good news" for people who are poor, and consider ways you can embody such good news.**

This passage might cause us to raise some questions in addition to those related to yesterday's meditation. The physical location of the text is the temple in Jerusalem. Here Jesus has confronted Israel's religious leaders. Here he has attacked them for their false piety and their exploitation of the poor. It is from the Temple that he has driven the money changers. And it is here that he speaks about the total destruction of the Temple.

Is it by chance that Mark has the widow with her two small coins appear in the Temple immediately following Jesus' condemnation of the religious leaders for devouring the houses of widows? Why would Jesus commend the widow for giving to a Temple whose destruction lies at hand? Might the writer of Mark tell this story as an example of how the Temple authorities victimized the poor and innocent? Is Jesus in fact lamenting the widow's plight and further illustrating the exploitation of which the religious leaders are guilty? Is this a continuation of Jesus' denunciation of the scribes who, rather than caring for the poor as the law requires, rob them of their last pennies?

Maybe this story is a tale about the widow's total generosity as well as the guilt of those who exploited her. In any case, Christian stewardship obviously involves much more than "making donations."

PRAYER: Gracious God, teach us to practice justice and generosity in our lives each day. Amen.

I have heard the story of the widow's mite repeatedly since childhood, especially when stewardship season rolls around every year in our churches. But Jesus' words raise more questions than provide answers. Why would anyone, above all this poor widow, drop her last penny into the collection box?

Of course, the widow was raised in a religious community that valued charitable giving, and the Jerusalem temple depended upon such gifts for its very existence. But surely no one expected people to give until they had nothing left. A ten-percent tithe would have been quite sufficient.

So we are left to guess about the causes of this poor widow's generosity. Clearly Jesus is talking with religious leaders about the difference between appearances and pretensions and true matters of the heart. It is the widow's heart that finds such favor with Jesus. The widow gives, we might surmise, because her heart is full of gratitude to God. She does not have material wealth, but a richness in her life allows her to open her hands and give life away, even as life has been given to her.

We might also conclude that this woman has learned to trust God with her life. She knows that God, faithful and trustworthy, will continue to sustain her. I further contend that this woman knows God can take the little that she has and cause amazing things to happen—to both the giver and the gift.

I have seen examples of these things in my own church ministry. The most recent is the extraordinary generosity of some children in the aftermath of the tsunami. I think of those children who baked and sold cookies, who made and sold lemonade, who shoveled snow and ran errands because they cared about human beings who were in deep trouble. These children gave sacrificially and their combined gifts made a difference—to them as well as to the victims of the disaster.

SUGGESTION FOR MEDITATION: Meditate on the sources of gratitude in your life and ponder how these sources can find expression in graceful giving.

What does it mean to wait eagerly for the Lord, to await his second coming? We are all aware of cults and movements in American history, past and present, that have set particular dates for such an event and organized their life in anticipation of it. Few of us perceive this as a helpful way to understand what it means to wait eagerly for the Lord.

I live in a city full of pain and suffering caused by deep racial divisions that have existed for a long time. I teach in an inner-city ecumenical seminary whose faculty and student body includes everyone from Roman Catholics to Pentecostals. A diverse community of women and men, we reflect the racial, ethnic, and economic composition of the city itself. In the midst of our city's conflicts, the seminary provides a "safe place" where people can dare to tell one another the stories of their pain. Not long ago I happened upon two women tearfully embracing each other after an extended after-class conversation in which one had shared with the other her own painful experiences of growing up as a black person in our city.

In this special community we are learning that God loves our city with all of its brokenness and that Christ gave his life for the life of the whole world. To wait eagerly for the Lord is to do what Jesus taught us—to actively love God and one another. When we seek to do that with all our hearts we experience the healing presence of Christ in our midst. His coming into our midst to reconcile us to God and one another is the gift that God intends for our city. Ours must be an active waiting.

PRAYER: Loving God, give us courage to cross boundaries in order to know and love all your children. Amen.

The Path of Life

November 13–19, 2006 • Ann Svennungsen[‡]

MONDAY, NOVEMBER 13 • Read Psalm 16

You lead me in the path of life.

On confirmation Sunday, the preacher invited the confirmands to show the congregation their feet—to stick them out in the aisles so everyone could see. He proclaimed that the promises they would make that morning were promises to walk in a particular way, to follow a particular path. It is the path of discipleship, the path of life. The psalmist affirms that God will show us this path of life. Indeed, God has shown us most profoundly in the life of Jesus—with his feet moving to the rhythms of worship and prayer, justice and mercy, welcome and generosity.

Sometimes we'd like more than a path. We'd like "to arrive," to see the finished product—something certain, a final destination. And, sometimes, we'd like the path to move in another direction, say to riches, fame, or power. But the path of life is a path of service and love, grace and generosity, freedom and joy.

And the journey cannot be made alone. It's within a community that God continues to reveal the path of life. Indeed, one of the earliest names for the Christian community was "the Way." It was a community on the move—following Jesus—walking in the way of life. For confirmands and for all Christians, young and old, life is not an individualistic journey. Our feet lead us to weekly worship and formation within a community, then to acts of justice and love in daily life. Though we never fully arrive, there is, through it all, something certain, something firm and secure: God will be with us every step of the way.

PRAYER: O God of love, draw me closer to you and your people, and show me the path of life that my thoughts, words, and actions might further your love on earth. Amen.

[‡]President, The Fund for Theological Education; Lutheran pastor; member, St. John's Lutheran Church (ELCA), Atlanta, Georgia.

In your presence there is fullness of joy.

A congregation welcomes its members each week with the word JOY splashed large and bright on a permanent banner. Though the psalmist affirms that God's presence brings "fullness of joy," I am ambivalent about the banner. What if we're not feeling much joy when we arrive for worship? What if we're sad, angry, or confused? Can we expect members to experience "fullness of joy" without creating a new law prescribing how a Christian should feel?

Amazingly, scripture often speaks about joy in passages that focus primarily on suffering. Paul proclaims in Second Corinthians, "We are . . . as sorrowful, yet always rejoicing" (6:10). In Acts, the persecuted apostles "rejoiced that they were considered worthy to suffer dishonor for the sake of [Christ's] name" (5:41).

In John's Gospel, Jesus states that his followers can experience joy even amidst struggle: "When a woman is in labor, she is sad that her hour has come. But once the baby is born, her joy makes her forget the suffering, because a child has been born into the world" (AT). The chapter closes with the same Greek word addressed to the disciples: "In the world you will find [birth pangs], but have courage, I have overcome the world" (AT).

When we struggle for the sake of life and experience birth pangs, then mixed in is the spirit of deep and profound joy. If we find ourselves without joy for a significant time, we need to look carefully at our lives, both physical and spiritual. Both medical and spiritual reasons exist for a long-held sadness. Fullness of joy does not result from our avoiding struggle. True joy is found in participating with God for the sake of life. True joy is found in the embrace of God.

PRAYER: O God, I praise you for your presence in the heights and depths. Today I lift up to you those who experience a long-held sadness (names) and pray that I will be an instrument of your healing love. Amen.

Tell us, when will this be?

Throughout history, Christians have wanted to know the time of Jesus' return. Perhaps the readers of Mark's Gospel worried that they might miss the event. Could Jesus somehow appear without their being aware? Jesus reassures them that the signs will be so obvious that no one will fail to notice. However, only God knows the exact date (Mark 13:32). Jesus makes it clear that our calling is not to make predictions about the end-time. Rather it is to remain faithful during every time.

Part of faithfulness comes in bearing witness to Christ. In the very next verse, Jesus reminds the disciples, "You will be beaten in synagogues; and you will stand before governors and kings because of me, as a testimony to them. And the good news must first be proclaimed to all nations [Gentiles]" (13:9). Our time and passion is not to be spent in calculations and predictions but rather in faithful proclamation, sharing the good news in our communities and even to the ends of the earth.

And, finally, it doesn't matter so much when Jesus returns. We will all face "the end" at some time, whether it's with trumpet sound or the silencing of our breathing when we die. We will all one day face the Lord.

The miracle of faith is that we have already faced the end that really matters. In baptism, we died to sin and were raised with Christ. In that new birth, the future has already broken into our lives. No, eternal life doesn't begin when we die—it begins now, today. So when we think about the end-times, we must first look backward, remembering an earlier death, a baptismal death and a raising to life. Trusting in that gift, we spend our lives sharing the good news, hopeful because our life is held secure in the eternal life of God.

Prayer: Living Christ, I praise you that in my relationship with you I am joined to a life that has no end. Fill me with hope and joy in this relationship that I may freely live in service to others. Amen.

Beware that no one leads you astray.

As part of a college seminar, I traveled to Cairo, Egypt. One evening, my professor's friend drove us through the city. Sitting in the front seat, I began to ask him about his life. I was oblivious to the fact that he had to translate each question into Arabic, think of his answer, translate the answer back into English, say it to me—all while negotiating the crazy traffic. Finally he said to me, "You will need to be quiet, or I will drive us off the road."

Jesus warns the disciples, "Beware that no one leads you astray." When walking in the path of life, we can easily be distracted. However, Jesus provides an amazing example of devotion. Immediately prior to this text, Jesus affirms the widow's offering: "Out of her poverty [she] has put in everything she had, her whole life" (12:44, RSV). Now Jesus prepares to offer "everything" he has, his whole life, in Jerusalem.

As Jesus speaks of tribulation in chapter 13, he is both preparing the disciples both for the suffering that awaits him in Jerusalem as well as for the tribulations they will face. His language is vivid and honest. This is a countercultural movement. There will be many reasons to veer from the path. So Jesus warns us, "Beware that no one leads you astray." Though we may not experience physical persecution for our faith, we do encounter powers that "lead us astray," especially the powers of consumerism, technology, and individualism. Perhaps the "cocoon of autonomy" leads us astray from love of God and neighbor.

God created us to live a good life. But the fullest life, the deepest joy, the most profound meaning, doesn't come through the latest recreational gadget. It comes through a relationship with Jesus, a relationship with his community, a life of love for the world.

PRAYER: God of light, open my eyes to recognize the powers that might lead me astray. Give me the courage to resist and to persevere in your path of justice and love. Amen.

And the LORD remembered her. . . .

In my twenty-two years as a parish pastor, I was amazed at the variety of losses that people experienced. Some were public—the loss of health, the loss of life. Many were private. All were times of anguish. When the oncologist says, "We've tried every treatment; there's nothing more we can do." When the letter arrives, the thin one, that says, "There were many excellent candidates for this job, this placement in grad school—we regret to inform you, you were not selected." When a long-term girlfriend says, "It's just not going to work. It's over." Or, when the banker looks across the desk, "There are no other financing options for your farm, your business, your dream—you'll have to let it go."

Hannah also suffered the loss of a dream—the dream of becoming pregnant, bearing a child, becoming a mother. Her deep anguish kept her from eating. What is more, her barrenness led to ostracism within her own family. Though her husband still cherished her, Elkanah's other wife taunted her, rejecting Hannah because of her barrenness.

Into this barren place God's word was spoken: "And the Lord remembered her. . . ." It was the word of hope and grace. In Hannah's case, God's remembrance also meant a change in her situation: she conceived and bore a son. Sometimes we too experience such miraculous change—a healing, a new job. But all the time we receive assurance of God's abiding presence. As the prophet Isaiah reminds us: "Can a woman forget her nursing child, or show no compassion for the child of her womb? Even these may forget, yet I will not forget you. See, I have inscribed you on the palms of my hands" (49:15-16). Yes, the path of life, the path of discipleship, still includes change and loss. But at no time will we be lost to God. You and I are inscribed on the palms of God's hands.

PRAYER: Living Christ, be present with all who live with loss or anguish (names). Inspire the members of my congregation that we may faithfully embody your healing presence. Amen.

I will remember their sins and their lawless deeds no more.

A parishioner once asked me why we had to begin each worship service with a confession of sin. Couldn't we just begin with a word of love? Sin is so negative, so depressing. By contrast, the author of Hebrews had little trouble speaking about sin. Indeed, he recognized that forgiveness of sin is our deepest need. He rejoiced that Christ "offered for all time a single sacrifice for sins." Unlike earlier priests, Christ's offering of himself on the cross is a once-for-all sacrifice for the world. Even Christ's posture indicates the permanence of this offering, for Jesus now sits at the right hand of God, whereas the priests continue standing—a transitory position.

Yes, it may seem odd to begin every worship service with a word of forgiveness. It may feel like going to the house of friends for dinner and having them greet you at the door, "Welcome, Ann, I forgive you." Still, perhaps only such a shocking word will startle us into an honest appraisal of things. God's love invites our honesty about our lives—admitting that we don't always get it right, that we don't have it all together. We struggle, we fail.

Oh, at times, it is enough simply to say, "God loves you. God welcomes you." But sometimes we need stronger words. If we just hear that God loves us, we might respond, "Yeah, you say you love me, God, but if you really knew me, you wouldn't. If you knew how I hoard my money, grasp for attention, envy others—if you knew my thoughts deep down, you wouldn't really love me." But God knows us, and God says something unambiguous to us: "I forgive you," which means, "I love you no matter what. I see it all, and I love you still. I see it all, and I love you enough to come in Resurrection power to forgive you, to heal you from the inside out."

PRAYER: O God, you know me through and through. You know how hard I try to change, how quickly I get stuck. Forgive me, gracious God, and renew me through your loving Spirit. Amen.

Let us consider how to provoke one another to love and good deeds.

We seek to walk in the path of life, a path that we believe is life-giving both for ourselves and the world. Yet, we do not make this journey alone. The Christian life is both corporate and communal—a hard concept to digest in our individualistic culture.

Any suggestion that we live the faith by ourselves is untrue. What we as *individual* Christians do is participate in that *communal* work. Often we struggle even to get to corporate worship each week. We "neglect to meet together," as the writer of Hebrews laments. Consumerism so infiltrates our society that we begin to think of worship as just another item for consumption, an experience we enjoy if a better opportunity doesn't come along. Indeed, a pastor struggles with the challenge of finding lectors, Communion assistants, and Sunday school teachers and wonders if laypeople hesitate because they want to keep their options open to a more inviting offer. Our society encourages us to be consumers of goods, and we want to make sure that worship is the best good to be had on Sunday.

However, the New Testament clearly emphasizes the importance of corporate worship. The New Testament has the audacity to call the community of believers the body of Christ, Christ's visible presence on earth. Within the gathered community the risen Christ continues his healing and transforming work, just as surely as Christ healed during his earthly life.

"Do not neglect to meet together," the writer of Hebrews reminds us. Our corporate gathering is where God's word is proclaimed, where we're drawn into the mystery of God, where we're reconnected in community and formed as disciples, where we're sent forth to do justice and love mercy.

PRAYER: Living Christ, through a community you have drawn me into abundant life. Inspire me to be truly present every week when my congregation gathers for worship. Amen.

Life in God's Reign

November 20–26, 2005 • Kwasi Kena[‡]

**MONDAY, NOVEMBER 20 • Read 2 Samuel 23:1-7;
Psalm 132:1-12**

"I may not be what I ought to be and I may not be what I'm going to be, but thank God I'm not what I used to be!" This prayer from the African American Christian community could have issued from the lips of King David, Israel's second king. He identifies himself as the "favorite" of God. His last words declare the virtues of serving justly as God's anointed king. Anyone familiar with David's sullied past might raise a questioning eyebrow.

Isn't this the same David who committed acts of adultery, murder, and deceit? How could such a person serve as God's mouthpiece? What gave David the audacity to believe that the spirit of the Lord would speak through him? Apparently David could embrace God's forgiveness for his misdeeds and refocus his spiritual gaze on God's ideal for leadership. In truth, David is not the sum of his good and bad deeds; neither are we.

With the confidence that comes with a clear conscience, David compares a just ruler to the welcoming light of the morning. Contemporary society, often darkened by scandal, needs the sacred light brought by righteous leaders. God's ideal remains the standard for Christians in leadership positions.

Where can we find an image of a just ruler? Look to David and his house. Again, the temptation is to point fingers at David and his unruly children and cry foul. The larger message to consider is God's faithfulness in honoring God's covenants with those who willingly repent and accept forgiveness.

SUGGESTION FOR MEDITATION: What unconfessed sin hampers your capacity to serve Christ? How have you learned to walk in wholeness after God has forgiven you?

[‡]Director, Evangelism Ministries, General Board of Discipleship, Nashville, Tennessee.

TUESDAY, NOVEMBER 21 • **Read Revelation 1:4b-8**

Captivating! That is a likely response once you allow the impact of today's reading to seep slowly into your soul. In the middle of a typical biblical greeting, joy erupts. The pages shout; Christ has freed us from sin and made us a kingdom of priests serving God! We have been made a kingdom? We are priests? At first glance, these two notions seem incomprehensible. That is why the words must seep into our souls. Beneath this eruption of joy lies a deeper message.

Why would a writer suddenly interject such an ebullient doxology? Perhaps because of what was said and to whom it was said. John, the attributed writer of Revelation, was an outcast on the isle of Patmos and, from all appearances, an insignificant person. Imagine the awe of learning that seemingly insignificant outcasts can experience God's reign as citizens and priests!

The raw joy of experiencing God's reign as both citizen and priest is our motivation for living and serving as Christians. Regardless of the country noted on our passports or the presence or absence of a seminary degree, Christ declares that his disciples are citizens and priests in *his* domain.

Today's passage underscores the importance of acknowledging God's grace while serving as Christ's priests. The sacrificial gift of Christ's life releases us from our sins. Our admittance as citizens of God's kingdom results from faith in Christ's redemptive act on the cross. Our status as "priests" is bestowed because Christ declares that his followers serve in that capacity.

Feeling outcast or insignificant? Take heart. In Christ, we are citizens and priests in God's reign.

SUGGESTION FOR MEDITATION: **How does being "made a kingdom" impact your life currently? What does it mean for you to be considered a priest who serves God?**

"Who says so?" Depending on the context, that question can be more than intimidating. Are you a leader in your church or community? Are you in a position of authority? Who says so? Does a title bestowed by a person or group make you a leader?

Pilate asks Jesus, "Are you the King of the Jews?" Behind Pilate's probing inquiry stands an insidious "Who says so?" The question of "who made Jesus king" is important. The person or group that bestows a title often believes they have the right to define the role the title-bearer should play. Bestowal of titles can carry a self-serving component.

Fear and outrage drive Pilate's interest in this question's answer. If the Jews consider Jesus their king, Rome will consider Jesus a power threat to the Roman Empire. Rome already has an emperor; there is no room for two.

Today people often elect leaders to power. In effect, the voters bestow the title. An elected leader's title puts him or her in position to lead—but who determines the rightful path of leadership? As stakeholders in the election, voters feel entitled to lobby and press the elected person to carry out the voters' will. Should an elected leader attempt the unorthodox, a "who says so" rebuttal usually is forthcoming.

The definition of a leader by Pilate and voters shares a common thread. Both definitions are earthbound. In each case leaders are determined by earthly means—military conquest or voter popularity. By contrast, Jesus tells Pilate, "My kingdom is not from this world." Jesus' kingdom does not adhere to earthly rules and expectations.

In Jesus' kingdom, might and popularity do not constitute sufficient qualifications for leadership. God bestows titles, roles, and purpose. Are you a Christian leader? "Who says so?"

SUGGESTION FOR MEDITATION: **What does it mean to be a Christian who serves as a leader in your church or community? What title, role, and purpose do you believe Jesus Christ has given you in life?**

THANKSGIVING DAY USA

Thanksgiving is no mere holiday. It is an annual reminder to thank God for the special things in life. On Thanksgiving it is tempting to offer a ritual rehearsal of our usual "thank-you list," before digging into dinner. Break away from the ordinary. Why not thank God for creation? There is just cause to do so.

Rich soil yields the produce we consume. Pastures and the wilderness teem with greenery that feeds the animals of the world. Trees give fruit that satisfies our hunger and delights our tastebuds. But what if creation faltered—exhausted from overuse, lifeless from excess pollution?

People regularly dismiss the ominous predictions of global warming, wars over water, and extinction of living creatures. People believe that the worst will only happen after we die. But what if creation had a say in the matter?

In today's reading, Joel serves as creation's voice. Do not fear soil but rejoice! The Lord has done great things. Do not fear animals. The pastures and wilderness are lush and green; the trees and vines bear their fruit. God cares for creation, and creation relies on God.

Creation's "confident proclamation" reveals one of God's most notable characteristics: care of creation. The Hebrews recognized God's reliability to replenish all of creation. One sign of good leadership is dependability. Regular care, offered consistently over time, builds trust and confidence. Joel expresses confidence in God's provision. He then takes the next logical leap: God will also take care of Israel.

If we fail to thank God for creation today, creation may choose to speak for itself.

SUGGESTION FOR MEDITATION: **How often do you pause to admire creation and thank God for the experience? Consider making a "thank-you" list of creation's goodness. How might you sustain your ongoing awareness and thankfulness?**

Frenzy and worry often harass twenty-first century Western culture. Such an environment tempts us to presume that we alone personify anxiety. In truth, scripture reveals that being anxious is a longstanding human preoccupation.

Jesus, as recorded in Matthew, urges us not to worry about anything. Jesus' message is more an observation about nature than a new prophetic revelation. In the spirit of yesterday's reading, Jesus reminds us that God is a faithful provider worthy of our absolute trust and confidence.

Jesus frames his message with two key arguments. First, God feeds the creatures of the earth and clothes the lilies of the field. They feel no neglect, so why would God neglect us humans who are of much more value to God than they? Second, striving for food and material goods is what the Gentiles do. In other words, striving consumerism characterizes people who have no relationship with God. Through relationship with God we learn to trust divine provision.

We, modern consumers, can benefit from the wisdom of Jesus' words. Advertisements assault our senses throughout the day enticing us to buy. Counteracting this assault requires a quick wit and determined spirit. The spirit of today's reading strikes at the core of consumerism. The message is not just for the rich who are subject to arrogance over their wealth. The message is also for the poor who lust after things. In both cases self-worth and the accumulation of things become indistinguishable. Material wealth is an intoxicating idol bent on luring us into its service. Resist striving for things—God provides.

SUGGESTION FOR MEDITATION: What clutter in your house is due to excess? Who might benefit from a donation of your excess goods? What prevents you from cleaning house and donating the excess as a spiritual act of worship?

God's people are always on a journey. Psalm 126 expresses the sentiment of the Hebrews on their pilgrimage to Jerusalem. They come to remember the restoration of Zion and their renewal as the people of God. Through faith in God the Hebrew pilgrims anticipate a radical change in their condition. Dreamily, the Hebrews reflect on the restoration of Zion, a time of laughter and joy, a time of abundance.

Our contemporary global village requires restoration. Much lies about us in ruins. What hope might we gain from sacred dreams today? Who "sees" beyond dire circumstances and declares confidence in God as Restorer today?

Like the Hebrew pilgrims, contemporary Christians are also on a journey. Unlike the Hebrew pilgrims, however, contemporary Christians cannot return to a single geographical location— Zion. We do not limit restoration of the land to one particular region, country, or nation. Given the worldwide scattering of the body of Christ, the restoration of the land now takes on a global perspective.

The Hebrews use an idiom that describes the restorative process they will experience. They use the idiom "restore the fortunes," a prophetic saying to indicate a dramatic change in condition. The change refers to the stark contrast between experiencing God's disfavor as an exiled people and being a restored people. The contrast spurs their thoughts of the way things used to be when they walked in God's favor. Their longing for that past experience directs their prayers.

What directs our prayers today? Does some golden past represent a time when we walked closely with God? What need do we have for restoration?

SUGGESTION FOR MEDITATION: **As a pilgrim where are you on the road of life—in exile or in restoration? Do you experience "sacred dreams" that allow you to see beyond dire circumstances? What does God need to restore in your life?**

The poor and rich, mighty and weak inhabit the global village. From outward appearance some people and nations appear to have a decided advantage over others. Yet despite one's standing in life there is one "technology" that all can access—prayer.

Paul opens with an apostolic exhortation, urging his audience to pray and intercede for everyone but particularly for those in high positions. Paul's apostolic urging is no mere request. Because of Paul's recognition as an apostle of Jesus Christ, his words carry more authoritative weight. When Paul says pray, he expects the Christians to take heed. Who carries that authority in our lives?

Paul lists various categories of prayer. These categories, while not exhaustive, do represent an approach to prayer. The community that offers supplication, prayer, and intercession focuses outwardly. Pray for everyone, especially leaders in high positions.

The outward focus on others revolutionizes our prayer life. Concern for more than our families and ourselves staves off selfish preoccupation. More importantly, each prayer offered for those outside the community of faith embeds evangelism into the DNA of the Christian praying community.

Paul's description of prayer is instructive: pray for others, for leaders, for those outside the faith community. And pray with a purpose in view.

The coarse, unruly behavior of leaders needed addressing. Paul himself had been a zealous Pharisee, unashamed in his persecution of Christians. Prayer, Paul discovered, can change demeanor. Accordingly, Paul urges Christians to pray "so that we may lead a quiet and peaceable life in all godliness and dignity."

A prayerful life bears rich fruit: selflessness, evangelism, peaceable and godly living. Life in God's reign demands different standards, and prayer can transform us into God's image.

SUGGESTION FOR MEDITATION: **For whom do you regularly pray? After reading Paul's exhortation, who else needs your prayers?**

Christ Is Coming! Christ Is Coming!

November 27–December 3, 2006 • *Mariellen Sawada Yoshino*[‡]

MONDAY, NOVEMBER 27 • **Read 1 Thessalonians 3:11-13**

I used to consider it a compliment when people would say to me, "How busy you are!" With my tightly scheduled calendar, I enjoyed hearing the comment, "Oh, you are always so busy!" I had grown up on the adage "busy hands, happy heart." I thought that translated into "busy life, fulfilled heart."

Then I learned the Japanese word for busy. It is *i-so-ga-shi*. When *i-so-ga-shi* is written in the kanji characters of Japanese writing, "busy" is translated to mean "to lose one's heart."

I had trouble believing this definition, but deep down, I knew it to be true. Busy-ness does take from one's life, one's essence. It robs the busied people of the enjoyment of each day, the richness of each hour, the holy-ness of each moment.

This Advent season, let us not lose our hearts. Instead, may our Lord "strengthen [our] hearts in holiness" each and every day.

This Advent season, let us not lose our hearts. Instead, may our hearts be found "blameless before our God" each and every hour.

This Advent season, let us not lose our hearts. Instead, may our hearts be readied for "the coming of our Lord Jesus with all his saints" each and every moment.

This Advent season, let us not lose our hearts. Instead, let us know this to be true: Christ is coming. Christ is coming.

PRAYER: How can we lose our hearts, Lord, when we know that you are coming? How can we be anything other than strengthened in heart, mind, and spirit? Thank you, Lord Jesus, that you are coming into our world and into our hearts. Amen.

[‡]Senior minister, Wesley United Methodist Church, San Jose, California.

After a season of watchful and active care, Yas Morimoto is ready to harvest the fig trees in her backyard. Every year at harvest time, Yas waits expectantly. She readies the necessary ingredients to bake with them. She sets up her special appliance to dry them, and she anticipates the moment she can eat a few of the precious figs fresh off the tree branch.

I never noticed Yas's fig trees, nor did I note when the fig branches sprouted tender leaves or when they needed tending. However, I did notice the trees when the branches became laden with fruit. "Wow," I exclaimed, when I saw the figs. "This fruit seems so . . . interesting. So lovely. But what are they?"

Yas is not surprised when the figs appear on her trees! She is instead joyful, thankful, and ready.

When Christ appears in our lives, when Christ comes face-to-face with us, when we see the light and life of Christ in our midst will we be unready and unaware? Will we unknowingly exclaim, "Wow!" Will we wonder, *This Christ is so . . . interesting. So lovely. But who is he?*

Christ seems to say to us, "Take some cues from Yas. Use this season of your lives to become aware, to get ready, and to give joy-filled thanks to God."

"Because," Christ says, "I am coming."

PRAYER: **Lord Jesus, when will I see and know the signs you are revealing to me? Will it be in this season? Lord, may it be in this season. Amen.**

In this country, where English is his second language, Rev. Junichi so often said, "Teach me." With the new American tradition of Halloween, he sighed and said, "Teach me." When the church group went fishing at "Family Camp," he asked, "Teach me?" When American "'slang" became confusing, he laughed, "Teach me!"

No matter the situation, Rev. Junichi's manner of humility in readiness to learn from others gave him the openness to receive new ideas, teachings, and understandings. The psalmist expresses that same humility when he too says "Teach me." The psalmist says, "Make me to know your ways, O LORD; teach me your paths. Lead me in your truth, and teach me."

This season of watching and waiting for Christ offers a tremendous opportunity for learning. There is so much to be known amidst the hope and joy of Advent. So much so, that like the psalm writer and Rev. Junichi, might we too say "teach me" when we wonder about the depth of God's love in sending us the Messiah? Might we too say "teach me" when we yearn to make time and space in our day to prepare for Christ's birth? Might we say "teach me" when we question how to respond this year to Christ's coming?

Lord, "teach me"—for Christ is coming. Christ is coming.

PRAYER: Teach me, O God. Teach me about the hope and joy of Christ, and allow me to be your trusting student. Amen.

In her late eighties, Mrs. Takaoka still walks in our Japantown neighborhood. It's not always easy, but she says she enjoys her walks to the market, to the church, and to the Senior Center. One day, when the cherry trees were in full bloom, I saw Mrs. Takaoka walking along, aided by her walker. She walked steadily until she paused and leaned on her walker. Then I saw her white hair flowing behind her as she lifted her face to the cherry blossoms that seemed to shower upon her. And I saw her smile and smile and smile.

Mrs. Takaoka's great joy brought a smile to my face. While the cherry blossoms graced her face and hair, she seemed to increase and abound in love and joy.

This overwhelming, overflowing love and joy is what the apostle Paul says we need in order to be ready for the coming of Jesus Christ. "What's more," implies Paul, "we must ask our God to strengthen our hearts that we might be made pure and blameless in order to meet the coming Christ."

"This isn't a hypothetical situation," Paul seems to say. "It is fact, as real as the cherry blossoms that shower upon you each year." So increase and abound in love, even and especially amidst the holiday stress and pressure to be everywhere and to do everything. Strengthen your hearts, even and especially amidst the holiday schedules and celebrations. Now. In this season. Because he is coming. Christ is coming.

PRAYER: O Lord, how might I become more and more ready for Jesus Christ? In what ways might I increase and abound in love? Amen.

Oh, for the childlike grace to "trust and obey" when we recognize the words of Jesus calling to us. Through today's scripture Jesus does call. He says, "Look up."

But in this busy season, even those simple words seem to be an unnecessary agenda item, an item for which there's no time, and so it doesn't get done. Jesus says, "Look up and see the signs and symbols of this season"; I look down into my tasks and agendas.

Jesus says, "Look up, and expect my coming in a cloud with power and great glory"; I look through my trials and tribulations.

Jesus says, "Look up, and know your redemption is near"; I look around to assess what others are thinking and to hear what they are saying.

And yet, when I say to one-year-old Jalen, "Look up," this baby child does just that. He looks up, stretching his neck until his head tilts back, and he sees the mistletoe hanging directly overhead. He points to it and squeals with joy.

Like this young one, Jesus points upward. He says, "Look up and see the signs that will be in the sun, the moon, and the stars. When you see these signs, stand up and raise your heads to see that which is worth squealing for joy. Look up and see. Point to me—for I am coming soon. I am coming soon."

PRAYER: O Lord, how might I take the time to look up, to really look up from my own agenda to see what you would have me see and know? How might I surrender to you, to so "trust and obey" your words of scripture? Help me to see you. Amen.

The gifts are wrapped: the crossword puzzle book for my father, the handmade candles for my cousins, the pajamas for Wendy, the "our-year-together" scrapbook for Steve. The church Christmas offering is in its envelope. The goodie bags for the children at the Farmers' Market are filled.

I am ready. I feel organized and accomplished. And yet, in the midst of my efficiency, in the midst of my wanting to remember everyone in a very special way, I have not readied my gift to God. I have neither wrapped nor organized God's gift. I have not prepared my gift to God in any special way because I do not know what gift to give God.

Certainly today's scripture offers me a hint. The psalm writer seems to suggest, "Just give to God your soul. Lift up your soul as God's Christmas gift."

My soul? My weary, weak, and washed-out soul? My too often faithless, fearful soul? Certainly not my soul!

But the psalm writer persists, "Just lift up your gift and say, 'to you, O Lord, I lift my soul. O, my God, in you I trust' . . . to make my gift special and complete."

So today, on this day before the first Sunday of Advent, I lift up to you, O God, this unorganized, unwrapped, inefficient gift of my soul. I lift my soul to you, hoping that you will find it an acceptable gift. Hoping that you will hold my soul with your love and your nurture. Hoping that this soul might become more and more a faithful gift for you, a gift readied for this time of Christ's coming.

PRAYER: Dear God, how do you feel about this soul that I lift up today? In your hands, may my soul become an acceptable "Christ is coming" gift. Amen.

FIRST SUNDAY OF ADVENT

Many of us made pilgrimage to the ruin of Ground Zero, the site where the World Trade Center towers once stood. We felt awash in horror and grief as we witnessed this place of death and devastation. Many of us had a sense that this place signaled that the future was hopeless.

Yet, a banner at Ground Zero proclaimed this message: "Remember, Reconnect, Rebuild." With these words, the banner seemed to say, "Continue on! There is a hope-filled future."

The Advent lesson tells of a biblical place of devastation that scripture describes as "a waste without human beings or animals" (Jer. 33:6). To this place and to the people sensing a hopeless future, God sends a banner in the form of the prophet Jeremiah. This Jeremiah-banner proclaims God's desire to "heal and reveal"(Jer. 33:6), to "restore and rebuild"(Jer. 33:7), and to "cleanse and forgive"(Jer. 33:7). God sent this banner to the people of Bible times so they might not give up, so they might realize that "there is a hope-filled future."

After the Bible-times people received this banner-message, God sent to the people another banner-message. This message was the best of all. It held the greatest strength and hope! It told of the greatest reason to continue on.

This banner-message said to the Bible-times people, "Continue on!" because, "The days are surely coming . . . when a righteous branch . . . will spring up. . . ." It said, "Continue on, fully with life, because the righteous branch, Christ, is coming."

Amidst any brokenness, any loss, any despair, there is good reason to remember, reconnect, and rebuild. Christ is coming. Christ is coming!

PRAYER: You are coming, aren't you, O Lord? How can I live more fully, this day, in the joy of your coming? Amen.

God's Purifying Initiative

December 4–10, 2006 • John D. Copenhaver Jr.[‡]

MONDAY, DECEMBER 4 • Read Malachi 3:1-4

The prophecies of Malachi come at a difficult time in Israel's history. The glorious prophecies of the restoration prophets have not been realized. The people complain, "All who do evil are good in the sight of the LORD, and [God] delights in them" (Mal. 2:17). They ask if God cares: "Where is the God of justice?" (Mal. 2:17).

To this weary and discouraged remnant, Malachi brings the bracing revelation that God will come suddenly to the Temple. But before the Lord comes, God will send a messenger to cleanse the priests, the descendants of Levi, with fuller's soap and to purify them with fire as a refiner purifies gold and silver.

God will also bring judgment upon those who oppress workers in their wages, who take advantage of widows and orphans, who mistreat aliens and immigrants, who cheat on their spouses, and who bear false witness. The people who complain and question may well get more than they bargain for.

These words may not offer the comfort the people desire, but they will help them renew their faithfulness to the covenant. The people hope for a restoration of the golden age, when Israel enjoyed prosperity, peace, and security; but it appears that God is more interested in covenant faithfulness.

During the Advent season, we examine our faithfulness to our covenant with God (our baptismal and membership vows). Let us renew those vows today and ask God to purify and cleanse our hearts.

SUGGESTION FOR MEDITATION: I invite you to renew your vows to God. If you have a hymnal or book of worship, find the vows of baptism and membership and renew your commitment to them.

[‡]Professor of Religion and Philosophy, Shenandoah University, Winchester, Virginia.

I appreciate the Christian year, especially the penitential seasons of Advent and Lent. I need their reflective themes, and I delight in anticipation of Christmas and Easter.

The first two weeks of Advent are especially penitential. They call for an unsparing examination of conscience, a thorough moral inventory in the light of God's mercy. Malachi proclaims that the Holy One is coming and that we need to put our lives in order. Business as usual is not enough; we need to reexamine our priorities.

Malachi raises a special concern about the integrity of the priesthood. How can the priests lead Israel in worship if they are corrupt? So God's first initiative in sending the messenger is to purify the priests. All of us who hold positions of leadership in the church, whether lay or ordained, should embrace God's purifying effort.

If God takes the initiative, what part do we play? Our part is wonderful—we let ourselves be loved! In the language of John Wesley, we make use of the "means of grace." Besides corporate worship and the sacraments, I think the season of Advent lends itself to the disciplines of confession and reconciliation, silence and solitude, fasting and meditation. Some churches now offer Advent quiet days and retreats to cultivate these disciplines. But think how foreign these disciplines are to our extended cultural celebration of Christmas. Let us be among those who recover the contemplative nature of this sacred season.

To those who wondered where God was, Malachi proclaims that God is coming to set things right. "The day is coming, burning like an oven." The arrogant and wicked will be burned—root and branch. But on those who observe the covenant, "the sun of righteousness shall rise, with healing in its wings. You shall go out leaping like calves from the stall."

PRAYER: Holy God, have mercy on me. Give me courage to open every area of my life to your transforming grace. And, send me out leaping like a calf! Amen.

Years before Paul wrote this letter, he had a vision of a Macedonian man pleading with him, "Come over to Macedonia and help us" (Acts 16:9). True to the vision, Paul traveled to Philippi, a Roman colony in Macedonia along a major road linking Rome and Byzantium. There Paul planted the first Christian community in Europe.

As was his practice, Paul first looked for the synagogue. The Jewish community in Philippi, being rather small in number, did not have synagogue; they met at a "place of prayer." Paul finds a receptive audience there, especially among the women. During his time in Philippi, Paul and Silas are jailed for "disturbing the city" by exorcising a slave girl with a "spirit of divination" and thereby depriving her owners of income.

Now, years later, Paul once again finds himself in prison but not in Philippi. He sends this letter by way of Epaphroditus whom the Philippians had sent to Paul to care for him. As was his custom, Paul begins his letters with a salutation followed by thanksgiving.

Probably the best-known verse in this passage is verse 6: "I am confident of this, that the one who began a good work among you will bring it to completion by the day of Jesus Christ." Notice the word *among*. Every other translation I have read used the preposition *in*. I checked six popular translations and paraphrases; each uses *in*. But against the weight of tradition, I think the New Revised Standard Version (NRSV) translators got it right. Why? Paul's deep concern in writing to the Philippians is for the unity of the church while suffering opposition. The work of God is to bring the church to completion. We cannot be holy by ourselves; rather our holiness consists in being an integral part of the body of Christ. Thanks be to God who has made us members of Christ's body.

PRAYER: Holy God, thank you for grafting us into the vine that bears such beautiful, nourishing fruit. Help us abide in the true vine, our Lord Jesus Christ. Amen.

THURSDAY, DECEMBER 7 • **Read Philippians 1:3-11**

Paul is imprisoned, not knowing what awaits him, and yet he writes this stunning letter of thanksgiving and joy. He evidences no trace of bitterness or anxiety. Rather Paul's deepest concern is for the welfare of the church in Philippi. The church was experiencing opposition and persecution from outside and painful division from within. Along with Paul, they have been graciously granted the privilege "not only of believing in Christ, but of suffering for him as well" (1:29).

Paul and the Christians at Philippi have been partaking of the same grace, grace that has sustained them in their suffering and in their defense and confirmation of the gospel. Paul rejoices in this fellowship but is distressed to hear of divisions in the church and believes the only cure is greater love. "My prayer is that your love for each other may increase more and more and never stop improving" (1:9, JB). This overflowing love, along with insight and knowledge, will preserve them "pure and blameless" in the day of Christ. Toward the end of this letter, Paul pleads with Euodia and Syntyche, two women who probably lead house-churches, to exercise this love and be reconciled.

Disunity and division are a scandal and blot on the church. Let us examine ourselves. Do we secretly bear a grudge against someone in our church? Do we despise and avoid those of a different theological perspective? Do we allow old wounds to fester and poison fellowship? During this Advent, let us reach out to those we may have alienated or to those from whom we feel estranged. Seek them out when you "pass the peace" or go out of your way to greet them. As Paul wrote the Christians in Rome, "Do all you can to live at peace with everyone" (Rom. 12:18, JB).

PRAYER: Triune God, heal your church and make us one as you are one. May our love for one another increase more and more and never stop improving. Amen.

Waiting. Waiting. Waiting. With Christians of all ages, we await the fullness of God's reign. But it is not a passive waiting; rather we seek to anticipate God's reign in the here and now, in this present age where injustice and violence seem the norm. In resisting oppression and working for peace, we become, along with Zechariah, Elizabeth, John, and Mary, heralds of God's coming reign.

In this passage Zechariah becomes our model for waiting. For nine long months he has waited in mute expectancy for his promised son's birth. Evidently, this divinely imposed muteness does not embitter Zechariah. When he finally speaks, he lets loose a torrent of praise that closes with the words of this prophetic hymn.

One critic called the history of Christianity a long "theological filibuster." We are often too quick to speak and too slow to listen, both in our witness and in our prayers. Let us add Zechariah's muteness to our spiritual disciplines this Advent. In addition to fasting from food, let us add a fast of words. If we can't observe an Advent silent retreat or "quiet day," perhaps we can at least add a few minutes to our daily devotions to pause from composing our prayers to wait in expectant silence, resting in God's grace. As we listen to the heart of God, we may find renewed compassion for God's suffering children and courage to speak up for those who are oppressed. Indeed, after his long fast from words, Zechariah prophesied the "dawn from on high will break upon us, to give light to those who sit in darkness and in the shadow of death, to guide our feet into the way of peace." Perhaps if we listened more and spoke less, our words would have the immediacy and power of Zechariah's.

SUGGESTION FOR MEDITATION: At the end of your verbal prayer, set aside a few minutes for silence. You may want to repeat the phrase, "Guide our feet into the way of peace" several times as an entrance into the silence.

This is the quintessential message of Advent: "Prepare the way of the Lord." When we hear these bracing words, we feel the weight of centuries of prophecies and expectant waiting. Now the waiting is over; the reign of God is breaking upon us! But how shall we prepare?

Repent! We began the week by remembering our baptismal vows. Today our text brings us back to baptism but not to Christian baptism. Most churches view Christian baptism as a regenerating sacrament that confers the Holy Spirit, the spirit of life. John comes preaching a baptism of repentance for the forgiveness of sins. As baptized Christians our sins have been forgiven, and we are in right relationship with God. What meaning then can John's demand for repentance have for us, who are "washed in the blood of the Lamb"?

In his book, *The Monastic Journey* (1977), Thomas Merton writes about the Benedictine vow of *conversatio morum* (conversion of life). Of all the monastic vows (including poverty, chastity, obedience, and stability), Merton considered the conversion of life the most demanding and all-encompassing. It reflects a commitment to bring every area of life into conformity with the gospel, to orient all of life toward God. In many ways, it brings to mind Wesley's belief that all Christians, not just clergy, should be "going on to perfection." Essentially, conversion of life (and Wesley's Christian perfection) is continuous growth in love, love of God and neighbor. The root word for repentance is the Hebrew word for "turn." We heed John's call by a continuous turning to God and to those in need. In the words of the Shaker hymn, "To turn, turn will be our delight, till by turning, turning we come round right."

PRAYER: Merciful God, during this holy season of Advent, grant me genuine repentance. Wherever I may have strayed from your love, strengthen my resolve to get back on the path to holiness. Amen.

SECOND SUNDAY OF ADVENT

Make straight the way of the Lord! What must we do in our homes, our places of work, and our churches to prepare the way of the Lord? What stands in the way of God's will? How can we do the works of God? "We are what he has made us, created in Christ Jesus for good works, which God prepared beforehand to be our way of life" (Eph. 2:10).

What do we do? John offers us a good place to start: clothe the poor and feed the hungry. When John demands that his hearers "bear fruit worthy of repentance," (3:8) his conscience-stricken hearers ask what they should do. "Whoever has two coats must share with anyone who has none, and whoever has food must do likewise" (3:11). It is interesting that John does not tell them to pray or fast or retreat, the disciplines that foster repentance. The fruit of repentance turns us to neighbors in need. The fruit of repentance are the works of justice and mercy.

Apparently John sees feeding the hungry and clothing the poor as a work of justice. If we have more than enough, our excess belongs to the poor and needy. The needs of our sisters and brothers make claims upon us. Only our hardness of heart keeps us from responding to their need. So justice demands it, but love enables us to see the hungry and poor as family. Love compels us to share from our abundance.

This text helps us see that our goal during Advent is not our growth in personal piety or personal purity but self-forgetfulness in responding to the needs of others. The most purifying actions are those that turn us from preoccupation with ourselves or our spiritual progress to God and our neighbor.

PRAYER: God of justice and compassion, give us such love for the needy and most vulnerable that we forget ourselves in their service. Amen.

God's Song, Our Song

December 11–17, 200 • Heather Murray Elkins[‡]

MONDAY, DECEMBER 11 • Read Philippians 4:4-7

I'm working on the third week in Advent, but it's still Indian summer outside my window. Months before you opened to this page, someone somewhere in the world prepared a text for this day and no other. It is not an accidental meeting on a page. These are texts designed to travel over distance and through time. This meditation is meant to send Christian greetings, to encourage devotion, to illuminate scripture. It stands in the tradition of Paul who wrote a friendship letter to a community in Philippi. His words link to this page and continue to support the communities of Christ everywhere. Those who first heard the letter are connected over the centuries with those who now study these verses at home or hear them read aloud when they gather to worship.

An ancient way of telling time is the liturgical calendar that uses a pattern of readings from scripture as a discipline to shape our lives *imago Christi*, in the image of Christ. But how can something written long ago be of any use in a world that's shapeshifting by the hour?

This day's reading instructs us to shape our lives by joy. "Rejoice in the Lord always; again I will say, Rejoice." In the power of this holy joy, we are asked to make peace among ourselves. We are encouraged not to worry and are taught how to pray. We are given a blessing, "the peace of God, which surpasses all understanding, will guard your hearts and your minds in Christ Jesus."

SUGGESTION FOR MEDITATION: These are the words of life whether it's the third week in August or Advent, whether it's the first or the twenty-first century, whether it's the Upper Room in Jerusalem or Nashville, whether we're in Palestine, West Virginia, or Palestine. May this give us joy.

[‡]Academic Dean, Drew Theological School, Madison, New Jersey.

Good news? Hardly. The wild-haired street preacher/anarchist starts by calling the religious establishment a snake pit and ends up consigning God-knows-who to unquenchable fire. It certainly makes for news. It would still make headlines today. But what qualifies this news as "good"? Why is this at the heart of the evangel of Jesus the Christ? Who's disturbing our peace? The clue to this week's Advent adventure is John.

If clothes make a man, John is somewhat underdressed according to ancient and modern standards. He's definitely not short on words, however. He roars out of the wilderness like a flash flood, words spilling out of him, sweeping everything up in his path. Those who get caught in the current hear the words of Amos in the undercurrent: "Let justice roll down like waters, and righteousness like an ever-flowing stream" (5:24).

Here is a word from the Lord that disturbs our peace, thanks be to God. John breaks what seems to be the long, hard silence of God. It's not the first time. The evangel/angel's news of John's arrival leaves father, Zechariah, at a loss for words. The good news leaves him speechless. He only finds his voice after he holds his newborn son and names him John.

Unlike his father, John is not at a loss for words when it comes to good news. His gift, his genius, comes in his ability to recognize its arrival. The Baptist knows how to name the Holy. It's a gift that requires more than being good with words. It's a willingness to proclaim what you believe in whatever fashion you can. It's not a matter of language but life. John, after all, first danced in his mother's womb to let her know when Mary and the Word of life walked in.

PRAYER: Holy One, send us such good news that we're willing to disturb the peace for God's sake. Amen.

John the Baptist is the Advent adventurer, stalking through the wilderness of his time on the trail of the messiah. He's the original hellfire-and-brimstone preacher, but he also offers hope to the community he rakes over the coals. A willingness to hope is a willingness to enter the wilderness. Hope is not a domesticated state of mind. It seems to camp out in odd places, crops up at the worst possible times. Just as we resign ourselves to the minimum wages of life with no benefits, hope whispers that we shouldn't settle for despair's bottom line. Hope thrives in the barren places of our lives.

When hope comes out of the wilderness, it turns what we take for granted upside down making us restless and setting our teeth on edge. It wakes us up, stirs our imagination, and energizes our wide-awake dreams. It affects everyone: soldiers and farmers, sailors, tailors, cooks, collectors, and cabinet makers. It's contagious because hope-filled humans refuse to recognize boundaries.

Take the people who gather down by the riverside. They're at the bottom of the empire's food chain. They're controlled by a very efficient occupation army. Their religious leaders have either been co-opted or killed. They've been conquered too many times to count; yet they refuse to believe that they've been abandoned by the Holy One, maker of heaven and earth. Surrounded by sophisticated systems of civil religion where Caesar is both God and Caesar, they pray for Emmanuel, God with us: a fervent prayer for apparently godforsaken people who are starving for some sense of purpose, thirsting for some meaning for their pain. Somewhere in the waters of repentance and the voice from the wilderness, hope's deep roots take hold in their hearts. Down by the riverside God's wilderness wheat begins to spring up, wild and green.

PRAYER: Holy One, calm my heart with hope and trouble my prayers with love. Amen.

"Surely God is my salvation: I will trust, and will not be afraid, for the LORD GOD is my strength and my might; he has become my salvation." This sentence first caught my attention because of the grammar. "Has become" implies a history as well as a future. It makes salvation a process, not a product; it's a relationship, not a possession. "I've been saved," conveys a different sound and sense to me than "God has become my salvation." This is what "being perfected in love" involves, a holy/human relationship that deepens over time until human time itself is transformed into eternity.

One of my friends, a famous Christian musician, hates the hymn "Amazing Grace." Whenever he imagines heaven, he pictures many rooms filled with music; in one of those rooms angels will be singing this hymn forever. He says he will know he's in heaven if he's not in that room.

I, on the other hand, have limited musical gifts. I'm one of the really high-risk humans who need amazing grace just to get through the day, let alone the pearly gates. The older I grow, the greater my need for the one whose name means "God is salvation." Whenever I remember the grace that "taught my heart to fear," I give thanks for the Living One who relieved those fears. This grace is amazing, part of the saving history of all God's children. It's at the center of this season of joyful song and sober prayer as we who are baptized seek justice and resist evil in Christ's name. We anticipate and remember the "grace that brought us safe thus far" as we watch for the homecoming of God.

SUGGESTION FOR MEDITATION: **In this season we hear angelic sounds in elevators and grocery stores. Sing along with the angels, out loud. It's one way to reclaim a few tunes for God.**

"With joy you will draw water from the wells of salvation." These are words of life, a promise that matters as much to those who first heard it as it matters to those who hear it today. A promise of water, a promise of life. Sweet, clear, pure living water from deep wells of wellness. Just hearing it makes us thirsty. Water has served as a natural symbol of holiness in every religion, one of the most ancient and universal of human dreams.

Throughout Hebrew Scriptures God is known as the One who transforms the waters of chaos and death into waters of life. The story of these living waters flows through the salvation history that we recite over our baptismal fonts and pools. We are bathed in this promise as we prepare for the coming of the Christ who brings us life by water and the Spirit.

There's a break in this waterline, however. What happens when that dream is polluted? We're having to learn what Isaiah's community knew about water. Over a billion people in the world don't have access to a single glass of clean water. Water is a priceless gift of God, but human sin has poisoned the wells, the rivers, and the springs. Those with means buy living water and those without the means go thirsty and dream.

Isaiah is pouring words of comfort for a struggling community on the margins of a great empire. For us to hear what they heard, we need to be reimmersed in the waters of our baptism. We need to know what it means to thirst for righteousness, and how it feels to share a cup of cool water with a child, a community, or one billion people. We need to remember Christ's words, "I thirst."

SUGGESTION FOR MEDITATION: World War I poet Wilfred Owen reminds us in "Strange Meeting" that the sweet well water of peace comes from truths too deep to be tainted.

How long does a song last? The scripture passage today reads like the journal of a songwriter who starts by jotting down the lyrics of one of his favorite songs: "God is my strength and my song, and has become my salvation." He then moves into a future tense when countless voices will shout and sing for joy. In this passage the writer shifts from recording his own testimony (God as strength-song-salvation) to invoking the harmonies of a community that he loves.

To grasp the power of these words we have to believe, as this writer did, that God is coming into the world and coming soon. The songwriter has to make the people listen. His task is to restore their memory. They're suffering a crisis. They've lost their sense of being chosen. They've forgotten the songs of Zion. They doubt that the god who calls them is the God of all time and space. They're in the process of deserting their post, falling silent, extinguishing the light.

So what does the songwriter do? He sings them a song about everything they've forgotten, about God's promises and the one who is coming to fulfill those promises. He sings to them of home and the holy history that they and their children's children have received as a treasure. He sings to restore their memory and to recreate a sense of the future. The last thing he does is invite them to sing; no, he *commands* them to sing.

How long has this song lasted? It stretches over us like a sacred canopy. It makes room for those of Isaiah's time and those who have been adopted into this covenant by Christ. It binds alien and native alike into a seamless song of praise.

SUGGESTION FOR MEDITATION: **Today I will remember to sing with the angels and archangels and all the heavenly hosts.**

THIRD SUNDAY OF ADVENT

The small book that bears the name Zephaniah is a revelation of time. It interrupts this season of purple Sundays with a red-letter day: the day of the Lord. For those who hear this text as originally intended, read aloud in its entirety to a community, this means Judgment Day. It begins with a dateline, the reign of Josiah, the last of the godly kings of Judah. It proclaims the coming of "the day of the Lord" when "soiled, defiled, oppressing" cities will be leveled and all the "proudly exultant ones" will be removed from the midst of those who survive. This passage ends with a love song by the Holy One for "a people humble and lowly."

How we interpret this text depends on who we think we are and what we know about what precedes the "song of joy." Judgment Day brings justice as well as mercy. The poor, the homeless, the leftover people will find comfort in this word. All those who have prayed without ceasing will have their prayers answered. The angry Judge of Judgment Day comforts a war-weary people with a promise of homecoming, a song of freedom from fear, and a peaceful sleep.

It is a text filled with unexpected graces. The prophet has been shouting at us, demanding that we come to our senses before we're destroyed. Now he tells us to sing and rejoice. His words push us beyond our insistence on business as usual. This text tells time differently than the world clock. This is a radical shift in consciousness that makes sense of this season of preparing for the birth of a savior and praying fervently for Christ to come again. We don't know exactly what we're praying for beyond asking God to come into our midst, and that's the point.

PRAYER: Come, Lord Jesus. Change our empty words into pure speech. Renew us with your love. Amen.

Celebrating with Mary

December 18–24, 2006 • J. Marshall Jenkins[‡]

MONDAY, DECEMBER 18 • Read Luke 1:46-55

In joyous anticipation of her firstborn, Mary sings revolution. Enraptured that God chose her, a maiden of no prominence, a woman with no voice, to bear the world's savior, her joy calls up visions of the rich tasting the dust of poverty, the powerful limping with the burden of oppression. Such angry bliss speaks of painful memories: Perhaps a high-society girl snubbed her. Or a powerful boy tried to toy with her body. Maybe taunting, well-heeled brats humiliated her father. Or drunkards with Roman privilege soiled her people's land.

Do we ease her anger by celebrating her son's birth in ways that only the wealthy and powerful can enjoy? Of course not. Can we who are rich and powerful be merry this season as she was? Only if we invite Mary into our homes and let her direct the party. After all, she is his mother.

Mary would, I suspect, have us dream dreams and tell tales of hope, the kind of hope that the rich and powerful are too busy and satisfied to entertain, the kind of hope that sustains us in our poverty. That takes knowing our poverty, if not poverty of money, then poverty of intimacy and belonging—the very things our souls need most, the very things that require setting aside possessions and power. Mary's anger frees us to truly celebrate her son's birth. Let her in.

PRAYER: Father of our Lord, we welcome your favored one Mary, not as our guest but as our host celebrating the birth of your son. In Jesus' name. Amen.

[‡]Author and psychologist; Director of Counseling, Berry College; member, Westminster Presbyterian Church, Rome, Georgia.

People in my country worry about many things. Exile is not one of them. Bounded east and west by vast oceans, protected by history's mightiest military, we fear terrorism; but we don't fear mass uprooting. This anguished psalm of one spent by dislocation or depressed by coming home to ruins does not seem to concern us.

If we reduce ourselves to beings motivated only by economics and security, the psalm does not touch us. But having made us in God's image, God bids us love as Christ loves. The world is full of exiles, from Asian girls kidnapped for prostitution to entire ethnic groups blown about in developing countries with no government that welcomes them. God bids us suffer and pray with them. We cannot walk away from this psalm.

We do not claim to know how exiles feel. Mary, the humble maiden carrying God's son in occupied territory, knew a bit more about those feelings. Mother Teresa often said that along with the material poverty of a significant minority in America, she observed a more pervasive poverty of connection and mutual commitment. She saw loneliness everywhere: people exiled in their suburban neighborhoods, even in their marriage beds.

We cannot walk away from this psalm. We cannot celebrate the birth of Mary's son without it. His suffering love is at least as old as the first life form struggling to survive. But his palpable suffering-with-us is at least as old as Christmas. His suffering love nourishes us and shelters us in our poverty. His suffering love calls us to share our suffering love as our greatest Christmas gift.

PRAYER: Lord, through the suffering love of Jesus, we receive meaning and hope. Through our own suffering love, give good gifts to your children. In Jesus' name. Amen.

In the angry joy of the Magnificat (Luke 1:47-55), Mary celebrated her pregnancy not only against the dark background of painful personal memories but of national loss and longing. She sang like Micah, the prophet who held fast to mourning the northern kingdom's exile, to anxiety over the southern kingdom's vulnerability and to hope in God's promises. God helped him hold all that pathos in one heart.

Micah offered a heart large with suffering and hope and a mind gleeful over the irony of God overshadowing the great with the small. A place like Bethlehem, not Jerusalem, will usher in the Messiah.

Mary, in true prophetic form, took Micah's prophecy once told—"Israel will be abandoned until the time when she who is in labor gives birth" (NIV)—and pushed it farther than words can go. She embodied it. She was the hourglass that marked her people's agonized waiting for the Lord.

Mary also marked the impending arrival joyfully, as she should. But did she know what to expect from her long-awaited son? Micah knew to expect one from a small place leading as a lowly shepherd, but he expected the Messiah to rule with military might, not the kind of power Mary's son ultimately used. Did Mary know any better than Micah? Do we?

Micah saw the Messiah through a glass dimly. Mary saw face-to-face, but only as the messianic story unfolded, confounding every witness including her. We know the story in retrospect, but we really know it no better unless we let it shape us. If we do, then like Micah and Mary before us, we will hold suffering and hope in our hearts. We will hold them with love.

PRAYER: Lord, enlarge our hearts that we may embody the suffering, hope, and love of those who waited patiently and passionately for Jesus' first coming. In Jesus' name. Amen.

If Mary sang the Magnificat to Jesus in the cradle, on his birthdays, or whenever the sight of him touched her, her angry joy may have shaped him. Phrases like "He has scattered the proud in the thoughts of their hearts" (Luke 1:51) may have replayed in his mind. He would later declare society's last first and the first last in his Father's kingdom. He would refuse to play politics-as-usual. Moreover, he reserved his hottest anger for religion-as-usual.

For Jesus saw religious leaders take God's blessings for booty. People looked to them for words of hope and consolation, but they kept God as their crony and held grace at a distance. They reduced sacrificial rituals from worship to appeasement. They reduced moral practices from celebrations of freedom to burdens that kept people in their places. In the spirit of Mary's Magnificat, Jesus attacked their love of status and held up children, aliens, even sinners as examples of righteousness exceeding theirs.

In the ultimate act of faith, Jesus put his body on the line like a sacrificial lamb. In the same act, the ultimate act of love, he assured the redemption that religion-as-usual cannot reach. He still works and sacrifices to cultivate in us a radical religion of responding to God from the heart. His religion does not reserve power for a spiritual elite. It makes the power of God available to all who ask in humble expectation and brave hope.

Religion-as-usual is easier, so we fill Christmas with it. But Jesus' own radical religion frees us to celebrate his coming every time the Spirit moves us to have faith like his, to love like him.

PRAYER: Lord, send your Holy Spirit to build faith and love in our hearts. In Jesus' name. Amen.

In her blessings for Mary, Elizabeth concludes, "Blessed is she who believed that there would be a fulfillment of what was spoken to her by the Lord." She knows the darker side of that blessing. When the same angel who visited Mary visited her husband, the priest Zechariah, he stumbled over his own doubt and asked for proof that the angel wasn't kidding. The angel proved it by striking him mute.

As with Mary, the angel promised a child under unlikely circumstances: Zechariah and Elizabeth were long of tooth and short on youth. A humble man, Zechariah needed a moment to grasp how God could choose such unlikely candidates for bearing and rearing any child, not to mention a child with a bold mission ahead. He asked an honest question, an all-too-human question, but in his worries about his and Elizabeth's limitations, he took too long before considering God's infinite possibilities.

So Elizabeth, wiser and sadder about angel visits, joyfully breaks the lonely silence, and Mary chimes in. Mary instinctively knows that her humble state is not an occasion for doubt but for praise, that the lower she is, the greater the wonder of God's choosing her. When Elizabeth bore John, Zechariah got the point and joined the chorus (Luke 1:67–79).

But even before his birth, Elizabeth and Zechariah's son John prophesied with a leap in the womb. This visitor carries the one worth waiting for, worth leaping for. This visitor carries the fulfillment of Israel's hopes, from those of old Zechariah waiting for the ancient story to unfold to those of the unborn prophet John waiting to be born. This visitor, so full of faith, is the fulfillment of faith.

PRAYER: Lord, build our confidence that you will fulfill your promises. In Jesus' name. Amen.

When we observe an apple, how we see it depends on the colors, shapes, and configurations in the background. We see an apple in a pigpen differently than we see an apple in a bowl of fruit. Gestalt psychologists call the object to which we attend—the apple in this case—the "figure," and the background, the "ground."

As she sings, Mary's lowliness is the ground against which we perceive the might, mercy, and faithfulness of God. Her lyrics make God the figure, herself the ground. Mary reveals God by being Mary.

We see God's glory against the background of Mary's humility. Her joy highlights God's faithfulness. Her anger illumines God's wrath and places God's mercy in bold relief. Her seeming insignificance accentuates God's call. Her hopeful expectation brightens God's promises.

This picture has three dimensions. God turns it, and we see Mary as figure, God as ground. God reveals Mary by being God. God calls her, and we see her anew. Otherwise, would Elizabeth have called her, "Blessed . . . mother of my Lord"? Would unborn John have leaped?

God turns the picture again as God does whenever a child is born, and the child is the figure. Mary retreats to the ground joyfully, as parents do. She invites us there to celebrate his birth with the rotting hay, teeming flies, grunting creatures, and uncouth shepherds without which and whom we could not see the child right. By going in lowliness, anger, joy, and love for him, we share in the task of revealing him to a world groaning in travail. And the child will reveal God to us and us to ourselves in one turn of the picture.

PRAYER: God, take the colors, shapes, and configurations of our lives and use them to reveal your son to a searching world. In Jesus' name. Amen.

Third Sunday of Advent/Christmas Eve

Sandwiched between tales of angelic visitations, this verse understates the one event we cannot overstate. "And she gave birth to her firstborn son," a joyous event in its own right. But in this case heaven descended to earth, the Word became flesh, the divine became human—all unthinkable.

Mary gives birth, and Luke leaves out her labor even though earth, wind, and fire labor, all creatures labor, all things groan with Mary in anticipation (Rom. 8:22-23). She wraps him in bands of cloth to keep him warm. But her child is the light of the world, the one who will bring fire, the one who will rage against the high and mighty. Mary, not yet seeing the grown man living prophetic anger and joy, only knows the baby in a cold, exposed, dark place. She wraps him, holds him; warmth fills her spent body.

Mary lays him in a manger, confusing the animals, confusing all people who look for their salvation where they make reservations in advance. She lays him there "because there was no place at the inn," or anywhere else for that matter. There will never be a place for him in his mortal walk: "He was in the world, and the world came into being through him; yet the world did not know him. He came to what was his own, and his own people did not accept him" (John 1:10-11).

Annually we decorate, shop, travel, sing, eat, and drink in anticipation. Somewhere in the blur of it all, Mary holds out her son to us. Do we know him? Do we accept him?

PRAYER: Lord, I want to know Jesus and to love him. I open my arms to embrace the child. Open my heart, that I may embrace the man. In Jesus' name. Amen.

Welcoming God's Incarnate Presence

December 25–31, 2006 • Joseph N. Davis[‡]

CHRISTMAS DAY

Though we live in a culture that places great emphasis on physical beauty, we do not normally marvel at the beauty of anyone's feet. But Isaiah tells us, "How beautiful on the mountains are the feet of those who bring good news!" This is a poetic way of saying that people rejoice at the coming of messengers who bring good news.

When I come home from work, the first thing I hear when I walk in the door is the jingling of my dog Bo's collar tags. As soon as he knows I am home, he runs to greet me, wags his tail vigorously, and tries to jump up and lick my hand. It never fails. No matter how gloomy my day, Bo greets me with an abundance of doggy joy.

Can Bo be so grateful for the little things I do? I make sure he has food and shelter and that his basic needs are met. Yet he greets me with joy that knows no bounds. He manifests the joy we often experience when anyone comes to us bearing news of salvation, of peace—the message that our God reigns.

All too often we fail in our attempts to find the joy we should feel during Christmas. One way to recover this joy is to celebrate whenever anyone—from the preacher at the Christmas service to the shop clerk who says, "Merry Christmas!"—brings us the good news of Christ's coming into the world.

SUGGESTION FOR MEDITATION: Who in your life brings tidings of joy? Who makes Christ known to you and those you love? Praise God for the messengers who bring you news of Christ. Greet them with joy the next time you see them. And check out their feet. Aren't they beautiful?

[‡]Episcopal priest; rector, St. Philip Church, Memphis, Tennessee.

The prologue to John's Gospel (John 1:1-18) takes us from before creation ("In the beginning was the Word") to the crucifixion ("his own people received him not") to the latest baptism at the local church down the street ("But to all who received him, who believed in his name, he gave power to become children of God"). At Christmas we celebrate the fact that "the Word became flesh and dwelt among us." But we must not stop there. We must let this Word rule our hearts, which gives us "power to become children of God."

The Gospel writer points out the importance of human actions, the consequences of freedom abused and properly exercised. When we receive God's Word, we receive God. When we reject God's Word, we reject God. How we respond to the ways God speaks to us and comes to us in the world determines whether we will be among God's faithful children or among those who reject divine authority and the lordship of Christ.

Christmas is an ideal time to consider how the Word of God came into our world as a tiny, helpless baby. Mary and Joseph received him gladly, as did shepherds and wise men. Herod did not. As God's children by faith and grace, are we willing to let God's Word bring us love, truth, hope, and shelter? Are we willing to receive God's Word eagerly and, by doing so, find life, strength, and joy?

SUGGESTION FOR PRAYER: Consider how you have failed to receive God's Word in the last week. Ask forgiveness. Consider how have you welcomed that Word into the world. Give thanks.

Though Hannah has given up her son Samuel to the service of the Lord in the house of the Lord at Shiloh, she continues to make him "a little robe and to take it to him each year." I can imagine a row of robes hanging in the room where the boy Samuel vested for the service. The row would have been added to each year, and each robe would be several inches longer than the last. This row of vestments signals Hannah's love and support for her son as he offers his service to the Lord over the years.

Like Hannah, we offer our children to the service of God. After that offering, they still need our steady support to grow in years and in stature. They depend on us not only for vestments but also for instruction in God's word, moral teaching, musical training, food, opportunities to enjoy Christian fellowship, and chances to give of themselves to others. They need our love, our encouragement, and our dedication to help them become the servants of God they are called to be. They need our help as they try to become faithful servants of the Lord, emulating Samuel rather than the sons of Eli who "had no regard for the LORD."

Though we may never see the fruit of our actions of support, we can expect to find an unrecognized Samuel in our midst who needs our help to grow into a powerful servant God.

SUGGESTION FOR PRAYER: **How can you help the young Christians you know grow up in the service of the Lord? Decide on one action you can take to support at least one of God's young servants, and then follow through.**

What does it mean to have the word of Christ dwell in you richly? It means to obey the command from "Joy to the World," which tells us, "Let every heart prepare him room."

In my city a classical music radio station helps the word of Christ dwell in its listeners richly. Such a situation is rare in these days when so many secular businesses seem to be fleeing from public recognition of Christ at Christmas or any other time. But what is a classical music station supposed to do? All the good Christmas music is about the birth of Christ, and listeners of all faiths want to hear the best seasonal music when appropriate.

In the days around Christmas, this station plays the glorious choral and instrumental music of the past thousand years—music that renders the songs of angels in ecstatic harmonies, that honors the humility of the Virgin Mary and Joseph, that pays homage to shepherds and wise men. Most of all, this music wraps the message of the birth of Christ around our hearts with bonds that will never weaken.

Driving in my car at night during these days around Christmas, I turn my radio on and listen to hear if the music of the angels is going on around me—and most often, during these special days, I find that it is. I can hear it, ringing forth with glory to bring light into our darkness. Oh, that we could hear the angel choirs all year round!

We can if we embrace these words from Colossians: "As God's chosen ones, holy and beloved, clothe yourselves with compassion, kindness, humility, meekness, and patience. . . . Above all, clothe yourselves with love. . . . Let the peace of Christ rule in your hearts." The message of Christmas encourages us to live gently in the world, to be mindful of others, and to live in love. This Christmastide, take these words from Colossians with you.

PRAYER: **Lord God, thank you for the ways the music of the season has caught me up in the glory of Christ. Open my heart to his word, and let the joy of the angels dwell in me always. Amen.**

FRIDAY, DECEMBER 29 • **Read Colossians 3:17**

During the Christmas season, we ponder the gift quality of Christian life and faith. Because Christ came into our world, we have the grace to "put on" (Col. 3:12) the virtues of Christian life and treat one another as Christ has treated us. Once we receive Christ, we have a responsibility and mission to serve him in the world, so much so that Paul actually tells us to do everything "in the name of the Lord Jesus."

To act in the name of someone is to act as that person's special representative. Sometimes my father would give me, while still in my teenage years, his credit card and tell me to buy gasoline or pick up an item at the store. He said I should sign for him on the piece of paper. Little did I comprehend the trust and power (for good and evil) that he had put in my hands with that little piece of plastic. Now that I have my own teenage son and my own pieces of plastic, I have begun to grasp how much my father entrusted to me when he gave me his credit card.

Now that we have received Christ, God wants us to act in Christ's name, to spend ourselves and our possessions for Christ. All our words and deeds will ideally reflect what Christ would have us say and do. He is counting on us.

PRAYER: Thank you, Lord Jesus, for the gift of your life in me. May my words and deeds always show forth your presence and power for good. Turn me away from anything that would bring dishonor to your holy name. Give me joy in your love, rather than fear of failure, as I seek to represent you in the world. Amen.

When Jesus is twelve years old, Joseph and Mary lose him. How could they let that happen? How could he wander off? We expect such things with our own children but not with Jesus! Isn't he too precious, too good, too obedient to get lost? On the third day, "they found him in the Temple, sitting among the teachers, listening to them and asking them questions."

How could Jesus treat his parents that way? His answer reveals a unique perspective. "Did you not know that I must be in my Father's house?" Another translation reads, "Did you not know that I must be about My Father's business?" (NKJV). Jesus has no idea that he is lost. He is quite at home in the Temple, sitting among the teachers, learning about his Father. He is getting a taste of his true home—more so than when he is with his mother and foster father in Nazareth.

Here's another experience for Mary to ponder in her heart and for us to ponder in ours. We strive so hard to create a home for our children, to make them comfortable and well-adjusted people in this life. Yet they have a truer, more permanent home away from us and beyond us. All Christians have a duty to help children feel at home in their heavenly Father's house and to consider it normal to be about God's business. How can we make it easier for children to worship and learn about God through a way of life that prepares them for eternal life?

PRAYER: O God, guide me that I may help the children I know be at home in your house and be about your business in this world. Amen.

How did you spend the week after Christmas? Maybe you visited family. You may have had some time off from work or school. Did you take in more movies, sporting events, or other forms of entertainment? Maybe you cleaned house and tried to restore order. Perhaps you wrote thank-you notes. You may have returned to the normal routine of your job.

I mention all of this to make a point: even after Christmas, life goes on. But it goes on with a dramatic difference: Life goes on in the midst of celebration and praise for the birth of Christ in the world. Psalm 148 is a beautiful song of praise. In stunning poetry the psalmist proclaims God's reign in the world and calls everything on earth to praise God. Angels, sun and moon, shining stars, mountains, wild animals, young men and women, old and young—everyone and everything on earth must praise God.

We have an opportunity to make a huge difference in the world simply by praising God. And we have every reason to praise God: the creation of the world and its redemption by Jesus Christ. God's gift to us of Jesus showers all the world with light and love. This is what we celebrate every Christmas.

All that we are and have comes from God. Praise turns daily life into celebration. It turns our hearts toward joy in the hope of God's work through Christ in our world.

PRAYER: Come, Holy Spirit; inspire my heart with praise for the Lord Jesus Christ. Let me remember him at morning and evening, in work and rest, when I am alone and when I am with others.

The Revised Common Lectionary[‡] for 2006
Year B – Advent / Christmas Year C
(Disciplines Edition)

January 1

January 6
EPIPHANY
*(These readings are used for
Sunday, January 1.)*
Isaiah 60:1-6
Psalm 72:1-7, 10-14
Ephesians 3:1-12
Matthew 2:1-12

January 2–8
BAPTISM OF THE LORD
Genesis 1:1-5
Psalm 29
Acts 19:1-7
Mark 1:4-11

January 9–15
1 Samuel 3:1-20
Psalm 139:1-6, 13-18
1 Corinthians 6:12-20
John 1:43-51

January 16–22
Jonah 3:1-5, 10
Psalm 62:5-12
1 Corinthians 7:29-31
Mark 1:14-20

January 23–29
Deuteronomy 18:15-20
Psalm 111
1 Corinthians 8:1-13
Mark 1:21-28

January 30–February 5
Isaiah 40:21-31
Psalm 147:1-11, 20c
1 Corinthians 9:16-23
Mark 1:29-39

February 6–12
2 Kings 5:1-14
Psalm 30
1 Corinthians 9:24-27
Mark 1:40-45

February 13–19
Isaiah 43:18-25
Psalm 41
2 Corinthians 1:18-22
Mark 2:1-12

February 20–26
TRANSFIGURATION
2 Kings 2:1-12
Psalm 50:1-6
2 Corinthians 4:3-6
Mark 9:2-9

February 27–March 5
FIRST SUNDAY IN LENT
Genesis 9:8-17
Psalm 25:1-10
1 Peter 3:18-22
Mark 1:9-15

March 1
ASH WEDNESDAY
Joel 2:1-2, 12-17 (*or* Isaiah 58:1-12)
Psalm 51:1-17
2 Corinthians 5:20*b*–6:10
Matthew 6:1-6, 16-21

March 6–12
SECOND SUNDAY IN LENT
Genesis 17:1-7, 15-16
Psalm 22:23-31
Romans 4:13-25
Mark 8:31-38 (*or* Mark 9:2-9)

March 13–19
THIRD SUNDAY IN LENT
Exodus 20:1-17
Psalm 19
1 Corinthians 1:18-25
John 2:13-22

March 20–26
FOURTH SUNDAY IN LENT
Numbers 21:4-9
Psalm 107:1-3, 17-22
Ephesians 2:1-10
John 3:14-21

March 27–April 2
FIFTH SUNDAY IN LENT
Jeremiah 31:31-34
Psalm 51:1-12
(*or* Psalm 119:9-16)
Hebrews 5:5-10
John 12:20-33

April 3–9
PASSION/PALM SUNDAY

Liturgy of the Palms
Mark 11:1-11
(*or* John 12:12-16)
Psalm 118:1-2, 19-29

Liturgy of the Passion
Isaiah 50:4-9*a*
Psalm 31:9-16
Philippians 2:5-11
Mark 14:1–15:47
(*or* Mark 15:1-47)

April 10–16
EASTER
Acts 10:34-43
Psalm 118:1-2, 14-24
1 Corinthians 15:1-11
John 20:1-18
(*or* Mark 16:1-8)

HOLY WEEK

Holy Monday
Isaiah 42:1-9
Psalm 36:5-11
Hebrews 9:11-15
John 12:1-11

Holy Tuesday
Isaiah 49:1-7
Psalm 71:1-14
1 Corinthians 1:18-31
John 12:20-36

Holy Wednesday
Isaiah 50:4-9*a*
Psalm 70
Hebrews 12:1-3
John 13:21-32

Maundy Thursday

Exodus 12:1-14
Psalm 116:1-4, 12-19
1 Corinthians 11:23-26
John 13:1-17, 31b-35

Good Friday

Isaiah 52:13–53:12
Psalm 22
Hebrews 10:16-25
John 18:1–19:42

Holy Saturday

Job 14:1-14
Psalm 31:1-4, 15-16
1 Peter 4:1-8
Matthew 27:57-66
  or John 19:38-42

April 17–23

Acts 4:32-35
Psalm 133
1 John 1:1–2:2
John 20:19-31

April 24–30

Acts 3:12-19
Psalm 4
1 John 3:1-7
Luke 24:36b-48

May 1–7

Acts 4:5-12
Psalm 23
1 John 3:16-24
John 10:11-18

May 8–14

Acts 8:26-40
Psalm 22:25-31
1 John 4:7-21
John 15:1-8

May 15–21

Acts 10:44-48
Psalm 98
1 John 5:1-6
John 15:9-17

May 22–28

Acts 1:15-17, 21-26
Psalm 1
1 John 5:9-13
John 17:6-19

MAY 25
ASCENSION DAY

Acts 1:1-11
Psalm 47
Ephesians 1:15-23
Luke 24:44-53

May 29–June 4
PENTECOST

Acts 2:1-21
Psalm 104:24-34, 35b
Romans 8:22-27
John 15:26-27; 16:4b-15

June 5–11
TRINITY

Isaiah 6:1-8
Psalm 29
Romans 8:12-17
John 3:1-17

June 12–18

1 Samuel 15:34–16:13
Psalm 20
2 Corinthians 5:6-17
Mark 4:26-34

June 19–25
1 Samuel 17:1*a*, 4-11,
  19-23, 32-49
Psalm 9:9-20
2 Corinthians 6:1-13
Mark 4:35-41

June 26–July 2
2 Samuel 1:1, 17-27
Psalm 130
2 Corinthians 8:7-15
Mark 5:21-43

July 3–9
2 Samuel 5:1-5, 9-10
Psalm 48
2 Corinthians 12:2-10
Mark 6:1-13

July 10–16
2 Samuel 6:1-5, 12*b*-19
Psalm 24
Ephesians 1:3-14
Mark 6:14-29

July 17–23
2 Samuel 7:1-14*a*
Psalm 89:20-37
Ephesians 2:11-22
Mark 6:30-34, 53-56

July 24–30
2 Samuel 11:1-15
Psalm 14
Ephesians 3:14-21
John 6:1-21

July 31–August 6
2 Samuel 11:26–12:13*a*
Psalm 51:1-12
Ephesians 4:1-16
John 6:24-35

August 7–13
2 Samuel 18:5-9, 15, 31-33
Psalm 130
Ephesians 4:25–5:2
John 6:35, 41-51

August 14–20
1 Kings 2:10-12; 3:3-14
Psalm 111
Ephesians 5:15-20
John 6:51-58

August 21–27
1 Kings 8:1, 6, 10-11,
  22-30, 41-43
Psalm 84
Ephesians 6:10-20
John 6:56-69

August 28–September 3
Song of Solomon 2:8-13
Psalm 45:1-2, 6-9
James 1:17-27
Mark 7:1-8, 14-15, 21-23

September 4–10
Proverbs 22:1-2, 8-9, 22-23
Psalm 125
James 2:1-17
Mark 7:24-37

September 11–17
Proverbs 1:20-33
Psalm 19
James 3:1-12
Mark 8:27-38

September 18–24
Proverbs 31:10-31
Psalm 1
  (*or* Psalm 54)
James 3:13–4:3, 7-8*a*
Mark 9:30-37

September 25–October 1
Esther 7:1-6, 9-10; 9:20-22
Psalm 124
James 5:13-20
Mark 9:38-50

October 2–8
Job 1:1; 2:1-10
Psalm 26
Hebrews 1:1-4; 2:5-12
Mark 10:2-16

October 9–15
Job 23:1-9, 16-17
Psalm 22:1-15
Hebrews 4:12-16
Mark 10:17-31

> **October 9**
> **THANKSGIVING DAY**
> **CANADA**
> Joel 2:21-27
> Psalm 126
> 1 Timothy 2:1-7
> Matthew 6:25-33

October 16–22
Job 38:1-7, 34-41
Psalm 104:1-9, 24, 35c
Hebrews 5:1-10
Mark 10:35-45

October 23–29
Job 42:1-6, 10-17
Psalm 34:1-8, 19-22
Hebrews 7:23-28
Mark 10:46-52

October 30–November 5
Ruth 1:1-18
Psalm 146
Hebrews 9:11-14
Mark 12:28-34

November 1
ALL SAINTS DAY
Isaiah 25:6-9
Psalm 24
Revelation 21:1-6a
John 11:32-44

November 6–12
Ruth 3:1-5; 4:13-17
Psalm 127
Hebrews 9:24-28
Mark 12:38-44

November 13–19
1 Samuel 1:4-20
Psalm 16
Hebrews 10:11-25
Mark 13:1-8

November 20–26
THE REIGN OF CHRIST
2 Samuel 23:1-7
Psalm 132:1-12
Revelation 1:4b-8
John 18:33-37

> **November 23**
> **THANKSGIVING DAY, USA**
> Joel 2:21-27
> Psalm 126
> 1 Timothy 2:1-7
> Matthew 6:25-33

November 27–December 3
FIRST SUNDAY OF ADVENT
Jeremiah 33:14-16
Psalm 25:1-10
1 Thessalonians 3:9-13
Luke 21:25-36

December 4–10
SECOND SUNDAY OF ADVENT
Malachi 3:1-4
Luke 1:68-79
Philippians 1:3-11
Luke 3:1-6

December 11–17
THIRD SUNDAY OF ADVENT
Zephaniah 3:14-20
Isaiah 12:2-6
Philippians 4:4-7
Luke 3:7-18

December 18–24
FOURTH SUNDAY OF ADVENT
Micah 5:2-5*a*
Luke 1:47-55
  (*or* Psalm 80:1-7)
Hebrews 10:5-10
Luke 1:39-45

December 24
CHRISTMAS EVE
Isaiah 9:2-7
Psalm 96
Titus 2:11-14
Luke 2:1-20

December 25–31
FIRST SUNDAY AFTER
CHRISTMAS
1 Samuel 2:18-20, 26
Psalm 148
Colossians 3:12-17
Luke 2:41-52

December 25
CHRISTMAS DAY
Isaiah 52:7-10
Psalm 98
Hebrews 1:1-12
John 1:1-14